Hands-On JavaScript High Performance

Build faster web apps using Node.js, Svelte.js, and WebAssembly

Justin Scherer

BIRMINGHAM - MUMBAI

Hands-On JavaScript High Performance

Commissioning Editor: Pavan Ramchandani
Acquisition Editor: Ashitosh Gupta
Content Development Editor: Keagan Carneiro
Senior Editor: Hayden Edwards
Technical Editor: Jane Dsouza
Copy Editor: Safis Editing
Project Coordinator: Manthan Patel
Proofreader: Safis Editing
Indexer: Tejal Daruwale Soni
Production Designer: Alishon Mendonsa

First published: February 2020

Production reference: 1280220

Published by Packt Publishing Ltd.
Livery Place
35 Livery Street
Birmingham
B3 2PB, UK.

ISBN 978-1-83882-109-8

www.packt.com

To my mother, Kristi, and to my father, Jerry, for their love, determination, and sacrifice throughout life. To my wife, Vlasta, for being my loving spouse and partner in life.

– Justin Scherer

Packt.com

Subscribe to our online digital library for full access to over 7,000 books and videos, as well as industry leading tools to help you plan your personal development and advance your career. For more information, please visit our website.

Why subscribe?

- Spend less time learning and more time coding with practical eBooks and Videos from over 4,000 industry professionals

- Improve your learning with Skill Plans built especially for you

- Get a free eBook or video every month

- Fully searchable for easy access to vital information

- Copy and paste, print, and bookmark content

Did you know that Packt offers eBook versions of every book published, with PDF and ePub files available? You can upgrade to the eBook version at www.packt.com and as a print book customer, you are entitled to a discount on the eBook copy. Get in touch with us at customercare@packtpub.com for more details.

At www.packt.com, you can also read a collection of free technical articles, sign up for a range of free newsletters, and receive exclusive discounts and offers on Packt books and eBooks.

Contributors

About the author

Justin Scherer has been professionally developing JavaScript applications for over 10 years. On top of this, he has worked in a variety of fields, ranging from embedded systems to high-performance cluster applications. Utilizing JavaScript to cluster simulation models, write RFID tracking systems, and even to hook Fortran code together, Justin brought JavaScript to Argonne National Laboratory as a way of quickly prototyping and building out ideas.

Justin then went on to work for an e-learning start-up and lead the frontend development team. He currently works for a large financial institution, where he is leading the charge on developing a highly performant frontend and middleware through the use of JavaScript.

During his time off, he has a handful of hobbies, including but not limited to playing the piano, going to concerts, repairing watches, reading, and spending time with his wife. He enjoys his time with his wife and their cat and dog. His mind is constantly wandering to new areas where technology, especially web technology, could prove useful.

I would first like to thank my wife for being the wonderful person she is. If it were not for her, I would still be wondering whether I could even write a book in the first place. She has always pushed me to be the best person, even when she does not realize she is doing it. I would also like to thank my mom for always being the most wonderful person I have ever known and for always being the biggest supporter no matter what I decided to do. I would like to thank my dad for always being one step ahead of me and keeping me on my toes; he is my role model and I strive to be as good of a man as he is. Finally, I would like to thank my brother. While he may not realize the impact he has had on me, he has always shown me what it means to work hard and to achieve your goals.

About the reviewer

Jean-Sébastien Goupil is a web developer with more than 15 years of experience. He previously worked for Microsoft and is now a web architect consultant for his own company, working with new clients on web products. He champions quality and consistency at every opportunity and is driven to help others through teaching and blogging.

In his free time, he codes barcode software. He loves sports, hiking, canoeing, crabbing, and chatting about technology.

Packt is searching for authors like you

If you're interested in becoming an author for Packt, please visit `authors.packtpub.com` and apply today. We have worked with thousands of developers and tech professionals, just like you, to help them share their insight with the global tech community. You can make a general application, apply for a specific hot topic that we are recruiting an author for, or submit your own idea.

Table of Contents

Preface

Much of today's web environment has changed dramatically – not only in terms of creating web applications but also when it comes to creating server-side applications. A frontend ecosystem that was dominated by jQuery and CSS frameworks such as Bootstrap has been replaced with reactive, fully fledged applications that could be mistaken for an application running on the desktop.

The language we write these applications in has also changed in a dramatic fashion. What was once a mess of `var` and scope issues has turned into a fast and easy-to-program language. JavaScript has not only changed the way we write our frontend, it has also changed the backend programming experience.

We are now able to write server-side applications in the language that we write our frontend in. JavaScript has also modernized, and possibly even popularized, the event-driven system with Node.js. We can now write code for both our frontend and backend in JavaScript and possibly even share the JavaScript files we generate between the two.

However, while the application landscape has evolved and many people have moved onto modern frameworks, such as React and Vue.js for the frontend and Express and Sails for the backend, many of these developers do not understand the inner workings. While this showcases just how simple it is to enter into the ecosystem, it also showcases how easy it is to not understand how to optimize our code bases.

This book focuses on teaching highly performant JavaScript. This not only means fast execution speeds, but also a lower memory footprint. This means that any frontend system will get to the user faster, and we will be able to start our applications that much faster. On top of this, we have many new technologies that have moved the web forward, such as Web Workers.

Who this book is for

This book is for those who are interested in all the latest features of the modern web. On top of this, it's also for those with an interest in reducing memory costs while increasing speed. People who are interested in how a computer works and even how a JavaScript compiler works will be interested in the contents of this book. Finally, for those who are interested in WebAssembly but do not know where to start, this is a good jumping-off point in learning the essentials.

What this book covers

Chapter 1, *Tools for High Performance on the Web*, will cover the various browsers that our applications can run on. We will also take a look at the various tools that help us to debug, profile, and even run ad hoc code to test the functionality of our JavaScript.

Chapter 2, *Immutability versus Mutability – The Balance between Safety and Speed*, will take a look at the concepts of mutable/immutable state. We will cover when and where to use each. On top of this, we will cover how to create the illusion of immutability while having a mutable data structure.

Chapter 3, *Vanilla Land – Looking at the Modern Web*, will take a look at how far JavaScript has come and all of the new and notable features up to ECMAScript 2020. On top of this, we will look at various advanced features, such as currying and writing in a functional manner.

Chapter 4, *Practical Example – A Look at Svelte and Being Vanilla*, will cover a fairly new framework called Svelte. It will go over this compile to Vanilla JavaScript framework and explore how it achieves lightning-fast results with an intuitive framework.

Chapter 5, *Switching Contexts – No DOM, Different Vanilla*, will cover the low-level Node.js work. This means taking a look at the various modules available to us. We will also take a look at how we can achieve amazing results with no extra libraries.

Chapter 6, *Message Passing – Learning about the Different Types*, will take a look at different ways to talk among different processes. We will cover unnamed pipes, named pipes, sockets, and transmission via TCP/UDP. We will also take a look at HTTP/2 and briefly look at HTTP/3.

Chapter 7, *Streams – Understanding Stream and Non-Blocking I/O*, will cover the Stream API and how to utilize it. We will cover each type of stream and the use cases for each. On top of this, we will implement some practical streams that, with some modification, could be used in other projects.

Chapter 8, *Data Formats – Looking at Different Data Types Other Than JSON*, will look into schema and schema-less data types. We will look into implementing a data format and then see popular data formats in action.

Chapter 9, *Practical Example – Building a Static Server*, will take the previous four chapters and apply these concepts and build a static site generator. While it may not be as powerful as GatsbyJS, it will have most of the features we expect from a static site generator.

Chapter 10, *Workers – Learning about Dedicated and Shared Workers*, will move back to the frontend and take a look at two of the web worker types. We will utilize these to process data from the main thread. On top of this, we will take a look at how we can talk among our workers and the main process.

Chapter 11, *Service Workers – Caching and Making Things Faster*, will look at the service worker and the life cycle of the service worker. On top of this, we will look at practical examples of how to utilize a service worker in a progressive web application.

Chapter 12, *Building and Deploying a Full Web Application*, will look at **continuous integration/continuous deployment (CI/CD)** with the tool CircleCI. We will see how we can use it to deploy our web application built in Chapter 9, *Practical Example – Building a Static Server*, to a server. We will even take a look at adding some security checks to our application before deployment.

Chapter 13, *WebAssembly – A Brief Look into Native Code on the Web*, will look at this relatively new technology. We will see how to write low-level WebAssembly and how it runs on the web. We will then turn our attention to writing C++ for the browser. Finally, we will take a look at a ported application and the WebAssembly that is behind it.

To get the most out of this book

In general, the requirements to run most of the code are minimal. A computer that is capable of handling Chrome, Node.js, and a C compiler is needed. The C compiler that we will be utilizing near the end of this book will be CMake. These systems should work on all modern operating systems.

For Chrome, having the latest versions will be helpful as we will be utilizing some features that are either in the proposal stage or in ECMAScript 2020. We are using the latest LTS version of Node.js (v12.16.1), and are avoiding the use of Node.js 13 as it won't be promoted to LTS. On top of this, the command-line tool for Windows is not that great, so it is recommended to download Cmder, from https://cmder.net/, to have a Bash-like shell for Windows.

Finally, a modern IDE or editor is needed. We will be utilizing Visual Studio Code throughout this book, but many other alternatives, such as Visual Studio, IntelliJ, Sublime Text 3, and so on, can be used.

Software/hardware covered in the book	Operating system requirements
Svelte.js v3	Windows 10/OSX/Linux
ECMAScript 2020	Windows 10/OSX/Linux
Node.js v12.16.1 LTS	Windows 10/OSX/Linux
WebAssembly	Windows 10/OSX/Linux

Download the example code files

You can download the example code files for this book from your account at www.packt.com. If you purchased this book elsewhere, you can visit www.packtpub.com/support and register to have the files emailed directly to you.

You can download the code files by following these steps:

1. Log in or register at www.packt.com.
2. Select the **Support** tab.
3. Click on **Code Downloads**.
4. Enter the name of the book in the **Search** box and follow the onscreen instructions.

Once the file is downloaded, please make sure that you unzip or extract the folder using the latest version of:

- WinRAR/7-Zip for Windows
- Zipeg/iZip/UnRarX for Mac
- 7-Zip/PeaZip for Linux

The code bundle for the book is also hosted on GitHub at https://github.com/PacktPublishing/Hands-On-High-Performance-Web-Development-with-JavaScript. In case there's an update to the code, it will be updated on the existing GitHub repository.

We also have other code bundles from our rich catalog of books and videos available at https://github.com/PacktPublishing/. Check them out!

Conventions used

There are a number of text conventions used throughout this book.

`CodeInText`: Indicates code words in text, database table names, folder names, filenames, file extensions, pathnames, dummy URLs, user input, and Twitter handles. Here is an example: "This is very similar to `console.time` and `timeEnd` but it should showcase what is available with generators."

A block of code is set as follows:

```
for(let i = 0; i < 100000; i++) {
    const j = Library.outerFun(true);
}
```

Any command-line input or output is written as follows:

```
> npm install what-the-pack
```

Bold: Indicates a new term, an important word, or words that you see onscreen. For example, words in menus or dialog boxes appear in the text like this. Here is an example: "If we open the DevTools by pressing *F12* in Windows, we may see the **Shader Editor** tab already."

Warnings or important notes appear like this.

Tips and tricks appear like this.

Get in touch

Feedback from our readers is always welcome.

General feedback: If you have questions about any aspect of this book, mention the book title in the subject of your message and email us at `customercare@packtpub.com`.

Errata: Although we have taken every care to ensure the accuracy of our content, mistakes do happen. If you have found a mistake in this book, we would be grateful if you would report this to us. Please visit www.packtpub.com/support/errata, selecting your book, clicking on the Errata Submission Form link, and entering the details.

Piracy: If you come across any illegal copies of our works in any form on the Internet, we would be grateful if you would provide us with the location address or website name. Please contact us at copyright@packt.com with a link to the material.

If you are interested in becoming an author: If there is a topic that you have expertise in and you are interested in either writing or contributing to a book, please visit authors.packtpub.com.

Reviews

Please leave a review. Once you have read and used this book, why not leave a review on the site that you purchased it from? Potential readers can then see and use your unbiased opinion to make purchase decisions, we at Packt can understand what you think about our products, and our authors can see your feedback on their book. Thank you!

For more information about Packt, please visit packt.com.

1
Tools for High Performance on the Web

JavaScript has become the mainstay language of the web. There is no extra runtime needed, and there is no compilation process required to run an application in JavaScript. Any user can open up a web browser and start typing in the console to learn the language. In addition to this, there have been many advancements in the language along with the **Document Object Model (DOM)**. All of this has led to a rich environment for developers to take and create.

On top of this, we can see the web as a *build once, deploy anywhere* environment. The code that works on one operating system will work on another. There is some variation that will need to happen if we want to target all browsers, but it can be seen as a *develop once, deploy anywhere* platform. However, all of this has led to applications that have become bloated, with expensive frameworks and unnecessary polyfills. The necessity for these frameworks can be seen in most job postings, but sometimes we don't need them to create rich applications.

This chapter focuses on the tools that we will use to help us build and profile high-performance web applications. We will take a look at the different modern browsers and their unique contributions. We will then take a deep dive into the Chrome developer tools. Overall, we will learn the following:

- The different development tools embedded in each browser
- An in depth look at the following Chrome tools:
  - The Performance tab
  - The Memory tab
  - The Renderer tab
- jsPerf and benchmarking code

Technical requirements

The following are prerequisites for this chapter:

- A web browser, preferably Chrome.
- An editor; VS Code is preferred.
- Knowledge of JavaScript and some of the DOM APIs.
- The relevant code can be found at `https://github.com/PacktPublishing/`
  `Hands-On-High-Performance-Web-Development-with-JavaScript/tree/master/`
  `Chapter01`.

DevTools for different environments

There are four browsers that are considered modern browsers. These are Edge, Chrome, Firefox, and Safari. These browsers uphold the latest in standards and are being actively developed. We will take a look at how each is developing and some of their unique features.

 Internet Explorer is getting close to the end of its life cycle. The only development that will be happening with the browser is critical security fixes. New applications should try to deprecate this browser, but if there is a client base still utilizing it, then we may need to develop for it. We will not be focusing on polyfills for it in this book.

Edge

Microsoft's Edge browser was their take on the modern web. With the EdgeHTML renderer and the Chakra JavaScript engine, it performs well in many benchmarks. While the Chakra engine does have different optimizations for it than Chrome or Firefox, it is an interesting browser to look at from a pure JavaScript perspective.

 As of the time of writing of this book, Microsoft was changing the rendering engine of Edge to the Chromium system. This has many implications for web developers. First, this means that more browsers will be running the Chromium system. This means less to worry about in terms of cross-browser development. While support for the current form of Edge is required, it may disappear in the coming year.

In terms of features, Edge is light compared to the other browsers. If we need to perform any type of performance testing for it, the best bet is to profile code with jsPerf or others instead of the built-in tools. On top of this, the Chakra engine utilizes different optimization techniques, so what may work with Chrome or Safari may be less optimized for Edge. To get to the developer tools on Windows, we can press *F12*. This will pull up the usual console dialog, shown as follows:

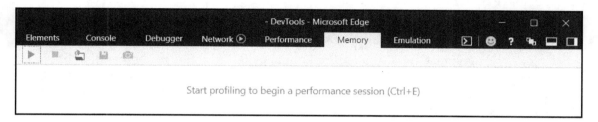

We will not be going through any interesting features specific to Edge since most, if not all, of the features in their developer tools are the same as those found in other browsers.

With the latest Edge browser based on Chromium, OS X users will be happy to note that the browser is supposed to be supported. This means cross-browser development will get easier for those on OS X versus Windows or Linux.

Safari

Apple's Safari browser is based on the WebKit rendering engine and the JavaScriptCore engine. The WebKit engine is what Chrome's Blink engine is based on, and the JavaScriptCore engine is used in a few places for the OS X operating system. An interesting point regarding Safari is the fact that if we are running Windows or Linux, we will not be able to access it directly.

To get access to Safari, we will need to utilize an online service. BrowserStack or LambdaTest, along with a host of others, can do this job for us. With any of these, we now have access to browsers that we may not otherwise have had. Thanks to LambdaTest, we will utilize their free service to take a brief look at Safari.

Again, we will notice that there is not too much to the Safari browser development tools. All of the same tools are also available in the other browsers and they are usually more powerful in these other browsers. Getting familiar with each of the interfaces can help when debugging in that specific browser, but not a lot of time needs to be dedicated to looking at the browsers that do not have any specific features unique to them.

Firefox

Mozilla's Firefox utilizes the SpiderMonkey JavaScript engine and the enhanced Gecko engine. The Gecko engine got some nice improvements when they added parts of their project Servo code base to it to give a nice multithreaded renderer. Mozilla has been at the forefront of the latest web technologies. They were one of the first to implement WebGL and they have been one of the first to implement WebAssembly and the **WebAssembly System Interface** (**WASI**) standard.

 What follows is a fairly technical discussion about shaders and the shader language, **OpenGL Shading Language** (**GLSL**). It is recommended that you read on to find out more about this, but for those of you who are lost, it may be helpful to visit the documentation to learn more about this technology, at `https://developer.mozilla.org/en-US/docs/Games/Techniques/3D_on_the_web/GLSL_Shaders`.

If we open the DevTools, *F12* in Windows, we may see the **Shader Editor** tab already. If not, go to the triple-dot menu on the right and open up **Settings**. On the left-hand side, there should be a list of checkboxes with a heading of **Default Developer Tools**. Go ahead and select the **Shader Editor** option. Now, if we head into this tab, we should get something that looks like the following:

The tab is asking for a canvas context. Essentially, the tool is looking for a few items:

- A canvas element
- A 3D-enabled context
- Vertex and fragment shaders

A file in our repository called `shader_editor.html` has the necessary code to get the canvas set up and also has the shaders set up so we can utilize them with the shader editor. These shaders are the way to programmatically use the GPU on the web. They utilize a version of the OpenGL specification called OpenGL ES 3.0. This allows us to use almost everything in that specification, specifically, the vertex and fragment shaders.

To program with these shaders, we use a language called **GL Shading Language** (GLSL). This is a C-like language that has a bunch of features that are specific to it, such as swizzling. Swizzling is the ability to utilize the vector components (up to four) and combine them in any shape or form that we choose. An example of this looks like the following:

```
vec2 item = vec2(1.0, 1.0);
vec4 other_item = item.xyxx;
```

This creates a four-element vector and sets the x, y, z, and w components to the x, y, x, and x items, respectively, from the two-element vector. The nomenclature can take a while to get used to, but it makes certain things a lot easier. An example is shown above, where we need to create a four-element vector from a two-element vector. In basic JavaScript, we would have to do the following:

```
const item = [1.0, 1.0];
const other_item = [item[0], item[1], item[0], item[0]];
```

Instead of writing the preceding, we are able to utilize the shorthand syntax of swizzling. There are other features in the GLSL system that we will look at in later chapters, but this should give a taste of how different the languages are.

Now, if we open up the `shader_editor.html` file and reload the page, we should be greeted with what looks like a white page. If we look at the **Shader Editor**, we can see on the right-hand side that we are setting a variable called `gl_FragColor` to a four-element vector, all of which are set to `1.0`. What happens if we set it to `vec4(0.0, 0.0, 0.0, 1.0)`? We should now see a black box in the top-left corner. This showcases the fact that the four components of the vector are the red, green, blue, and alpha components of color, ranging from `0.0` to `1.0`, just like the `rgba` system for CSS.

Are there other color combinations besides a single flat color? Well, each shader comes with a few global variables that are defined ahead of time. One of these, in the fragment shader, is called `gl_FragCoord`. This is the lower left-hand coordinate in the window space ranging from `0.0` to `1.0` (there should be a theme developing here for what values are considered good in GLSL). If we set the four-vector x element to the x element of `gl_FragCoord`, and the y element to the y element of `gl_FragCoord`, we should get a simple white box, but with a single-pixel border on the left, and one on the bottom.

Besides swizzling and global variables, we also get other mathematical functions that we can use in these shaders. Let's wrap these x and y elements in a `sin` function. If we do this, we should get a nice plaid pattern on the screen. This should give a hint as to what the fragment shader is actually doing. It is trying to paint that location in the 3D space, based on various inputs, one being the location from the vertex shader.

It is then trying to draw every single pixel that makes up the inside of the mesh that we declared with the vertex shader. Also, these fragments are calculated all at the same time (or as much as the graphics card is capable of), so this is a highly parallelized operation.

This should give a nice sneak peek into the world of GLSL programming, and the possibilities besides 3D work that the GLSL language can provide for us. For now, we can play a bit more with these concepts and move onto the last browser, Chrome.

Chrome

Google's Chrome browser utilizes the Blink engine and uses the famous V8 JavaScript runtime. This is the same runtime that is used inside Node.js, so getting familiar with the development tools will help us in a lot of ways.

Chrome has been at the forefront of web technologies, just like Firefox. They have been the first to implement various ideas, such as the QUIC protocol, which the HTTP/3 standard is loosely based on. They created the **Native Plugin Interface** (**NaCL**) that helped, alongside asm.js, to create the standard for WebAssembly. They have even been pioneers in making web applications start to become more native-like by giving us APIs such as the Bluetooth, Gamepad, and Notifications APIs.

We will be specifically looking at the Lighthouse feature that comes with Chrome. The Lighthouse feature can be accessed from the **Audits** tab in the Chrome browser. Once we are here, we can set up our audit with a myriad of settings:

- First, we can audit our page based on it running from a mobile device or desktop. We can then audit various features of our site.
- If we are developing a progressive web application, we may decide that SEO is not needed. On the other hand, if we are developing a marketing site, we could decide that the progressive web app check is not needed. We can simulate a throttled connection.
- Finally, we can start off with clean storage. This is especially helpful if our application utilizes caching systems that are built into browsers, such as session storage or local storage.

As an example, let's look at an external site and see how well it stacks up in the audit application. The site we will be looking at is Amazon, located at https://www.amazon.com. The site should be a good example for us to follow. We are going to look at it as a desktop application, without any throttling. If we run the audit, we should get something that looks like the following:

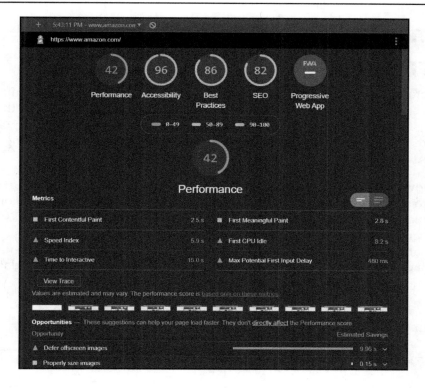

As we can see, the main page does well in performance and best practices, but Chrome is warning us about accessibility and SEO performance. In terms of accessibility, it seems that images do not have `alt` attributes, which means screen readers are not going to work well. Also, it seems that the developers have `tabindexes` higher than 0, possibly causing the tab order to not follow the normal page flow.

If we wanted to set up our own system to test, we would need to host our pages locally. There are many great static site hosting solutions (we will be building one later in the book), but if we needed to host content, one of the easiest methods would be to download Node.js and install the `static-server` module. We will go into depth later on how to get Node.js up and running and how to create our own servers, but for now, this is the best bet.

We have looked at the main modern web browsers that are out there and that we should target. Each of them has its own capabilities and limitations, which means we should be testing our applications on all of them. However, the focus of this book will be the Chrome browser and the developer tools that come with it. Since Node.js is built with the V8 engine, and with many other new browsers being based on the Chromium engine, such as Brave, it would make sense to utilize this. We are going to go into detail regarding three specific features that the Chrome developer tools give us.

Chrome – an in-depth look at the Performance tab

As stated before, except for a select few tools inside Firefox, Chrome has become widely ubiquitous as the browser of choice for users and developers. For developers, this can be in large part thanks to its wonderful developer tools. The following sections are going to take a look at three critical tools that are important to any developer when designing web applications. We will start with the performance tool.

This tool allows us to run performance tests while our application is running. This is great if we want to see how our application behaves when certain things are done. For example, we can profile our application's launch state and see where possible bottlenecks are located. Or, when user interaction happens, such as a submit on a form, we can see the call hierarchy that we go through to post the information and return it back to the user. On top of this, it can even help profile code when we use a web worker and how the data transfer works between our application contexts.

Following is a screenshot of the **Performance** tab from the latest version of Chrome at the time of writing:

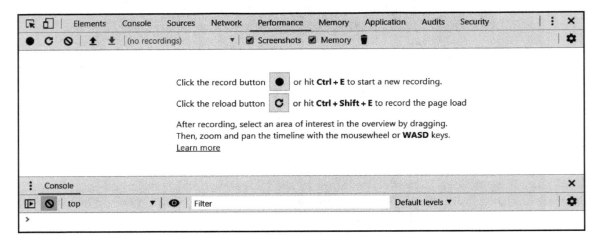

There are a couple of sections that are of interest. First, the bar below our developer tool tabs is our main toolbar. The left two buttons are probably the most important, the record and the record on reload tools. These will allow us to profile our application and see what happens at critical junctures in our code. After these come selection tools to grab profiles that you may have run before.

Next up are two options that I usually have turned on at all times:

- First, the screenshot capability will grab screenshots for us when it sees something critical happening with the application, such as memory growth or a new document being added.
- The next option is the memory profiler. It will tell us how much memory is being consumed at that time.

Finally, there is the delete action. As many would surmise, this deletes the profile that you are currently on.

Let's do a test run on a simple test application. Grab the `chrome_performance.html` file from the repository. This file showcases a standard Todo application, but it is written with a very basic templating system and no libraries. No libraries will become a standard throughout this book.

If we run this application and run a performance test from reload, we should get something that looks like the following:

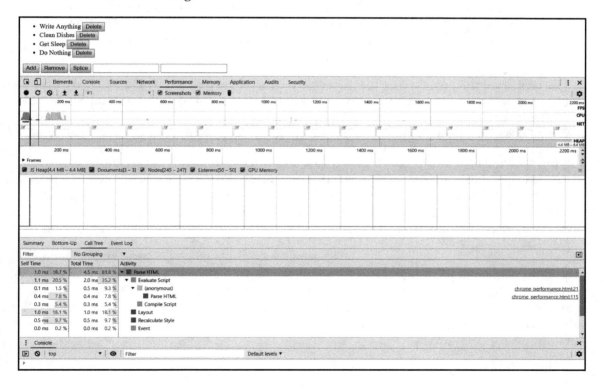

The page should be almost instant to load, but we still get some useful information here. Going from top to bottom, we get the following information:

- A timeline of pictures, along with graphing for FPS, CPU usage, network usage, and heap usage.
- A line graph of different statistics, such as JavaScript heap usage, the number of documents, the number of document nodes, the number of listeners, and the GPU memory that we are utilizing.
- Finally, we get a tabbed section that gives us all of the information about timings and a breakdown of where the time is allocated.

 Make sure you let the profiler run its course. It should automatically shut down after all operations are done on the page. This should ensure that you are getting as close to the correct information as possible on how your application is doing. The profiler may have to be run a couple of times to get an accurate picture also. The internal garbage collector is trying to hold onto some objects so that it can reuse them later, so getting an accurate picture means seeing what the low point is since that is most likely where the application baseline is following **Garbage Collection (GC)**. A good indicator of this is seeing a major GC and/or a DOM GC. This means we are starting afresh again.

In this basic example, we can see that most of the time was spent in the HTML. If we open this up, we will then see that evaluating our script took the majority of that time. Since most of our time was spent in evaluating the script and inserting our templated Todo application into the DOM, let's see what the statistics would look like if we did not have this behavior.

Comment out everything except for our basic tags, such as the `html`, `head`, and `body` tags. There are a few interesting elements regarding this run. First, the number of documents should have stayed the same or decreased. This will be touched upon later. Second, the number of nodes decreased dramatically and likely went down to around 12. Our JavaScript heap went down a little bit, and the number of listeners went down significantly.

Let's bring a single `div` tag back in. The number of documents, heap space, and listeners stayed the same, but the number of nodes increased again. Let's add in another `div` element and see how that affects the number of nodes. It should increase by four. One last time, let's add in another `div` element. Again, we should notice an increase of four DOM nodes being added. This gives us a bit of a clue into how the DOM is running and how we can make sure our profiling is correct.

First, the number of nodes is not directly equal to the number of DOM elements that are on the screen. DOM nodes are made up of several underlying basic nodes. As an example, if we add an element such as an `input` element, we may notice that the number of nodes increases by more than four. Second, the number of documents that are available is almost always going to be higher than a single document.

While some of this behavior can be attributed to bugs in the profiler, it also showcases the fact that there are things happening behind the scenes that are not available to the developer. When we touch on the **Memory** tab and look at call hierarchies, we will see how internal systems are creating and destroying nodes that a developer does not have full control of, along with documents that are invisible to the developer but are optimizations for the browser.

Let's add in our code block again and get back to what the original document was. If need be, go ahead and revert the Git branch (if this was pulled down from the repository) and run the profiler again. We specifically want to look at the **Call Tree** tab and the Parse HTML dropdown. There should be a hierarchy that looks something like the following:
Parse HTML > Evaluate Script > (anonymous) > runTemplate > runTemplate.

Let's change the code and turn our inner `for` loop into an array `map` function like this:

```
const tempFun = runTemplate.bind(null, loopTemp);
loopEls = data.items.map(tempFun);
```

Comment out both the `loopEls` array initialization and also the `for` loop. Run the profiler again and let's take a look at what this call stack looks like. We will notice that it is still profiling the `runTemplate` function as itself even though we bound it to a new function called `tempFun`. This is another piece that we have to keep in mind when we are looking at the call hierarchy. We may bind, call, or apply functions, but the development tools will still try to maintain the original definition of the function.

Finally, let's add a lot of items to our data list and see how this affects our profiling. Put the following code below the data section:

```
for(let i = 0; i < 10000; i++) {
    data.items.push({text : `Another item ${i}`});
}
```

We should now get a bit of a different picture than what we had before:

- First, where our time was close to being evenly split between layout by the GPU and the evaluation of our script, it now looks like we are spending most of our time running the layout engine. This makes sense since we are forcing the DOM to figure out the layout for each item when it gets added at the end of our script.
- Second, the **Evaluate Script** section should now contain quite a few more pieces than the simple call hierarchy that we saw before.
- We will also start to see different parts of the function being registered in the profiler. What this shows is that if something is below a certain threshold (it really depends on the machine and even the build of Chrome), it will not show that the function was considered important enough to be profiled.

Garbage collection is the process of our environment cleaning up unused items that we are no longer using. Since JavaScript is a memory-managed environment, meaning developers are not allocating/deallocating memory themselves like in languages such as C++ and Rust, we have a program that does this for us. V8, in particular, has two GCs, a minor GC called **Scavenger**, and a major one called **Mark-Compact**.

The scavenger goes through newly allocated objects and sees whether there are any objects that are ready to be cleaned up. Most of the time, our code is going to be written to use a lot of temporary variables for a short time span. This means that they are not going to be needed within a couple of statements of the variables being initialized. Take the following piece of code:

```
const markedEls = [];
for(let i = 0; i < 10000; i++) {
    const obj = els[i];
    if( obj.marked ) {
        markedEls.push(Object.assign({}, obj));
    }
}
```

In this hypothetical example, we want to get objects and clone them if they are marked for some procedure. We gather the ones that we want and the rest are now unused. The scavenger would notice a couple of things. First, it would seem that we are no longer using the old list, so it would automatically collect this memory. Second, it would notice that we have a bunch of unused object pointers (except for primitive types in JavaScript, everything is passed by reference) and it can clean these up.

This is a quick process and it gets either intertwined in our runtime, known as stop-and-go garbage collection, or it will run in parallel to our code, meaning that it will run at the exact same time in another thread of execution.

The Mark-Compact garbage collection runs for much longer but collects a lot more memory. It will go through the list of items that are currently still in the heap and see whether there are zero references to these items. If there are no more references, it will remove these objects from the heap. It will then try to compact all of the holes that are in the heap so that way, we do not have highly fragmented memory. This is especially useful for things such as arrays.

Arrays are contiguous in memory, so if the V8 engine can find a hole big enough for the array, then it will stick it there. Otherwise, it may have to grow the heap and allocate more memory for our runtime. This is what the Mark-Compact GC is trying to prevent from happening.

While a full understanding of how the garbage collector works is not needed in order to write highly performant JavaScript, a good understanding will go a long way into writing code that is not only easy to read but also performs well in the environment that you are using.

If you want to understand more about the V8 garbage collector, I would recommend going to the site at `https://v8.dev/blog`. It is always interesting to see how the V8 engine is working and how new optimizations lead to certain coding styles being more performant than they may have been in the past, such as the map function for arrays.

We did not go into full detail regarding the **Performance** tab, but this should give a good overview of how to utilize it when testing code. It should also showcase some of the internal workings of Chrome and the garbage collector.

There will be more discussion in the next section on memory, but it is highly recommended to run some tests against a current code base and notice what the performance is like when running these applications.

Chrome – an in-depth look at the Memory tab

As we move from the performance section to the memory section, we will revisit a good number of concepts from the performance tool. The V8 engine provides a great amount of support for developing applications that are both efficient in terms of CPU usage and also memory usage. A great way to test your memory usage and where it is being allocated is the memory profiling tool.

With the latest version of Chrome at the time of writing, the memory profiler appears as follows:

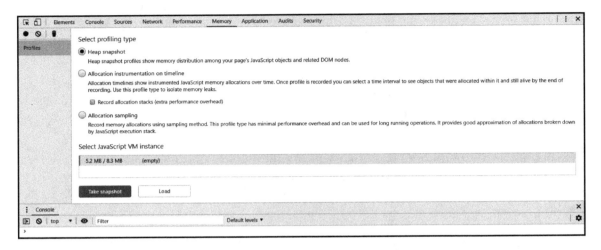

We will mainly be focusing on the first option that is selected, the **Heap snapshot** tool. The **Allocation instrumentation on timeline** tool is a great way to visualize and playback how the heap was being allocated and which objects were causing the allocations to occur. Finally, the **Allocation sampling** tool takes periodic snapshots instead of providing a continuous look, making it much lighter and able to perform memory tests while cumbersome operations are conducted.

The heap snapshot tool will allow us to see where memory is being allocated on the heap. From our previous example, let's run the heap snapshot tool (if you have not commented out the `for` loop that allocated 10,000 more DOM nodes, comment it out now). After the snapshot has run, you should get a table with a tree view on the left-hand side. Let's go looking for one of the *global* items that we are able to get to in the console.

We currently have items grouped by what they are or who they belong to. If we open up the **(closure)** list, we can find the `runTemplate()` function being held there. If we go into the **(string)** list, we can find the strings that were used to create our list. A question that may be raised is why some of these items are still being held on the heap even though we no longer need them. Well, this goes back to how the garbage collector works and who is currently referencing these items.

Take a look at the list items that are currently being held in memory. If you click on each of them, it shows us they are being referenced by `loopEls`. If we head back into our code, it can be noted that the only line of code that we use, `loopEls`, is in the following:

```
const tempFun = runTemplate.bind(null, loopTemp);
loopEls = data.items.map(tempFun);
```

Take this out and put the basic `for` loop back in. Run the heap snapshot and go back into the **(strings)** section. These strings are no longer there! Let's change the code one more time using the `map` function, but this time let's not use the bind function to create a new function. The code should look like the following:

```
const loopEls = data.items.map((item) => {
    return runTemplate(loopTemp, item);
});
```

Again, run a heap snapshot after changing out the code and we will notice that those strings are no longer there. An astute reader will notice that there is an error in the code from the first run; the `loopEls` variable does not have any variable type prefix added to it. This has caused the `loopEls` variable to go onto the global scope, which means that the garbage collector cannot collect it, since the garbage collector thinks that the variable is still in use.

Now, if we turn our attention to the first item in this list, we should observe that the entire template string is still being held. If we click on that element, we will notice that it is being held by the `template` variable. However, we may state that since the variable is a constant, it should automatically be collected. Again, the V8 compiler does not know this and has put it on the global scope for us.

There are two ways that we can fix this issue. First, we can use the old-school technique and wrap it in an **Immediately Invoked Function Expression (IIFE)**, which would look like the following:

```
(function() { })();
```

Or, if we wanted to and were writing our application only for browsers that support it, we could change the script type to a type of `module`. Both of these solutions make sure that our code is not now globally scoped. Let's put our entire code base in an IIFE since that is supported across all browsers. If we run a heap dump, we will see that that string is no longer there.

Finally, the last area that should be touched on is the working set of heap space and the amount it actually has allocated. Add the following line to the top of the HTML file:

```
<script type="text/javascript" src="./fake_library.js"></script>
```

This is a simple file that adds itself to the window to act as a library. Then, we are going to test two scenarios. First, run the following code:

```
for(let i = 0; i < 100000; i++) {
    const j = Library.outerFun(true);
    const k = Library.outerFun(true);
    const l = Library.outerFun(true);
    const m = Library.outerFun(true);
    const n = Library.outerFun(true);
}
```

Now, go to the performance section and check out the two numbers that are being displayed. If need be, go ahead and hit the garbage can. This causes the major garbage collector to run. It should be noted that the left-hand number is what is currently being used, and the right-hand number is what has been allocated. This means that the V8 engine has allocated around 6-6.5 MB of space for the heap.

Now, let's run the code in a similar fashion, but let's break each of these runs into their own loops, like the following:

```
for(let i = 0; i < 100000; i++) {
    const j = Library.outerFun(true);
}
```

Check the **Performance** tab again. The memory should be around 7 MB. Go ahead and click the trash can and it should drop back down to 5.8 MB, or around where the baseline heap should be at. What did this show us? Well, since it had to allocate items for each of those variables in the first `for` loop, it had to increase its heap space. Even though it only ran it once and the minor garbage collector should have collected it, it is going to keep that heap space due to heuristics built into the garbage collector. Since we decided to do that, the garbage collector will keep more memory in the heap because we are more than likely going to keep repeating that behavior in the short term.

Now, with the second set of code, we decided to use a bunch of `for` loops and only allocate a single variable at a time. While this may be slower, V8 saw that we were only allocating small chunks of space and that it could decrease the size of the main heap because we are more than likely to keep up the same behavior in the near future. The V8 system has a bunch of heuristics built into the system and it will try and guess what we are going to do based on what we have done in the past. The heap allocator can help show us what the V8 compiler is going to do and what our coding pattern is most like in terms of memory usage.

Go ahead and keep playing with the memory tab and add code in. Take a look at popular libraries (try to keep them small so you can track the memory allocations) and notice how they decided to write their code and how that causes the heap allocator to retain objects in memory and even keep a larger heap size around.

> It is generally good practice for a multitude of reasons, but writing small functions that do one thing very well is also great for the garbage collector. It will base its heuristics on the fact that a coder is writing these tiny functions and will decrease the overall heap space it will keep around. This, in turn, will cause the memory footprint of the application to also go down. Remember, it is not the working set size (the left-hand number) but the total heap space (the right-hand number) that is our memory usage.

Chrome – an in-depth look at the Rendering tab

The last section that we will look at in the developer tools is going to be the rendering section. This is usually not a default tab that is available. In the toolbar, you will notice a three-dot button next to the Close button. Click that, go to **More tools**, and click the **Rendering** option.

There should now be a tabbed item next to the **Console** tab that looks like the following:

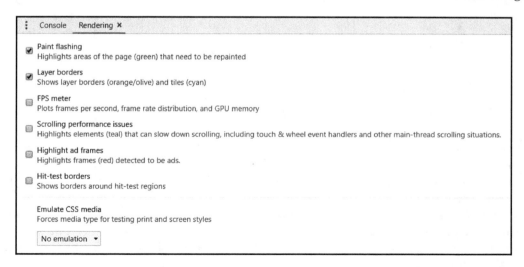

This tab can showcase a few items that we will be interested in when we are developing applications:

- First, when developing an application that is going to have a lot of data or a lot of eventing, it is suggested having the FPS meter turned on. This will not only let us know if our GPU is being utilized, but it will also show us if we are dropping frames due to constant repainting.
- Second, if we are developing an application that has a lot of scrolling (think of the infinite scrolling applications), then we will want to turn on the **Scrolling performance issues** section. This can notify us if there is an item or items in our application that can make the scrolling experience unresponsive.
- Finally, the **Paint flashing** option is great to see when there is a lot of dynamic content in our application. It will flash when a paint event has occurred and it will highlight the section that had to be repainted.

We are going to go through an application that is going to cause problems for most of these settings and see how we can improve the performance to make the user experience better. Open up the following file: `chrome_rendering.html`.

We should see a box in the top-left corner switching colors. If we turn on the **Paint flashing** option, we should now see a green box appearing whenever the box color changes.

This makes sense. Every time we recolor something, this means that the renderer has to repaint that location. Now, uncomment the following lines:

```
let appendCount = 0;
const append = function() {
    if( appendCount >= 100 ) {
        return clearInterval(append);
    }
    const temp = document.createElement('p');
    temp.textContent = `We are element ${appendCount}`;
    appendEl.appendChild(temp);
    appendCount += 1;
};
setInterval(append, 1000);
```

We should see elements being added at an interval of around 1 second. A couple of things are interesting. First, we still see that we are getting repainting done on the box that colors itself every second or so. But, on top of this, we will notice that the scrollbar is repainting itself. This means that the scrollbar is part of the rendering surface (some of you may know this since you can target scrollbars with CSS). But, what is also interesting is that when each element is added, it is not having to repaint the entire parent element; it is only painting where the child is being added.

So, a good question now would be: What happens if we prepend an element to our document? Comment out the lines of code that are changing the DOM and uncomment the following lines of code to see this in action:

```
setTimeout(() => {
    const prependElement = document.createElement('p');
    prependElement.textContent = 'we are being prepended to the entire
    DOM';
    document.body.prepend(prependElement);
}, 5000);
```

We can see that around five seconds into the lifetime of the document, both the element that we added and the red box that is sitting there have been repainted. Again, this makes sense. Chrome has to repaint anything that has changed when an update occurred. In terms of what our window looks like, this means it had to change the location of the box, and add in the text we added at the top, causing a repaint of both items.

Now, an interesting thing that we can look at is what happens if we make the element absolutely positioned with CSS. This would mean, in terms of what we see, that only the top portion of the rectangle and our text element should need a repaint. But, if we do this by making the position absolute, we will still see that Chrome had to repaint both elements.

Even if we change the line document.body.prepend to document.body.append, it will still paint both objects. Chrome has to do this because the box is one DOM object. It cannot repaint only parts of objects; it has to repaint the entire object.

A good thing to always remember is that when changing something in the document, what is it causing to reflow or repaint? Is adding a list item also causing other elements to move, change color, and so on? If it does, we may have to rethink our content hierarchy so we can ensure that we are causing the minimum amount of repainting in our document.

A final note on painting. We should see how painting works with the canvas element. The canvas element allows us to create 2D and 3D imagery through the 2D rendering context, or through the WebGL context. We will specifically focus on the 2D rendering context, but it should be noted that these rules also apply with the WebGL context.

Go ahead and comment out all of the code we have added so far and uncomment the following lines:

```
const context = canvasEl.getContext('2d');
context.fillStyle = 'green';
context.fillRect(10, 10, 10, 10);
context.fillStyle = 'red';
context.fillRect(20, 20, 10, 10);
setTimeout(() => {
```

```
    context.fillStyle = 'green';
    context.fillRect(30, 30, 10, 10);
}, 2000);
```

After about two seconds, we should see the addition of a green box to our little diagonal group of squares. What is interesting about this paint is that it only showed us a repaint for that little green square. Let's comment out that piece of code and add in the following code:

```
const fillStyles = ['green', 'red'];
const numOfRunsX = 15;
const numOfRunsY = 10;
const totalRuns = numOfRunsX * numOfRunsY;
let currX = 0;
let currY = 0;
let count = 0;
const paint = function() {
    context.fillStyle = fillStyles[count % 2];
    context.fillRect(currX, currY, 10, 10);
    if(!currX ) {
        currY += 10;
    }
    if( count === totalRuns ) {
        clearInterval(paint);
    }
}
setInterval(paint, 1000);
```

At intervals of about 1 second, we will see that it is truly only repainting where we say to paint. This can have huge implications for applications that need to be constantly changing the information that is on the page. If we find that we need to have something constantly update, it can actually be better to have it done in a canvas than to have it in the DOM. While the canvas API may not lend itself to being a rich environment, there are libraries out there that help with this.

 It is not suggested that every application out there is going to need the repainting capabilities of the canvas; it should be noted that most will not. However, every piece of technology that we talk through in this book is not going to solve 100% of the issues found in applications. One such issue is repainting problems and this can be solved with canvas-based solutions. Areas that the canvas is especially useful for are graphing and grid-based applications.

We will now look at the scroll option. This can help us when we have a long list of items. This may be in a tree-view, in an infinite scrolling application, or even in a grid-based application. At some point, we are going to run into serious slowdowns due to trying to render thousands of elements at a single time.

First, let's render 1,000,000 paragraph elements into our application with the following code:

```
for(let i = 0; i < 1000000; i++) {
    const temp = document.createElement('p');
    temp.textContent = `We are element ${i}`;
    appendEl.appendChild(temp);
}
```

While this may not seem like a real-world scenario, it does showcase how unfeasible infinitely loaded applications would be to run if we had to add everything to the DOM right away. So how would we handle this scenario? We would use something called deferred rendering. Essentially, we will have all of our objects in memory (in this case; for other use cases, we would continually make rest requests for more data) and we will add them as they should appear on the screen. We will need some code to do this.

 The following example is by no means a foolproof way of implementing deferred rendering. As with most of the code in this book, it takes a simple view to try to showcase a point. It can easily be built upon to create a real-world system for deferred rendering, but it is not something that should be copied and pasted.

A good way to start deferred rendering is to know how many elements we are going to have, or at least want to showcase in our list. For this, we are going to use a height of 460 pixels. On top of this, we are going to set our list elements to have a padding of 5 pixels and to be a height of 12 pixels with a 1-pixel border on the bottom. This means that each element will have a total height of 23 pixels. This would also mean that the number of elements that can be seen at one time is 20 (460 / 23).

Next, we set the height of our list by multiplying the number of items we have by the height of each item. This can be seen in the following code:

```
list.style.height = `${itemHeight * items.length}px`;
```

Now, we need to hold our index that we are currently at (the current 20 items on the screen) and measure when we get a scroll event. If we notice that we are above the threshold, we move to a new index and reset our list to hold that group of 20 elements. Finally, we set the top padding of our unordered list to the total height of the list minus what we have already scrolled by.

All of this can be seen in the following code:

```
const checkForNewIndex = function(loc) {
    let tIndex = Math.floor(Math.abs(loc) / ( itemHeight * numItemsOnScreen
     ));
    if( tIndex !== currIndex ) {
        currIndex = tIndex;
        const fragment = document.createDocumentFragment();
        fragment.append(...items.slice(currIndex * numItemsOnScreen,
         (currIndex + 2) * numItemsOnScreen));
        list.style.paddingTop = `${currIndex * containerHeight}px`;
        list.style.height = `${(itemHeight * items.length) - (currIndex *
         containerHeight)}px`;
        list.innerHTML = '';
        list.appendChild(fragment);
    }
}
```

So now that we have all of this, what do we put this function inside of? Well, since we are scrolling, logically, it would make sense to put it in the scroll handler of the list. Let's do that with the following code:

```
list.onwheel = function(ev) {
    checkForNewIndex(list.getBoundingClientRect().y);
}
```

Now, let's turn on the **Scrolling performance issues** option. If we reload the page, we will notice that it is highlighting our list and stating that the mousewheel event could be a potential bottleneck. This makes sense. Chrome notices that we are attaching a non-trivial piece of code to run on each wheel event so it shows us that we are going to potentially have issues.

Now, if we are on a regular desktop, we will most likely not have any issues, but if we add the following code, we can easily see what Chrome is trying to tell us:

```
const start = Date.now();
while( Date.now() < start + 1000 ) {; }
```

With that piece of code inside the wheel event, we can see the stuttering happen. Since we can now see stuttering and it being a potential bottleneck for scrolling, what's the next best option? Putting it in a setInterval, using requestAnimationFrame, or even using requestIdleCallback, with the last being the least optimal solution.

The **Rendering** tab can help flesh out quite a few issues that can crop up inside our applications and should become a regular tool for developers to figure out what is causing stuttering or performance problems in their applications.

These three tabs can help diagnose most problems and should be used quite frequently when developing an application.

jsPerf and benchmarking

We have come to the last section regarding high performance for the web and how we can easily assess whether our application is performing at peak efficiency. However, there are times when we are going to want to actually do true benchmarking, even if this may not give the best picture. jsPerf is one of these tools.

Now, great care has to be taken when creating a jsPerf test. First, we can run into optimizations that the browser does and that may skew results in favor of one implementation versus another. Next, we have to make sure that we run these tests in multiple browsers. As explained in a previous section, every browser runs a different JavaScript engine and this means that the creators have implemented them all differently. Finally, we need to make sure that we do not have any extraneous code in our tests, otherwise, the results can be skewed.

Let's look at a couple of scripts and see how they turn out based on running them inside jsPerf. So, let's begin:

1. Head on over to `https://jsperf.com`. If we want to create our own tests, we will have to sign in with our GitHub account, so go ahead and do this now.
2. Next, let's create our first performance test. The system is self-explanatory, but we will go over a couple of areas:

   - First, if we needed to add in some HTML code so that we could perform DOM manipulation, we would put this in the *preparation code HTML* section.
   - Next, we will put in any variables that we will need in all of our tests.
   - Finally, we can incorporate our test cases. Let's run a test.

3. The first test we will look at is utilizing a loop versus utilizing the `filter` function. We will not require any HTML for this, so we can leave this section blank.
4. Next, we will input the following code that will be needed by all of our test cases:

   ```
   const arr = new Array(10000);
   for(let i = 0; i < arr.length; i++) {
       arr[i] = i % 2 ? i : -1;
   }
   ```

5. Then, we will add in two different test cases, the `for` loop and the `filter` function. They should look like the following:

In the case of the loop:

```
const nArr = [];
for(let i = 0; i < arr.length; i++) {
    if( Math.abs(arr[i]) === arr[i]) {
        nArr.push(arr[i]);
    }
}
```

In the case of the filter:

```
const nArr = arr.filter(item => Math.abs(item) === item);
```

6. Now, we can save the test case and run the performance tester. Go ahead and hit the **Run** button and watch as the test runner goes over each piece of code multiple times. We should see something like the following:

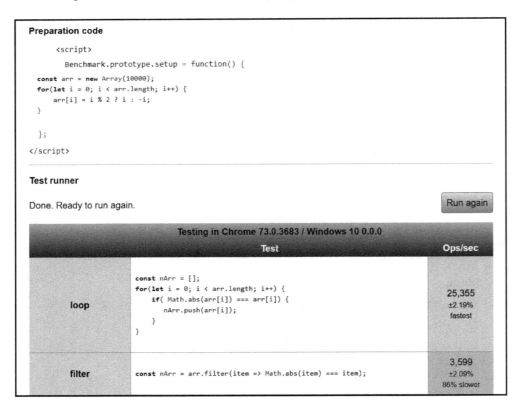

Well, as expected, the `for` loop performed better than the `filter` function. The breakdown of those three numbers on the right is as follows:

- The number of operations per second, or how many basic instructions the system could run in a single second.
- The variance in each test run for that specific test case. In the case of the `for` loop, it was plus or minus 2 percent.
- Finally, it will say whether it was the fastest, or how much slower than that it was. In the case of the filter, it was 86 percent slower.

Wow, that is quite significantly slower! In this case, we might think of a way for the filter to run more optimally. One way is that we might create the function ahead of time instead of creating an anonymous function. Near the bottom of our results, we will see a link for us to be able to add more tests. Let's head back into the test cases and add one for our new test.

Head near the bottom and there should be an **Add code snippet** button. Let's press this and fill in the details. We will call this new code snippet `filterFunctionDefined` and it should look something like the following:

```
const reducer = function(item) {
    return Math.abs(item) === item;
}
const nArr = arr.filter(reducer);
```

We can save this test case and rerun our results. The results seem to be almost exactly like the regular `filter` function. Some of this is due to our browsers optimizing our code for us. We can test these results in all of the browsers so we can get a better picture of how our code would function in each. But, even if we did run this elsewhere, we will see that the results are the same; the `filter` function is slower than a regular `for` loop.

 This is true for pretty much every array-based function. Helper functions are great, but they are also slower than regular loops. We will go into greater detail in the next chapter, but just realize ahead of time that most of the convenience that the browser gives us is going to be slower than just writing the function in a more straightforward manner.

Let's set up another test just to make sure we understand jsPerf.

First, create a new test. Let's perform a test on objects and see the difference between using a `for-in` loop versus a loop utilizing the `Object.keys()` method. Again, we will not need to utilize the DOM so we don't need to fill anything out for the HTML portion.

For our test setup, let's create a blank object and then fill it with a bunch of useless data utilizing the following code:

```
const obj = {};
for(let i = 0; i < 10000; i++) {
    obj[`item${i}`] = i;
}
```

Next, let's create two test cases, the first being call `for  in`, which should appear as follows:

```
const results = [];
for(let key in obj) {
    results.push([key, obj[key]]);
}
```

The second test case is the `Object.keys()` version, which appears as follows:

```
const results = [];
const keys = Object.keys(obj);
for(let i = 0; i < keys.length; i++) {
    results.push([keys[i], obj[keys[i]]]);
}
```

Now, if we run our test, we will notice that the `keys` version is able to do around 600 operations per second, while the `fo..in` version is able to do around 550. This one is fairly close so browser difference may actually come into play. When we start to get into minor differences, it is best to choose whichever was implemented later or is most likely to get optimizations.

 Most of the time, if something is just being implemented and the browser vendors agree to something being added, then it is probably in the early stages of development. If the performance results are within a tolerance that is allowed (usually around 5-10% difference), then it is best to go with the newer option. It is more likely to be optimized in the future.

All of this testing is amazing, and if we find something that we truly want to share with people, this is a great solution. But, what if we wanted to run these tests ourselves and not have to worry about an external site? Well, we can utilize the underlying library that jsPerf is using. It is called *Benchmark.js* and it is a great utility when we need to set up our own system for debugging code. We can find it at `https://benchmarkjs.com/`.

Let's grab the source code and set it as an external script in our HTML file. We will also need to add *Lodash* as a dependency. Next, let's write the same tests that we wrote before, but we are going to write them in our internal script and have it display the results on our screen. We will also only have it display the title of our script along with these results.

We can obviously make this a little fancier, but the focus will be on getting the library to properly benchmark for us.

We will have some setup code that will have an array of objects. These objects will have only two properties, the name of the test and the function that we want to run. In the case of our `for` loop versus our `filter` test, it would look like the following:

```
const forTest = Object.assign({}, testBaseObj);
forTest.title = 'for loop';
forTest.fun = function() {
    const arr = [];
    for(let i = 0; i < startup.length; i++) {
        if( Math.abs(startup[i]) === startup[i] ) {
            arr.push(startup[i]);
        }
    }
}
const filterTest = Object.assign({}, testBaseObj);
filterTest.title = 'filter';
filterTest.fun = function() {
    const arr = startup.filter((item) => Math.abs(item) === item);
}
const tests = [forTest, filterTest];
```

From here, we set up a benchmark suite and loop through our tests, adding them to the suite. We then add two listeners, one for a complete cycle so we can display it in our list, and the other on completion, so we can highlight the fastest running entry. It should look like the following:

```
const suite = new Benchmark.Suite;
for(let i = 0; i < tests.length; i++) {
    suite.add(tests[i].title, tests[i].fun);
}
suite.on('cycle', function(event) {
    const el = document.createElement('li');
    el.textContent = event.target;
    el.id = event.target.name;
    appendEl.appendChild(el);
})
.on('complete', function() {
    const fastest = this.filter('fastest').map('name');
    document.getElementById(fastest[0]).style.backgroundColor = 'green';
})
.run({ 'async' : true });
```

If we set all of this up, or if we run `benchmark.html`, we will see the output. There are many other cool statistics that we can get from the benchmark library. One of these is the standard deviation for each test. In the case of the `for` loop test that was run in Edge, it came out to around 0.004. Another interesting note is that we can look at each run and see the amount of time it took. Again, taking the `for` loop example, the Edge browser is slowly optimizing our code and also likely putting it into cache since the time keeps decreasing.

Summary

This chapter introduced many concepts for profiling and debugging our code. It took into account the various modern browsers that are out there and even the special features that each of them may or may not have. We specifically looked at the Chrome browser, since a good many developers use it as their main development browser. In addition to this, the V8 engine is used in Node.js, which means all of our Node.js code will use the V8 debugger. Finally, we took a look at utilizing jsPerf to find out what may be the best implementation of some piece of code. We even looked at the possibilities of running it in our own system and how we can implement this.

Looking forward, the remainder of the book will not specifically talk about any of these topics in such detail again, but these tools should be used when developing the code for the rest of the book. On top of this, we will be running almost all of the code in the Chrome browser, except for when we write GLSL, since Firefox has one of the best components for actually testing this code out. In the next chapter, we will be looking at immutability and when we should utilize it in development.

2
Immutability versus Mutability - The Balance between Safety and Speed

In recent years, development practices have moved to a more functional style of programming. This means less focus on mutable programming (changing variables instead of creating new ones when we want to modify something). Mutability happens when we change a variable from one thing to another. This could be updating a number, changing what the message says, or even changing the item from a string to a number. A mutable state leads to quite a few areas of programming pitfalls, such as undetermined state, deadlocking in multithreaded environments, and even the changing of data types when we did not mean to (also known as side effects). Now, we have many libraries and languages that help us curtail this behavior.

All of this has caused a push toward the use of immutable data structures and functions that create new objects based on the input. While this leads to fewer errors in terms of mutable state, it presents a host of other issues, predominantly, higher memory usage and lower speeds. Most JavaScript runtimes do not have optimizations that allow for this style of programming. When we are concerned with memory and speed, we need to have as much of an advantage as possible, and this is the advantage mutable programming gives us.

In this chapter, we are going to focus on the following topics:

- Current trends with immutability on the web
- Writing safe mutable code
- Functional-like programming on the web

Technical requirements

The following are prerequisites for this chapter:

- A web browser, preferably Chrome
- An editor; VS Code is preferred
- Knowledge of current state libraries such as Redux or Vuex
- The relevant code can be found at `https://github.com/PacktPublishing/Hands-On-High-Performance-Web-Development-with-JavaScript/tree/master/Chapter02`.

The current fascination with immutability

A look at current web trends shows the fascination with utilizing immutability. Libraries such as React can be used without their immutable state counterparts, but they are usually used along with Redux or Facebook's Flow library. Any of these libraries will showcase how immutability can lead to safer code and fewer bugs.

 For those of you who do not know, immutability means that we cannot change the variable once it has been set with data. This means that once we assign something to a variable, we can no longer change that variable. This helps prevent unwanted changes from happening, and can also lead to a concept called **pure functions**. We will not be going into what pure functions are, but just be aware that it is a concept that many functional programmers have been bringing to JavaScript.

But, does that mean we need it and does it lead to a faster system? In the case of JavaScript, it can depend. A well-managed project with documentation and testing can easily showcase how we would possibly not need these libraries. On top of this, we may need to actually mutate the state of an object. We may write to an object in one location, but have many other parts read from that object.

There are many patterns of development that can give us similar benefits to what immutability can without the overhead of creating a lot of temporary objects or even going into a fully pure functional style of programming. We can utilize systems such as **Resource Acquisition Is Initialization** (RAII). We may find that we want to use some immutability, and in this case, we can utilize built-in browser tools such as `Object.freeze()` or `Object.seal()`.

However, we are getting ahead of ourselves. Let's take a look at a couple of the libraries mentioned and see how they handle immutable states and how it could potentially lead to problems when we are coding.

A dive into Redux

Redux is a great state management system. When we are developing complex systems such as Google Docs or a reporting system that lets us look up various user statistics in real time, it can manage the state of our application. However, it can lead to some overly complicated systems that may not need the state management that it represents.

Redux takes the philosophy that no one object should be able to mutate the state of an application. All of that state needs to be hosted in a single location and there should be functions that handle state changes. This would mean a single location for writes, and multiple locations able to read the data. This is similar to some concepts that we will want to utilize later.

However, it does take things a step further and many articles will want us to pass back brand-new objects. There is a reason for this. Many objects, especially those that have multiple layers, are not easy to copy off. Simple copy operations, such as using `Object.assign({}, obj)` or utilizing the spread operator for arrays, will just copy the references that they hold inside. Let's take a look at an example of this before we write a Redux-based application.

If we open up `not_deep_copy.html` from our repository, we will see that the console prints the same thing. If we take a look at the code, we will see a very common case of copying objects and arrays:

```
const newObj = Object.assign({}, obj);
const newArr = [...arr];
```

If we make this only a single layer deep, we will see that it actually executes a copy. The following code will showcase this:

```
const obj2 = {item : 'thing', another : 'what'};
const arr2 = ['yes', 'no', 'nope'];

const newObj2 = Object.assign({}, obj2);
const newArr2 = [...arr2]
```

We will go into more detail regarding this case and how to truly execute a deep copy, but we can begin to see how Redux may hide problems that are still in our system. Let's build out a simple Todo application to at least showcase Redux and what it is capable of. So, let's begin:

1. First, we will need to pull down Redux. We can do this by utilizing **Node Package Manager** (**npm**) and installing it in our system. It is as simple as npm install redux.

2. We will now go into the newly created folder and grab the redux.min.js file and put it into our working directory.

3. We now will create a file called todo_redux.html. This will house all of our main logic.

4. At the top of it, we will add the Redux library as a dependency.

5. We will then add in the actions that we are going to perform on our store.

6. We will then set up the reducers that we want to use for our application.

7. We will then set up the store and prepare it for data changes.

8. We will then subscribe to those data changes and make updates to the UI.

   The example that we are working on is a slightly modified version of the Todo application from the Redux example. The one nice thing is that we will be utilizing the vanilla DOM and not utilizing another library such as React, so we can see how Redux can fit into any application if the need arises.

9. So, our actions are going to be adding a todo element, toggling a todo element to complete or not complete, and setting the todo elements that we want to see. This code appears as follows:

```
const addTodo = function(test) {
    return { type : ACTIONS.ADD_TODO, text };
}
const toggleTodo = function(index) {
    return { type : ACTIONS.TOGGLE_TODO, index };
}
const setVisibilityFilter = function(filter) {
    return { type : ACTIONS.SET_VISIBILITY_FILTER, filter };
}
```

10. Next, the reducers will be separated, with one for our visibility filter and another for the actual todo elements.

The visibility reducer is quite simple. It checks the type of action and, if it is a type of SET_VISIBILITY_FILTER, we will handle it, otherwise, we just pass the state object on. For our todo reducer, if we see an action of ADD_TODO, we will return a new list of items with our item at the bottom. If we toggle one of the items, we return a new list with that item set to the opposite of what it was set to. Otherwise, we just pass the state object on. All of this looks like the following:

```
const visibilityFilter = function(state = 'SHOW_ALL', action) {
    switch(action.type) {
        case 'SET_VISIBILITY_FILTER': {
            return action.filter;
        }
        default: {
            return state;
        }
    }
}

const todo = function(state = [], action) {
    switch(action.type) {
        case 'ADD_TODO': {
            return [
                ...state,
                {
                    text : action.text,
                    completed : false
                }
            ]
        }
        case 'TOGGLE_TODO': {
            return state.map((todo, index) => {
                if( index === action.index ) {
                    return Object.assign({}, todo, {
                        completed : !todo.completed
                    });
                }
                return todo;
            }
        }
        default: {
            return state;
        }
    }
}
```

11. After this, we put both reducers into a single reducer and set up the `state` object.

The heart of our logic lies in UI implementation. Notice that we set this up to work off the data. This means that data could be passed into our function and the UI would update accordingly. We could make it the other way around, but making the UI be driven by data is a good paradigm to live by. We first have a previous state store. We can utilize this further by only updating what was actually updated, but we only use it for the first check. We grab the current state and check the differences between the two. If we see that the length has changed, we know that we should add a `todo` item. If we see that the visibility filter was changed, we will update the UI accordingly. Finally, if neither of these is true, we will go through and check which item was checked or unchecked. The code looks like the following:

```
store.subscribe(() =>
    const state = store.getState();
    // first type of actions ADD_TODO
    if( prevState.todo.length !== state.todo.length ) {
     container.appendChild(createTodo(state.todo[state.todo.length
     - 1].text));
    // second type of action SET_VISIBILITY_FILTER
    } else if( prevState.visibilityFilter !==
      state.visibilityFilter ) {
        setVisibility(container.children, state);
    // final type of action TOGGLE_TODO
    } else {
        const todos = container.children;
        for(let i = 0; i < todos.length; i++) {
            if( state.todo[i].completed ) {
                todos[i].classList.add('completed');
            } else {
                todos[i].classList.remove('completed');
            }
        }
    }
    prevState = state;
});
```

If we run this, we should get a simple UI that we can interact with in the following ways:

- Add `todo` items.
- Mark existing `todo` items as complete.

We are also able to have a different view of it by clicking on one of the three buttons at the bottom as seen in the following screenshot. If we only want to see all of our completed tasks, we can click the Update button.

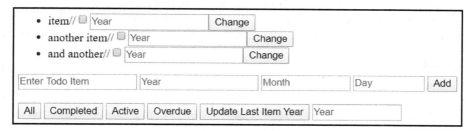

Now, we are able to save the state for offline storage if we wanted to, or we could send the state back to a server for constant updates. This is what makes Redux quite nice. However, there are some caveats when working with Redux that relate to what we stated previously:

1. First, we are going to need to add something to our Todo application to be able to handle nested objects in our state. A piece of information that has been left out of this Todo application is setting a date by when we want to complete that item. So, let's add some fields for us to fill out to set a completion date. We will add in three new number inputs like so:

   ```
   <input id="year" type="number" placeholder="Year" />
   <input id="month" type="number" placeholder="Month" />
   <input id="day" type="number" placeholder="Day" />
   ```

2. Then, we will add in another filter type of `Overdue`:

   ```
   <button id="SHOW_OVERDUE">Overdue</button>
   ```

3. Make sure to add this to the `visibilityFilters` object. Now, we need to update our `addTodo` action. We are also going to pass on a `Date` object. This also means we will need to update our `ADD_TODO` case to add the `action.date` to our new `todo` object. We will then update our `onclick` handler for our **Add** button and adjust it with the following:

   ```
   const year = document.getElementById('year');
   const month = document.getElementById('month');
   const day = document.getElementById('day');
   store.dispatch(addTodo(input.value), {year : year.value, month :
   month.value, day : day.value}));
   year.value = "";
   month.value = "";
   day.value = "";
   ```

4. We could hold the date as a `Date` object (this would make more sense), but to showcase the issue that can arise, we are just going to hold a new object with `year`, `month`, and `day` fields. We will then showcase this date on the Todo application by adding another `span` element and populating it with the values from these fields. Finally, we will need to update our `setVisibility` method with the logic to show our overdue items. It should look like the following:

```
case visibilityFilters.SHOW_OVERDUE: {
    const currTodo = state.todo[i];
    const tempTime = currTodo.date;
    const tempDate = new
Date(`${tempTime.year}/${tempTime.month}/${tempTime.day}`);
    if( tempDate < currDay && !currTodo.completed ) {
        todos[i].classList.remove('hide');
    } else {
        todos[i].classList.add('hide');
    }
}
```

With all of this, we should now have a working Todo application, along with showcasing our overdue items. Now, this is where it can get messy working with state management systems such as Redux. What happens when we want to make modifications to an already created item and it is not a simple flat object? Well, we could just get that item and update it in the state system. Let's add the code for this:

1. First, we are going to create a new button and input that will change the year of the last entry. We will add a click handler for the **Update** button:

```
document.getElementById('UPDATE_LAST_YEAR').onclick = function(e) {
    store.dispatch({ type : ACTIONS.UPDATE_LAST_YEAR, year :
      document.getElementById('updateYear').value });
}
```

2. We will then add in this new action handler for the `todo` system:

```
case 'UPDATE_LAST_YEAR': {
    const prevState = state;
    const tempObj = Object.assign({}, state[state.length -
      1].date);
    tempObj.year = action.year;
    state[state.length - 1].date = tempObj;
    return state;
}
```

Now, if we run our code with our system, we will notice something. Our code is not getting past the check object condition in our subscription:

```
if( prevState === state ) {
    return;
}
```

We updated the state directly, and so Redux never created a new object because it did not detect a change (we updated an object's value that we do not have a reducer on directly). Now, we could create another reducer specifically for the date, but we can also just recreate the array and pass it through:

```
case 'UPDATE_LAST_YEAR': {
    const prevState = state;
    const tempObj = Object.assign({}, state[state.length - 1].date);
    tempObj.year = action.year;
    state[state.length - 1].date = tempObj;
    return [...state];
}
```

Now, our system detects that there was a change and we are able to go through our methods to update the code.

> The better implementation would be to split out our `todo` reducer into two separate reducers. But, since we are working on an example, it was made as simple as possible.

With all of this, we can see how we need to play by the rules that Redux has laid out for us. While this tool can be of great benefit for us in large-scale applications, for smaller state systems or even componentized systems, we may find it better to have a true mutable state and work on it directly. As long as we control access to that mutable state, then we are able to fully utilize a mutable state to our advantage.

> This is not to take anything away from Redux. It is a wonderful library and it performs well even under heavier loads. But, there are times when we want to work directly with a dataset and mutate it directly. Redux can do this and gives us its event system, but we are able to build this ourselves without all of the other pieces that Redux gives us. Remember that we want to slim the codebase down as much as possible and make it as efficient as possible. Extra methods and extra calls can add up when we are working with tens to hundreds of thousands of data items.

With this introduction into Redux and state management systems complete, we should also take a look at a library that makes immutable systems a requirement: Immutable.js.

Immutable.js

Again, utilizing immutability, we can code in an easier-to-understand fashion. However, it will usually mean we can't scale to the levels that we need for truly high-performance applications.

First, Immutable.js takes a great stab at the functional-style data structures and methods needed to create a functional system in JavaScript. This usually leads to cleaner code and cleaner architecture. But, what we get in terms of these advantages leads to a decrease in speed and/or an increase in memory.

Remember, when we're working with JavaScript, we have a single-threaded environment. This means that we do not really have deadlocks, race conditions, or read/write access problems.

 We can actually run into these issues when utilizing something like `SharedArrayBuffers` between workers or different tabs, but that is a discussion for later chapters. For now, we are working in a single-threaded environment where the issues of multi-core systems do not really crop up.

Let's take a real-world example of a use case that can come up. We want to turn a list of lists into a list of objects (think of a CSV). What might the code look like to build this data structure in plain old JavaScript, and another one utilizing the Immutable.js library? Our Vanilla JavaScript version may appear as follows:

```
const fArr = new Array(fillArr.length - 1);
const rowSize = fillArr[0].length;
const keys = new Array(rowSize);
for(let i = 0; i < rowSize; i++) {
    keys[i] = fillArr[0][i];
}
for(let i = 1; i < fillArr.length; i++) {
    const obj = {};
    for(let j = 0; j < rowSize; j++) {
        obj[keys[j]] = fillArr[i][j];
    }
    fArr[i - 1] = obj;
}
```

We construct a new array of the size of the input list minus one (the first row is the keys). We then store the row size instead of computing that each time for the inner loop later. Then, we create another array to hold the keys and we grab those from the first index of the input array. Next, we loop through the rest of the entries in the input and create objects. We then loop through each inner array and set the key to the value and location j, and set the value to the input's i and j values.

Reading in data through nested arrays and loops can be confusing, but results in fast read times. On a dual-core processor with 8 GB of RAM, this code took 83 ms.

Now, let's build something similar in Immutable.js. It should look like the following:

```
const l = Immutable.List(fillArr);
const _k = Immutable.List(fillArr[0]);
const tFinal = l.map((val, index) => {
    if(!index ) return;
    return Immutable.Map(_k.zip(val));
});
const final = tfinal.shift();
```

This is much easier to interpret if we understand functional concepts. First, we want to create a list based on our input. We then create another temporary list for the keys called _k. For our temporary final list, we utilize the map function. If we are at the 0 index, we just return from the function (since this is the keys). Otherwise, we return a new map that is created by zipping the keys list with the current value. Finally, we remove the front of the final list since it will be undefined.

This code is wonderful in terms of readability, but what are the performance characteristics of this? On a current machine, this ran in around 1 second. This is a big difference in terms of speed. Let's see how they compare in terms of memory usage.

Settled memory (what the memory goes back to after running the code) appears to be the same, settling back to around 1.2 MB. However, the peak memory for the immutable version is around 110 MB, whereas the Vanilla JavaScript version only gets to 48 MB, so a little under half the memory usage. Let's take a look at another example and see the results that transpire.

We are going to create an array of values, except we want one of the values to be incorrect. So, we will set the 50,000th index to be wrong with the following code:

```
const tempArr = new Array(100000);
for(let i = 0; i < tempArr.length; i++) {
    if( i === 50000 ) { tempArr[i] = 'wrong'; }
    else { tempArr[i] = i; }
}
```

Then, we will loop over a new array with a simple `for` loop like so:

```
const mutArr = Array.apply([], tempArr);
const errs = [];
for(let i = 0; i < mutArr.length; i++) {
    if( mutArr[i] !== i ) {
        errs.push(`Error at loc ${i}. Value : ${mutArr[i]}`);
        mutArr[i] = i;
    }
}
```

We will also test the built-in `map` function:

```
const mut2Arr = Array.apply([], tempArr);
const errs2 = [];
const fArr = mut2Arr.map((val, index) => {
    if( val !== index ) {
        errs2.push(`Error at loc: ${index}. Value : ${val}`);
        return index;
    }
    return val;
});
```

Finally, here's the immutable version:

```
const immArr = Immutable.List(tempArr);
const ierrs = [];
const corrArr = immArr.map((item, index) => {
    if( item !== index ) {
        ierrs.push(`Error at loc ${index}. Value : ${item}`);
        return index;
    }
    return item;
});
```

If we run these instances, we will see that the fastest will go between the basic `for` loop and the built-in `map` function. The immutable version is still eight times slower than the others. What happens when we increase the number of incorrect values? Let's add a random number generator for building our temporary array to give a random number of errors and see how they perform. The code should appear as follows:

```
for(let i = 0; i < tempArr.length; i++) {
    if( Math.random() < 0.4 ) {
        tempArr[i] = 'wrong';
    } else {
        tempArr[i] = i;
    }
}
```

Running the same test, we get roughly an average of a tenfold slowdown with the immutable version. Now, this is not to say that the immutable version will not run faster in certain cases since we only touched on the map and list features of it, but it does bring up the point that immutability comes at a cost in terms of memory and speed when applying it to JavaScript libraries.

We will look in the next section at why mutability can lead to some issues, but also at how we can handle it by utilizing similar ideas to how Redux works with data.

 There is always a time and a place for different libraries, and this is not to say that Immutable.js or libraries like it are bad. If we find that our datasets are small or other considerations come into play, Immutable.js might work for us. But, when we are working on high-performance applications, this usually means two things. One, we will get a large amount of data in a single hit or second, and second, we will get a bunch of events that lead to a lot of data build-up. We need to use the most efficient means possible and these are usually built into the runtime that we are utilizing.

Writing safe mutable code

Before we move on to writing safe mutable code, we need to discuss references and values. A value can be considered anything that is a primitive type. Primitive types, in JavaScript, are anything that are not considered objects. To put it simply, numbers, strings, Booleans, null, and undefined are values. This means that if you create a new variable and assign it to the original, it will actually give it a new value. What does this mean for our code then? Well, we saw earlier with Redux that it was not able to see that we updated a property in our state system, so our previous state and current state showed they were the same. This is due to a shallow equality test. This basic test tests whether the two variables that were passed in are pointing to the same object. A simple example of this is seen with the following code:

```
let x = {};
let y = x;
console.log( x === y );
y = Object.assign({}, x);
console.log( x === y );
```

We will see that the first version says that the two items are equal. But, when we create a copy of the object, it states that they are not equal. y now has a brand-new object and this means that it points to a new location in memory. While a deeper understanding of *pass by value* and *pass by reference* can be good, this should be sufficient to move on to mutable code.

When writing safe mutable code, we want to give the illusion that we are writing immutable code. In other words, the interface should look like we are utilizing immutable systems, but we are instead utilizing mutable systems internally. Hence, there is a separation of the interface from the implementation.

We can make the implementation very fast by writing in a mutable way but give an interface that looks immutable. An example of this is as follows:

```
Array.prototype._map = function(fun) {
    if( typeof fun !== 'function' ) {
        return null;
    }
    const arr = new Array(this.length);
    for(let i = 0; i < this.length; i++) {
        arr[i] = fun(this[i]);
    }
    return arr;
}
```

We have written a _map function on the array prototype so that every array gets it and we write a simple map function. If we now test run this code, we will see that some browsers perform better with this, while others perform better with the built-in option. As stated before, the built-ins will eventually get faster, but, more often than not, a simple loop is going to be faster. Let's now look at another example of a mutable implementation, but with an immutable interface:

```
Array.prototype._reduce = function(fun, initial=null) {
    if( typeof fun !== 'function' ) {
        return null;
    }
    let val = initial ? initial : this[0];
    const startIndex = initial ? 0 : 1;
    for(let i = startIndex; i < this.length; i++) {
        val = fun(val, this[i], i, this);
    }
    return val;
}
```

We wrote a reduce function that performs better in every browser. Now, it does not have the same amount of type checking, which could lead to better performance, but it does showcase how we can write functions that can perform better but give the same type of interface that a user of our system expects.

What we have talked about so far is if we were writing a library for someone to use to make their lives easier. What happens if we are writing something that we or an internal team is going to utilize, as is the case for most application developers?

We have two options in this case. First, we may find that we are working on a legacy system and that we are going to have to try to program in a similar style to what has already been done, or we are developing something rather new and we are able to start off from scratch.

 Writing legacy code is a hard job and most people will usually get it wrong. While we should be aiming to improve on the code base, we are also trying to match the style. It is especially difficult for developers to walk through the code and see 10 different code choices used because 10 different developers have worked on the project over its lifespan. If we are working on something that someone else has written, it is usually better to match the code style than to come up with something completely different.

With a new system, we are able to write how we want and, with proper documentation, we can write something that is quite fast but is also easy for someone else to pick up. In this case, we can write mutable code that may have side effects in the functions, but we are able to document these cases.

Side effects are conditions that occur when a function does not just return a new variable or even a reference that the variable passed in. It is when we update another variable that we do not have current scope over that this constitutes a side effect. An example of this is as follows:

```
var glob = 'a single point system';
const implement = function(x) {
    glob = glob.concat(' more');
    return x += 2;
}
```

We have a global variable called `glob` that we are changing inside our function. Technically, this function has scope over `glob`, but we should try to define the scope of implement to be only what was passed into it and the temporary variables that implement have defined inside. Since we are mutating `glob`, we have introduced a side effect into our code base.

Now, in some situations, side effects are needed. We may need to update a single point, or we may need to store something in a single location, but we should try to implement an interface that does this for us instead of us directly affecting the global item (this should start to sound a lot like Redux). By writing a function or two to affect the out-of-scope items, we can now diagnose where an issue may come in because we have those single points of entry.

So what might this look like? We could create a state object just as a plain old object. Then, we could write a function on the global scope called `updateState` that would look like the following:

```
const updateState = function(update) {
    const x = Object.keys(update);
    for(let i = 0; i < x.length; i++) {
        state[x[i]] = update[x[i]];
    }
}
```

Now, while this may be good, we are still vulnerable to someone updating our state object through the actual global property. Luckily, by making our state object and our function `const`, we can make sure that erroneous code cannot touch these actual names. Let's update our code so our state is protected from being updated directly. There are two ways that we could do this. The first approach would be to code with modules and then our state objects which will be scoped to that module. We will look at modules and the import syntax further in the book. Instead, on this occasion, we are going to use the second method, code the **Immediately Invoked Function Expression (IIFE)** way. The following showcases this implementation:

```
const state = {};
(function(scope) {
    const _state = {};
    scope.update = function(obj) {
        const x = Object.keys(obj);
        for(let i = 0; i < x.length; i++) {
            _state[x[i]] = obj[x[i]];
        }
    }
    scope.set = function(key, val) {
        _state[key] = val;
    }
    scope.get = function(key) {
        return _state[key];
    }
    scope.getAll = function() {
        return Object.assign({}, _state);
    }
}) (state);
Object.freeze(state);
```

First, we create a constant state. We then IIFE and pass in the state object, setting a bunch of functions on it. It works on an internally `scoped _state` variable. We then have all the basic functions that we would expect for an internal state system. We also freeze the external state object so it can no longer be messed with. One question that may arise is why we are passing back a new object instead of a reference. If we are trying to make sure that we don't want anyone able to touch the internal state, then we cannot pass a reference out; we have to pass a new object.

We still have a problem. What happens if we want to update more than one layer deep? We will start running into reference issues again. That means that we will need to update our update function to perform a deep update. We can do this in a variety of ways, but one way would be to pass the value in as a string and we will split on the decimal point.

 This is not the best way to handle this since we could technically have a property of an object be named with decimal points, but it will allow us to write something quickly. Balancing between writing something that is functional, and what is considered a complete solution, are two different things and they have to be balanced when writing high-performance code bases.

So, we will have a method that will now look like the following:

```
const getNestedProperty = function(key) {
    const tempArr = key.split('.');
    let temp = _state;
    while( tempArr.length > 1 ) {
        temp = temp[tempArr.shift()];
        if( temp === undefined ) {
            throw new Error('Unable to find key!');
        }
    }
    return {obj : temp, finalKey : tempArr[0] };
}
scope.set = function(key, val) {
    const {obj, finalKey} = getNestedProperty(key);
    obj[finalKey] = val;
}
scope.get = function(key) {
    const {obj, finalKey} = getNestedProperty(key);
    return obj[finalKey];
}
```

What we are doing is breaking the key upon the decimal character. We are also grabbing a reference to the internal state object. While we still have items in the list, we move one level down in the object. If we find that it is undefined, then we will throw an error. Otherwise, once we are one level above where we want to be, we return an object with that reference and the final key. We will then use this in the getter and setter to replace those values.

Now, we still have a problem. What if we want to make a reference type be the property value for our internal state system? Well, we will run into the same issues that we saw before. We will have references outside the single state object. This means we will have to clone each step of the way to make sure that the external reference does not point to anything in the internal copy. We can create this system by adding a bunch of checks and making sure that when we get to a reference type, we clone it in a way that is efficient. This looks like the following code:

```
const _state = {},
checkPrimitives = function(item) {
    return item === null || typeof item === 'boolean' || typeof item ===
    'string' || typeof item === 'number' || typeof item === 'undefined';
},
cloneFunction = function(fun, scope=null) {
    return fun.bind(scope);
},
cloneObject = function(obj) {
    const newObj = {};
    const keys = Object.keys(obj);
    for(let i = 0; i < keys.length; i++) {
        const key = keys[i];
        const item = obj[key];
        newObj[key] = runUpdate(item);
    }
    return newObj;
},
cloneArray = function(arr) {
    const newArr = new Array(arr.length);
    for(let i = 0; i < arr.length; i++) {
        newArr[i] = runUpdate(arr[i]);
    }
    return newArr;
},
runUpdate = function(item) {
    return checkPrimitives(item) ?
        item :
        typeof item === 'function' ?
            cloneFunction(item) :
        Array.isArray(item) ?
            cloneArray(item) :
```

```
            cloneObject(item);
};

scope.update = function(obj) {
    const x = Object.keys(obj);
    for(let i = 0; i < x.length; i++) {
        _state[x[i]] = runUpdate(obj[x[i]]);
    }
}
```

What we have done is write a simple clone system. Our update function will go through the keys and run the update. We will then check for various conditions, such as if we are a primitive type. If we are, we just copy the value, otherwise, we need to figure out the complex type we are. We first search to see whether we are a function; if we are, we just bind the value. If we are an array, we will run through all of the values and make sure that none of them are complex types. Finally, if we are an object, we will run through all of the keys and try to update these running the same checks.

However, we have just done what we have been avoiding; we have created an immutable state system. We can add more bells and whistles to this centralized state system, such as eventing, or we can implement a coding standard that has been around for quite some time, called **Resource Allocation Is Initialization (RAII)**.

 There is a really nice built-in web API called **proxies**. These are essentially systems where we are able to do something when something happens on an object. At the time of writing, these are still quite slow and should not really be used unless it is on an object that we are not worried about for time-sensitive activities. We are not going to talk about them extensively, but they are available for those readers who want to check them out.

Resource allocation is initialization (RAII)

The idea of RAII comes from C++, where we have no such thing as a memory manager. We encapsulate logic where we potentially want to share resources that need to be freed after their use. This makes sure that we do not have memory leaks, and that objects that are utilizing the item are doing so in a safe manner. Another name for this is **scope-bound resource management (SBRM)**, and is also utilized in another recent language called Rust.

We can apply the same types of ideas that C++ and Rust do in terms of RAII in our JavaScript code. There are a couple of ways that we can handle this and we are going to look at them. The first is the idea that when we pass an object into a function, we can then null out that object from our calling function.

Now, we will have to use `let` instead of `const` in most cases for this to work, but it is a useful paradigm to make sure that we are only holding on to objects that we need.

This concept can be seen in the following code:

```
const getData = function() {
    return document.getElementById('container').value;
};
const encodeData = function(data) {
    let te = new TextEncoder();
    return te.encode(data);
};
const hashData = function(algorithm) {
    let str = getData();
    let finData = encodeData(str);
    str = null;
    return crypto.subtle.digest(algorithm, finData);
};
{
    let but = document.getElementById('submit');
    but.onclick = function(ev) {
        let algos = ['SHA-1', 'SHA-256', 'SHA-384', 'SHA-512'];
        let out = document.getElementById('output');
        for(let i = 0; i < algos.length; i++) {
            const newEl = document.createElement('li');
            hashData(algos[i]).then((res) => {
                let te = new TextDecoder();
                newEl.textContent = te.decode(res);
                out.append(newEl);
            });
        }
        out = null;
    }
    but = null;
}
```

If we run the following code, we will notice that we are trying to append to a `null`. This is where this design can get us into a bit of trouble. We have an asynchronous method and we are trying to use a value that we have nullified even though we still need it. What is the best way to handle this situation? One way is to `null` it out once we are done using it. Hence, we can change the code to look like the following:

```
for(let i = 0; i < algos.length; i++) {
    let temp = out;
    const newEl = document.createElement('li');
    hashData(algos[i]).then((res) => {
        let te = new TextDecoder();
```

```
        newEl.textContent = te.decode(res);
        temp.append(newEl);
        temp = null
    });
}
```

We still have a problem. Before the next part of the `Promise` (the `then` method) runs, we could still modify the value. One final good idea would be to wrap this input to output in a new function. This will give us the safety that we are looking for, while also making sure we are following the principle behind RAII. The following code is what comes out of this:

```
const showHashData = function(parent, algorithm) {
    const newEl = document.createElement('li');
    hashData(algorithm).then((res) => {
        let te = new TextDecoder();
        newEl.textContent = te.decode(res);
        parent.append(newEl);
    });
}
```

We can also get rid of some of the preceding nulls since the functions will take care of those temporary variables. While this example is rather trivial, it does showcase one way of handling RAII inside JavaScript.

On top of this paradigm, we can also add properties to the item that we are passing to say that it is a read-only version. This would ensure that we are not modifying the item, but we also do not need to `null` out the element on the calling function if we still want to read from it. This gives us the benefit of making sure our objects can be utilized and maintained without the worry that they will be modified.

We will take out the previous code example and update it to utilize this read-only property. We first define a function that will add it to any object that comes in like so:

```
const addReadableProperty = function(item) {
    Object.defineProperty(item, 'readonly', {
        value : true,
        writable :false
    });
    return item;
}
```

Next, in our `onclick` method, we pass our output into this method. This has now attached the `readonly` property to it. Finally, in our `showHashData` function, when we try to access it, we have put a guard on the `readonly` property. If we notice that the object has it, we will not try to append to it, like so:

```
if(!parent.readonly ) {
    parent.append(newEl);
}
```

We have also set this property to not be writable, so if a nefarious actor decided to manipulate our object's `readonly` property, they will still notice that we are no longer appending to the DOM. The `defineProperty` method is very powerful for writing APIs and libraries that cannot be easily manipulated. Another way of handling this is to freeze the object. With the `freeze` method, we are able to make sure that the shallow copy of an object is read-only. Remember that this is only for the shallow instance, not any other properties that hold reference types.

Finally, we can utilize a counter to see whether we can set the data. We are essentially creating a read-side lock. This means that while we are reading the data, we do not want to set the data. This means we have to take many precautions that we are properly releasing the data once we have read what we want. This can look like the following:

```
const ReaderWriter = function() {
    let data = {};
    let readers = 0;
    let readyForSet = new CustomEvent('readydata');
    this.getData = function() {
        readers += 1;
        return data;
    }
    this.releaseData = function() {
        if( readers ) {
            readers -= 1;
            if(!readers ) {
                document.dispatchEvent(readyForSet);
            }
        }
        return readers;
    }
    this.setData = function(d) {
        return new Promise((resolve, reject) => {
            if(!readers ) {
                data = d;
                resolve(true);
            } else {
                document.addEventListener('readydata', function(e) {
```

```
                data = d;
                resolve(true);
            }, { once : true });
        }
    });
    }
}
```

What we have done is set up a constructor function. We hold the data, the number of readers, and a custom event as private variables. We then create three methods. First, getData will grab the data and also add a counter to someone that is utilizing it. Next, we have the release method. This will decrement the counter, and if we are at 0, we will dispatch an event to tell the setData event that it can finally write to the mutable state. Finally, we have the setData function. A promise will be the return value. If there is no one that is holding the data, we will set it and resolve it right away. Otherwise, we will set up an event listener for our custom event. Once it fires, we will set the data and resolve the promise.

Now, this final method of locking mutable data should not be utilized in most contexts. There may only be a handful of times when you will want to utilize this, such as a hot cache where we need to make sure that we do not overwrite something while a reader is reading from this (this can happen on the Node.js side of things especially).

All of these methods help create a safe mutable state. With each of these, we are able to mutate an object directly and share that memory space. Most of the time, good documentation and careful control over our data will make it so we do not need to go to the extremes that we have here, but it is good to have these methods of RAII in our back pocket when we find something crops up and we are mutating something that we should not be.

Most of the time, the immutable and highly functional code will be more readable in the end and, if something does not need to be highly optimized, it is suggested to go for being readable. But, in high optimization cases, such as encoding and decoding or decorating columns in a table, we will need to squeeze out as much performance as we can. This will be seen later in the book where we utilize a mixture of programming techniques.

Even though mutable programming can be fast, sometimes, we want to implement things in a functional manner. The following section will explore ways to implement programs in this functional manner.

Functional style programming

Even after all of this talk about functional concepts not being the best in terms of raw speed, it can still be quite helpful to utilize them in JavaScript. There are many languages out there that are not purely functional and all of these give us the ability to utilize the best ideas from many paradigms. Languages such as F# and Scala come to mind. There are a few ideas that are great when it comes to this style of programming and we can utilize them in JavaScript with built-in concepts.

Lazy evaluation

In JavaScript, we can perform what is called lazy evaluation. Lazy evaluation means that the program does not run what it does not need to. One way of thinking about this is when someone is given a list of answers to a problem and they are told to put the correct answer to the problem. If they see that the answer was the second item that they looked at, they are not going to keep going through the rest of the answers they were given; they are going to stop at the second item. The way we use lazy evaluation in JavaScript is with generators.

Generators are functions that will pause execution until the `next` method is called on them. A simple example of this is shown as follows:

```
const simpleGenerator = function*() {
    let it = 0;
    for(;;) {
        yield it;
        it++;
    }
}

const sg = simpleGenerator();
for(let i = 0; i < 10; i++) {
    console.log(sg.next().value);
}
sg.return();
console.log(sg.next().value);
```

First, we notice that `function` has a star next to it. This shows that this is a generator function. Next, we set up a simple variable to hold our value and then we have an infinite loop. Some may think that this will run continuously, but lazy evaluation shows that we will only run up to the `yield`. This `yield` means we will pause execution here and that we can grab the value that we send back.

So, we start the function up. We have nothing to pass to it so we just simply start it. Next, we call `next` on the generator and grab the value. This gives us a single iteration and returns whatever was on the `yield` statement. Finally, we call `return` to say that we are done with this generator. If we wanted to, we can grab the final value here.

Now, we will notice that when we call next and try to grab the value, it returns undefined. We can take a look at the generator and notice that it has a property called `done`. This can allow us to see with finite generators if they are finished. So, how can this be helpful when we want to do something? A rather trivial example is a timing function. What we will do is start off the timer before we want to time something and then we will call it another time to calculate the time it took for something to run (very similar to `console.time` and `timeEnd`, but it should showcase what is available with generators).

This generator could look like the following:

```
const timing = function*(time) {
    yeild Date.now() - time;
}
const time = timing(Date.now());
let sum = 0;
for(let i = 0; i < 1000000; i++) {
    sum = sum + i;
}
console.log(time.next().value);
```

We are now timing a simple summing function. All this does is seed the timing generator with the current time. Once the next function is called, it runs the statements up to the `yield` and returns the value held in the `yield`. This will give us a new time against the time that we passed in. We now have a simple function for timings. This can be especially useful for environments where we may not have access to the console and we are going to log this information somewhere else.

Just as shown in the preceding code block, we can also work with many different types of lazy loading. One of the best types that utilize this interface is streams. Streams have been available inside Node.js for quite some time, but the stream interface for browsers has a basic standardization and certain parts are still under debate. A simple example of this type of lazy loading or lazy reading can be seen in the following code:

```
const nums = function*(fn=null) {
    let i = 0;
    for(;;) {
        yield i;
        if( fn ) {
            i += fn(i);
        } else {
```

```
            i += 1;
        }
    }
}
const data = {};
const gen = nums();
for(let i of gen) {
    console.log(i);
    if( i > 100 ) {
        break;
    }
    data.push(i);
}

const fakestream = function*(data) {
    const chunkSize = 10;
    const dataLength = data.length;
    let i = 0;
    while( i < dataLength) {
        const outData = [];
        for(let j = 0; j < chunkSize; j++) {
            outData.push(data[i]);
            i+=1;
        }
        yield outData;
    }
}

for(let i of fakestream(data)) {
    console.log(i);
}
```

This example shows the concept of lazy evaluation along with a couple of concepts for streaming that we will see in a later chapter. First, we create a generator that can take in a function and can utilize it for our logic function in creating numbers. In our case, we are just going to use the default case and have it generate one number at a time. Next, we are going to run this through a `for/of` loop to generate numbers up to 101.

Next, we create a `fakestream` generator that will chunk our data for us. This is similar to streams that allow us to work on a chunk of data at a time. We can transform this data if we want to (known as a `TransformStream`) or we can just let it pass through (a special type of `TransformStream` called a `PassThrough`). We create a fake chunk size at 10. We then run another `for/of` loop over the data we had before and simply log it. However, we could decide to do something with this data if we wanted to.

This is not the exact interface that streams utilize, but it does showcase how we can have lazy evaluation inside our code with generators and that it is also built into certain concepts such as streaming. There are many other potential uses for generators and lazy evaluation techniques that will not be covered here, but they are available to developers who are looking for a more functional-style approach to list and map comprehensions.

Tail-end recursion optimization

This is another concept that many functional languages have, but most JavaScript engines do not have (WebKit being the exception). Tail-end recursion optimizations allow recursive functions that are built in a certain way to run just like a simple loop. In pure functional languages, there is no such thing as a loop, so the only method of working over a collection is to recursively go through it. We can see that if we build a function as a tail-recursive function, it will break our stack. The following code illustrates this:

```
const _d = new Array(100000);
for(let i = 0; i < _d.length; i++) {
    _d[i] = i;
}
const recurseSummer = function(data, sum=0) {
    if(!data.length ) {
        return sum;
    }
    return recurseSummer(data.slice(1), sum + data[0]);
}
console.log(recurseSummer(_d));
```

We create an array of 100,000 items and assign them all the value that is at their index. We then try using a recursive function to sum all of the data in the array. Since the last call for the function is the function itself, some compilers are able to make an optimization here. If they notice that the last call is to the same function, they know that the current stack can be destroyed (there is nothing left for the function to do). However, non-optimized compilers (most JavaScript engines) will not make this optimization so we keep adding stacks to our call system. This leads to a call stack size exceedance and makes it so we cannot utilize this purely functional concept.

There is hope for JavaScript, however. A concept called trampolining can be utilized to make tail-end recursion possible by modifying the function a bit and how we call it. The following is the modified code to utilize trampolining and give us what we want:

```
const trampoline = (fun) => {
    return (...arguments) => {
        let result = fun(...arguments);
```

```
        while( typeof result === 'function' ) {
            result = result();
        }
        return result;
    }
}

const _d = new Array(100000);
for(let i = 0; i < _d.length; i++) {
    _d[i] = i;
}
const recurseSummer = function(data, sum=0) {
    if(!data.length ) {
        return sum;
    }
    return () => recurseSummer(data.slice(1), sum + data[0]);
}
const final = trampoline(recurseSummer);
console.log(final(_d));
```

What we are doing is wrapping our recursive function inside one that we run through in a simple loop. The `trampoline` function works like this:

- It takes in a function and returns a newly constructed function that will run our recursive function but loop through it, checking the return type.
- Inside this inner function, it starts the loop up by executing a first run of the function.
- While we still see a function as our return type, it will continue looping.
- Once we finally do not get a function, we will return the results.

We are now able to utilize tail-end recursion to do some of the things that we would do in a purely functional world. An example of this was seen previously (which could be seen as a simple reduce function). Another example is as follows:

```
const recurseFilter = function(data, con, filtered=[]) {
    if(!data.length ) {
        return filtered;
    }
    return () => recurseFilter(data.slice(1), con, con(data[0]) ?
      filtered.length ? new Array(...filtered), data[0]) : [data[0]] :
filtered);

const finalFilter = trampoline(recurseFilter);
console.log(finalFilter(_d, item => item % 2 === 0));
```

With this function, we are simulating what a filter-based operation may look like in a pure functional language. Again, if there is no length, we are at the end of the array and we return our filtered array. Otherwise, we return a new function that recursively calls itself with a new list, the function that we are going to filter with, and then the filtered list. There is a bit of weird syntax here. We have to pass back a single array with the new item if we have an empty list, otherwise, it will give us an empty array with the number of items that we pass in.

We can see that both of these functions pass what is known as tail-end recursion and are also functions that could be written in a purely functional language. But, we will also see that these run a lot slower than simple `for` loops or even the built-in array methods for these types of functions. At the end of the day, if we wanted to write purely functional programming using tail-end recursion, we could, but it is wise not to do this in JavaScript.

Currying

The final concept that we will be looking at is currying. Currying is the ability of a function that takes multiple arguments to actually be a series of functions that takes a single argument and returns either another function or the final value. Let's take a look at a simple example to see this concept in action:

```
const add = function(a) {
    return function(b) {
        return a + b;
    }
}
```

What we are doing is taking a function that accepts multiple arguments, such as the add function. We then return a function that takes a single argument, in this case, b. This function then adds the numbers a and b together. What this allows us to do is either use the function as we normally would (except we run the function that comes back to us and pass in the second argument) or we get the return value from running it on a single argument and then use that function to add whatever values come next. Each of these concepts can be seen in the following code:

```
console.log(add(2)(5), 'this will be 7');
const add5 = add(5);
console.log(add5(5), 'this will be 10');
```

There are a couple of uses for currying and they also show off a concept that can be used quite frequently. First, it shows off the idea of partial application. What this does is set some of our arguments for us and return a function. We can then pass this function along in the chain of statements and eventually use it to fill in the remaining functions.

Just remember that all currying functions are partially applied functions, but not all partially applied functions are currying functions.

An example of partial application can be seen in the following code:

```
const fullFun = function(a, b, c) {
    console.log('a', a);
    console.log('b', b);
    console.log('c', c);
}
const tempFun = fullFun.bind(null, 2);
setTimeout(() => {
    const temp2Fun = tempFun.bind(null, 3);
    setTimeout(() => {
        const temp3Fun = temp2Fun.bind(null, 5);
        setTimeout() => {
            console.log('temp3Fun');
            temp3Fun();
        }, 1000);
    }, 1000);
    console.log('temp2Fun');
    temp2Fun(5);
}, 1000);
console.log('tempFun');
tempFun(3, 5);
```

First, we create a function that takes three arguments. We then create a new temporary function that binds 2 to the first argument of that function. Bind is an interesting function. It takes the scope that we want as the first argument (what this points to) and then takes an arbitrary length of arguments to fill in for the arguments of the function we are working on. In our case, we only bind the first variable to the number 2. We then create a second temporary function where we bind the first variables of the first temporary function to 3. Finally, we create a third and final temporary function where we bind the first argument of the second function to the number 5.

We can see at each run that we are able to run each of these functions and that they take a different number of arguments depending on which version of the function we have used. bind is a very powerful tool and allows us to pass functions around that may get arguments filled in from other functions before the final function is used.

Currying is the idea that we will use partial application, but that we are going to compose a multi-argument function with multiple nested functions inside it. So what does currying give us that we cannot already do with other concepts? If we are in the pure functional world, we can actually get quite a bit. Take, for example, the map function on arrays. It wants a function definition of a single item (we are going to ignore the other parameters that we normally do not use) and wants the function to return a single item. What happens when we have a function such as the following one and it could be used inside the map function, but it has multiple arguments? The following code showcases what we are able to do with currying and this use case:

```
const calculateArtbitraryValueWithPrecision = function(prec=0, val) {
    return function(val) {
        return parseFloat((val / 1000).toFixed(prec));
    }
}
const arr = new Array(50000);
for(let i = 0; i < arr.length; i++) {
    arr[i] = i + 1000;
}
console.log(arr.map(calculatorArbitraryValueWithPrecision(2)));
```

What we are doing is taking a generic function (an arbitrary one at that) and utilizing it in the map function by making it more specific, in this case by giving the precision two decimal places. This allows us to write very generic functions that can work over arbitrary data and make specific functions out of them.

We will utilize partial application a bit in our code and we may use currying. In general, however, we will not utilize currying as is seen in purely functional languages as this can lead to a slowdown and higher memory consumption. The main ideas to take away are partial application and the idea of how variables on the outer scope can be used in an inner scoped location.

These three concepts are quite crucial to the idea of pure functional programming, but we will not utilize most of them. In highly performant code, we need to squeeze out every ounce of speed and memory that we can and most of these constructs take up more than we care for. Certain concepts can be used to great lengths in high-performance code. The following will be used in later chapters: partial application, streaming/lazy evaluation, and possibly some recursion. Being comfortable with seeing functional code will help when working with libraries that utilize these concepts, but as we have talked about at length, they are not as performant as our iterative methods.

Summary

In this chapter, we have looked at the ideas of mutability and immutability. We have seen how immutability can lead to slowdowns and higher memory consumption and can be an issue when we are writing high-performance code. We have taken a look at mutability and how to make sure we write code that utilizes it, but also makes it safe. On top of this, we have performed performance comparisons between mutable and immutable code and have seen where speed and memory consumption increases for the immutable types. Finally, we took a look at functional-style programming in JavaScript and how we can utilize these concepts. Functional programming can help with many issues, such as lock-free concurrency, but we also know that the JavaScript runtimes are single-threaded and so this does not give us an advantage. Overall, there are many concepts that we can borrow from the different paradigms of programming and having all of these in our toolkit can make us better programmers and help us write clean, safe, and high-performance code.

In the next chapter, we will take a look at how JavaScript has evolved as a language. We will also take a look at how browsers have changed to meet the demands of developers, with new APIs that cover everything from accessing the DOM to long-term storage.

3
Vanilla Land - Looking at the Modern Web

The landscape of the JavaScript language has changed quite a bit since the release of the ECMAScript 2015 standard. There are now many new features that make JavaScript a first-class language for all types of development. It has become much easier to use the language, and we can even see some syntactic sugar in it now.

From the ECMAScript 2015 standard and beyond, we have received classes, modules, more ways of declaring variables, variations of scope, and much more. All of these features and more are going to be explained throughout the rest of this chapter. This is an excellent chapter to read in full if you are new to the language or you may just want to check out the features that may be unfamiliar. We will also take a look at some older sections of the web with DOM queries and how we can utilize them to replace extraneous libraries that we may be currently using, such as jQuery.

In this chapter, the following topics will be covered:

- A dive into modern JavaScript
- Understanding classes and modules
- Working with the DOM
- Understanding the Fetch API

Technical requirements

The following are prerequisites for this chapter:

- An editor such as VS Code
- A system that is set up to use Node.js
- A browser, preferably Chrome
- A general understanding of JavaScript and its scope
- The relevant code can be found at `https://github.com/PacktPublishing/Hands-On-High-Performance-Web-Development-with-JavaScript/tree/master/Chapter03`.

A dive into modern JavaScript

As stated in the introduction, the language has changed for the better in a lot of ways. We now have proper scoping, better handling for `async` operations, more collection types, and even metaprogramming features such as reflection and proxies. All of these features lead to a more involved language, but they also lead to more effective problem-solving. We will be looking at a few of the best items to come out of the new standards and what they can be used for in our code.

One thing to also note moving forward is that any JavaScript code that is shown can be run in the following ways:

1. Adding it to the developer's console by hitting *F12* on the keyboard
2. Utilizing snippets in the developer's console that can be seen on the **Sources** tab, and in the left panel an option should be called **Snippets**
3. Writing a base level `index.html` that has a script element added to it

Let/const and block scoping

Before ECMAScript 2015, we only had the use of the `var` keyword for defining variables. The lifetime of a `var` keyword was from the function declaration to the end of it. This could lead to quite a few problems. The following code showcases one of the issues that we could run into with the `var` keyword:

```
var fun = function() {
    for(var i = 0; i < 10; i++) {
        state['this'] += 'what';
```

```
        }
        console.log('i', i);
    }
fun();
```

What would the console print out? In most languages, we would guess that this is an error or that it would print `null`. However, JavaScript's `var` keyword is function scoped, so the variable `i` will be `10`. This has led to many bugs popping up by accidentally forgetting to declare it a variable, or even the dreaded `switch` statement errors (these still happen with `let` and `const`). An example of a `switch` statement error is as follows:

```
var x = 'a';
switch(x) {
    case 'a':
        y = 'z';
        break;
    case 'b':
        y = 'y';
        break;
    default:
        y = 'b';
}
console.log(y);
```

From the preceding `switch` statement, we would expect `y` to be `null`, but because the `var` keyword is not block-scoped, it will be the letter `z`. We always had to stay on top of variables and make sure that we were not using something that was declared outside our scope and changing it, or we were making sure that we were redeclaring variables to stop leaks from happening.

With both `let` and `const`, we got block scoping. This means that the curly braces tell us how long our variables should live for. An example of this is seen here:

```
let x = 10;
let fun2 = function() {
    {
        let x = 20;
        console.log('inner scope', x);
    }
    console.log('outer scope', x);
    x += 10;
}
fun2();
console.log('this should be 20', x);
```

As we look at the printouts for the variable x, we can see that we have first declared it as 10 outside of the function. Inside the function, we have created a new scope with the curly braces and redeclared x as 20. Inside the block, the code will print out inner scope 20. But, outside of the block inside of fun2, we print out x and it is 10. The let keyword follows this block scope. Had we declared the variable as var, it would have stayed as 20 when we printed it out the second time. Finally, we add 10 to the outer x and we should see that x is 20.

In addition to getting block scoping, the const keyword gave us some immutability. If the types that we are working with are value types, we will not be able to mutate that value. If we have a reference type, the values inside the reference can be changed, but we cannot change the reference itself. This leads to some nice capabilities.

A great style of coding is to use const as much as possible and only use let when we need to mutate something at the base level, such as loops. Since an object, array, or a function can have its values mutated, we can set them to const. The only downside that this has is that they cannot be nulled out, but it still adds quite a bit of safety on top of possible performance gains that the compiler can utilize knowing a value is immutable.

Arrow functions

Another notable change to the language was the addition of arrow functions. With this, we have now gotten access to change this without having to resort to various hacks on the language. An example of this can be seen as follows:

```
const create = function() {
    this.x = 10;
    console.log('this', this);
    const innerFun = function() {
        console.log('inner this', this);
    }
    const innerArrowFun = () => {
        console.log('inner arrow this', this);
    }
    innerFun();
    innerArrowFun();
}
const item = new create();
```

We are creating a constructor function for a new object. We have two inner functions, one being a basic function call and the other being an arrow function. When we print this out, we notice that the basic function prints the window's scope. When we print the inner arrow function's scope, we get the scope of our parent.

We could solve this in a few ways for the basic inner function. First, we could declare a variable in the parent and utilize that for the inner function. Also, when we run the function, we could use call or `apply` to actually run the function.

However, neither of these is a good idea, especially when we now have arrow functions. A key point to remember is that the arrow function takes the scope of the parent, so whatever `this` points to for the parent, we are now going to do the same inside the arrow function. Now, we can always change that by utilizing `apply` on an arrow function, but it is best to only utilize `apply` and such for partial application reasons and not to call functions by changing its `this` keyword.

Collection types

An array and an object have been the two main types that JavaScript developers have used for quite some time. But, we now have two other collection types that help us do some things that we used to use these other types for. These are set and map. A set is an unordered collection of unique items. What this means is that if we try to put something in the set that is already there, we will notice that we only have a single item. We can easily simulate a set with an array like so:

```
const set = function(...items) {
    this._arr = [...items];
    this.add = function(item) {
        if( this._arr.includes(item) ) return false;
        this._arr.push(item);
        return true;
    }
    this.has = function(item) {
        return this._arr.includes(item);
    }
    this.values = function() {
        return this._arr;
    }
    this.clear = function() {
        this._arr = [];
    }
}
```

Since we now have the set system, we can just use that API. We also get access to the `for of` loop since the set is an iterable item (we can also use the next syntax if we get the iterator attached to the set). Sets also have an advantage of faster read access over arrays when we get into large datasets. The following example illustrates this point:

```
const data = new Array(10000000);
for(let i = 0; i < data.length; i++) {
    data[i] = i;
}
const setData = new Set();
for(let i = 0; i < data.length; i++) {
    setData.add(i);
}
data.includes(5000000);
setData.has(5000000);
```

While the set takes a bit longer to create, when it comes to looking for items or even grabbing them, the set will perform nearly 100 times faster than an array. This is mostly due to the way the array has to look items up. Since an array is purely linear, it has to go through each element to check, whereas the set is a simple constant time check.

 A set can be implemented in different ways depending on the engine. A set in the V8 engine is built utilizing hash dictionaries for the lookup. We will not go over the internals of this, but essentially, the lookup time is considered constant, or *O(1)*, for computer science folk, whereas the array lookup time is linear, or *O(n)*.

On top of the set, we also have maps. We can look at these and see them as just objects, but they have a couple of nice properties:

- First, we can use any value as the key, even an object. This can be great for adding other data that we do not want to tie directly to the object (private values come to mind).
- In addition to this, maps are also iterable, so we can utilize the `for of` loop just like a set.
- Finally, a map can give us performance benefits over a plain old object in the cases of large datasets and when the keys are the same types and so are the values.

The following example highlights many of the areas where maps are generally better than plain objects and where objects used to be used:

```
const map = new Map();
for(let i = 0; i < 10000; i++) {
```

```
        map.set(`${i}item`, i);
}
map.forEach((val, key) => console.log(val));
map.size();
map.has('0item');
map.clear();
```

On top of these two items, we also have weak versions of them. The weak versions have one major limitation: the values have to be objects. This makes sense once we understand what WeakSet and WeakMap do. They *weakly* store the reference to the items. This means that while the items they have stored are around, we can perform the methods that these interfaces give us. Once the garbage collector decides to collect them, the references will be removed from the weak versions. We may be wondering, why would we use these?

For a WeakMap, there are a few use cases:

- First, if we do not have private variables, we can utilize WeakMap to store values on the object without actually attaching the property to them. Now, when the object is eventually garbage collected, so is this private reference.
- We can also utilize weak maps to attach properties or data to the DOM without actually having to add attributes to the DOM. We get all of the benefits of data attributes without cluttering up the DOM.
- Finally, if we wanted to store reference data off to the side, but have it disappear when the data does, this is another use case.

All in all, WeakMap is used when we want to tie some sort of data to that object without having a tight coupling. We will be able to see this as follows:

```
const items = new WeakMap();
const container = document.getElementById('content');
for(let i = 0; i < 50000; i++) {
    const el = document.createElement('li');
    el.textContent = `we are element ${i}`;
    el.onclick = function(ev) {
        console.log(items.get(el));
    }
    items.set(el, i);
    container.appendChild(el);
}
const removeHalf = function() {
    const amount = Math.floor(container.children.length / 2);
    for(let i = 0; i < amount; i++) {
        container.removeChild(container.firstChild);
    }
}
```

First, we create a WeakMap to store the data we want against the DOM elements that we are creating. Next, we grab our unordered list and add a list element to each iteration. We then tie the number that we are on to the DOM element through the WeakMap. That way, the onclick handler can get the item and get back the data we stored against it.

With this, we can click on any of the elements and get the data back. This is cool since we used to add data attributes to the HTML elements directly in the DOM. Now we can just use WeakMap. But, we also get one more benefit that has been talked about. If we run the removeHalf function in the command line and garbage collect, we can take a look at how many items are in the WeakMap. If we do this and we check how many elements are in the WeakMap, we will notice the number of elements it has stored can range from 25,000 to the full 50,000 elements we started with. This is for the reason stated above; once a reference has been garbage collected, the WeakMap will no longer store it. It has a weak reference.

 The amount to be collected by the garbage collector is going to be up to the system that we are running. On some systems, the garbage collector may decide to not collect anything from the list. This all depends on how the V8 garbage collection has been set up for Chrome or Node.js.

We can easily see this if we replace WeakMap with a regular one. Let's go ahead and make this minor change. With this change, observe the same preceding steps. We will notice that the map still has all 50,000 items inside it. This is what we mean when we say something either has a strong reference or a weak reference. A weak reference will allow the item to be cleaned up by the garbage collector, whereas a strong reference will not. *WeakMaps* are great for these types of linking in terms of data to another data source. If we want the item decoration or the link to be cleaned up when the primary object is cleaned, a WeakMap is a go-to item.

A WeakSet has a more limited use case. One great use case is for checking for infinite loops in object properties or graphs. If we store all of the visited nodes in a WeakSet, we are able to check whether we have the items, but we also don't have to clear the set once we are done with the check. This means, once the data gets collected, so will all of the references that were stored in the WeakSet. Overall, a WeakSet should be used when we need to tag an object or a reference. This means that if we need to see whether we have it or whether it has been visited, a WeakSet is a likely candidate for this job.

We can utilize the deep copy example from the previous chapter. With it, we still run into one more use case that we did not think of. What happens if an item points to another item in the object and that same item decides to point back at the original item? This can be seen in the following code:

```
const a = {item1 : b};
const b = {item1 : a};
```

With each of these items pointing at one another, we would run into circular reference issues. A way to get around this is with a `WeakSet`. We could hold all the visited nodes, and if we come to a node that is already visited, we just return from the function. This can be seen in the modified version of the code:

```
const state = {};
(function(scope) {
    const _state = {},
        _held = new WeakSet(),
        checkPrimitives = function(item) {
            return item === null || typeof item === 'string' || typeof
            item === 'number' || typeof item === 'boolean' ||
            typeof item === 'undefined';
        },
        cloneFunction = function(fun, scope=null) {
            return fun.bind(scope);
        },
        cloneObject = function(obj) {
            const newObj = {},
            const keys = Object.keys(obj);
            for(let i = 0; i < keys.length; i++) {
                const key = keys[i];
                const item = obj[key];
                newObj[key] = runUpdate(item);
            }
            return newObj;
        },
        cloneArray = function(arr) {
            const newArr = new Array(arr.length);
            for(let i = 0; i < arr.length; i++) {
                newArr[i] = runUpdate(arr[i]);
            }
            return newArr;
        },
        runUpdate = function(item) {
            if( checkPrimitives(item) ) {
                return item;
            }
            if( typeof item === 'function' ) {
```

```
                        return cloneFunction(item);
                }
                if(!_held.has(item) ) {
                    _held.add(item);
                    if( item instanceof Array ) {
                        return cloneArray(item);
                    } else {
                        return cloneObject(item);
                    }
                }
            };
        scope.update = function(obj) {
            const x = Object.keys(obj);
            for(let i = 0; i < x.length; i++) {
                _state[x[i]] = runUpdate(obj[x[i]]);
            }
            _held = new WeakSet();
        }
    })(state);
    Object.freeze(state);
```

As we can see, we have added a new _held variable that will hold all of our references. Then, the runUpdate function has been modified to make sure that when an item is not a primitive type or a function, we check whether we already have it in our held list. If we do, then we skip the item, otherwise, we will just keep going. Finally, we replace the _held variable with a new WeakSet since the clear method is no longer available on *WeakSets*.

This does not keep the circular reference, which may be a problem, but it does solve our issue of the system going into an infinite loop because of objects referencing one another. Other than this use case, and maybe some more advanced ideas, there are not many other needs for a WeakSet. The main thing is if we need to track the existence of something. If we need to do this, the WeakSet is the perfect use case for us.

Most developers will not find a need for *WeakSets* or *WeakMaps*. These will likely be utilized by library authors. However, the conventions mentioned previously may come up in some cases so it is nice to know the reason for these items and why they are there. If we do not have a reason to use something, then we should most likely not use it, this is definitely the case with these two items since they have really specific use cases and one of the major use cases for *WeakMaps* is being delivered to us in the ECMAScript standard (private variables).

Reflection and proxies

One of the last major pieces of the ECMAScript standard we are going to touch on is two metaprogramming objects. Metaprogramming is the technique of having code that generates code. This could be for things such as compilers or parsers. It could also be for self-changing code. It can even be for runtime evaluation of another language (interpreting) and doing something with this. While this is probably the main feature that reflection and proxies give us, it also gives us the ability to listen to events on an object.

In the previous chapter, we talked about listening to events and we created a CustomEvent to listen for events on our object. Well, we can change that code and utilize proxies for that behavior. The following is some basic code to handle basic events on an object:

```
const item = new Proxy({}, {
    get: function(obj, prop) {
        console.log('getting the following property', prop);
        return Reflect.has(obj, prop) ? obj[prop] : null;
    },
    set: function(obj, prop, value) {
        console.log('trying to set the following prop with the following
         value', prop, value);
        if( typeof value === 'string' ) {
            obj[prop] = value;
        } else {
            throw new Error('Value type is not a string!');
        }
    }
});
item.one = 'what';
item.two = 'is';
console.log(item.one);
console.log(item.three);
item.three = 12;
```

What we have done is add some basic logging for the get and set methods on this object. We have extended the functionality of this object by also making the set method only take string values. With this, we have created an object that can be listened to and we can respond to those events.

Proxies are currently slower than adding a `CustomEvent` to the system. As stated previously, even though proxies were in the ECMAScript 2015 standard, their adoption has been slow, so browsers need some more time to optimize them. Also, it should be noted that we would not want to run the logging directly here. We would, instead, opt for the system to queue messages and utilize something called `requestIdleCallback` to run our logging code once the browser notices downtime in our application. This is still an experimental technology but should be added to all browsers soon.

Another interesting property of proxies is revocable methods. This is a proxy that we can eventually say is revoked and this will throw a `TypeError` when we try to use it after this method call. This can be very useful for anyone trying to implement the RAII pattern with objects. Instead of trying to `null` out the reference, we can revoke the proxy and we will no longer be able to utilize it.

This pattern of RAII will differ slightly from the null reference. Once we revoke a proxy, all references will no longer be able to use it. This may become an issue, but it would also give us the added benefit of failing fast, which is always a great property to have in code development. This means that when we are in development, it will throw a `TypeError` instead of just passing a null value. In this case, only try-catch blocks would allow this code to keep going instead of just simple null checks. Failing fast is a great way to protect ourselves in development and to catch bugs earlier.

An example of this is shown here with a modified version of the preceding code:

```
const isPrimitive = function(item) {
    return typeof item === 'string' || typeof item === 'number' || typeof
    item === 'boolean';
}
const item2 = Proxy.revocable({}, {
    get: function(obj, prop) {
        return Reflect.has(obj, prop) ? obj[prop] : null
    },
    set: function(obj, prop, value) {
        if( isPrimitive(value) ) {
            obj[prop] = value;
        } else {
            throw new Error('Value type is not a primitive!');
        }
    }
});
```

```
const item2Proxy = item2.proxy;
item2Proxy.one = 'this';
item2Proxy.two = 12;
item2Proxy.three = true;
item2.revoke();
(function(obj) {
    console.log(obj.one);
})(item2Proxy);
```

Now, instead of just throwing *TypeErrors* on the set, we also will throw a `TypeError` once we revoke the proxy. This can be of great use to us when we decide to write code that will protect itself. We also no longer need to write a bunch of guard clauses in our code when we are utilizing objects. If we utilize proxies and revocables instead, we are able to guard our sets.

 We did not go into the terminology of the proxy system. Technically, the methods we add in the handler for the proxies are called traps, similar to operating system traps, but we can really just think of them as simple events. Sometimes, the terminology can add a bit of confusion to things and is usually not needed.

Besides proxies, the Reflect API is a bunch of static methods that mirror the proxy handlers. We can utilize them in place of some familiar systems such as the `Function.prototype.apply` method. We can instead utilize the `Reflect.apply` method, which can be a bit clearer when writing our code. This looks like the following:

```
Math.max.apply(null, [1, 2, 3]);
Reflect.apply(Math.max, null, [1, 2, 3]);
item3 = {};
if( Reflect.set(item3, 'yep', 12) {
    console.log('value was set correctly!');
} else {
    console.log('value was not set!');
}
Reflect.defineProperty(item3, 'readonly', {value : 42});
if( Reflect.set(item3, 'readonly', 'nope') ) {
    console.log('we set the value');
} else {
    console.log('value should not be set!');
}
```

As we can see, we set a value on our object the first time and it was successful. But, the second property was first defined and it was set to non-writable (the default when we use `defineProperty`), and so we were not able to set a value on it.

With both of these APIs, we can write some nice functionality for accessing objects and even making mutations as safe as possible. We can utilize the RAII pattern very easily with these two APIs and we can even do some cool metaprogramming along with it.

Other notable changes

There are plenty of changes that have come with the advancement of the ECMAScript standard and we could devote an entire chapter to all of those changes, but we will lay out a few more here that can be seen in code written in this book and most likely seen elsewhere.

Spread operator

The spread operator allows us to pull apart arrays, iterable collections such as sets or maps, and even objects in the latest standard. This gives us a nicer syntax for performing some common operations such as the ones here:

```
// working with a variable amount of arguments
const oldVarArgs = function() {
    console.log('old variable amount of arguments', arguments);
}
const varArgs = function(...args) {
    console.log('variable amount of arguments', args);
}
// transform HTML list into a basic array so we have access to array
// operations
const domArr = [...document.getElementsByTagName('li')];
// clone array
const oldArr = [1, 2, 3, 4, 5];
const clonedArr = [...oldArr];
// clone object
const oldObj = {item1 : 'that', item2 : 'this'};
const cloneObj = {...oldObj};
```

What used to be `for` loops and other versions of iteration is now a simple one-line piece of code. Also, the first item is nice since it shows the reader of this code that we are utilizing the function as a variable argument function. Instead of needing documentation to lay this out, we can see this with the code.

 When dealing with arguments, if we are going to mutate them at all in the function, create a copy and then mutate. Certain de-optimizations happen if we decide to mutate the arguments directly.

Destructuring

Destructuring is the process of taking an array or an object and passing the items to the variable we are assigning to in an easier fashion. This can be seen with the following code:

```
//object
const desObj = {item1 : 'what', item2 : 'is', item3 : 'this'};
const {item1, item2} = desObj;
console.log(item1, item2);

//array
const arr = [1, 2, 3, 4, 5];
const [a, ,b, ...c] = arr;
console.log(a, b, c);
```

Both of these examples showcase some cool properties. First, we can pick and choose the items that we want from the object. We can also reassign the value to something else if we want to, on the left-hand side. On top of this, we can even do nested objects and destructuring.

For the array, we are able to pick and choose all of the items, some of the items, or even use the rest syntax by putting the rest of the array in a variable. In the preceding example, a will hold 1, b will hold 3, and c will be an array with 4 and 5 inside it. We skipped 2 by making that space empty. In other languages, we would use something like _ to showcase this, but we can just skip it here. Again, all of this is just syntactic sugar that enables tighter and cleaner code to be written.

Power operator

There is not much to say here other than the fact that we no longer need to utilize the Math.pow() function; we now have the power operator or **, leading to cleaner code and nicer-looking mathematical equations.

Parameter defaults

These allow us to put in default values if we do not have something for that position when calling a function. This may appear as follows:

```
const defParams = function(arg1, arg2=null, arg3=10) {
    if(!arg2 ) {
        console.log('nothing was passed in or we passed in a falsy value');
    }
    const pow = arg3;
```

```
if ( typeof arg1 === 'number' ) {
    return arg1 ** pow;
} else {
    throw new TypeError('argument 1 was not a number!');
}
}
```

One thing to note with parameter defaults is that once we start to utilize defaults in the chain of arguments, we can't stop using defaults. In the preceding example, if we gave argument 2 a default, we would have to give argument 3 a default, even if we just pass undefined or `null` to it. Again, this helps with the clarity of code and making sure that we no longer have to create default cases where we are looking at the arguments of the array.

A lot of code still utilizes the arguments section of a function. There are even other properties of a function that we can get at such as the caller. If we are in strict mode, a lot of this behavior will break. Strict mode is a way to not allow access to certain behaviors in the JavaScript engine. A good description of this can be found at `https://developer.mozilla.org/en-US/docs/Web/JavaScript/Reference/Strict_mode`. In addition to this, we should no longer be using the arguments section of the function since we have plenty of helpful alternatives with the new standard.

String templates

String templates allow us to pass in arbitrary code that will evaluate to a string or an object that has a `toString` function. This allows us, yet again, to write cleaner code instead of having to create a bunch of concatenated strings. It also allows us to write multiline strings without having to create escape sequences. This can be seen as follows:

```
const literal = `This is a string literal. It can hold multiple lines and
variables by denoting them with curly braces and prepended with the dollar
sign like so \$\{\}.
here is a value from before ${a}. We can also pass an arbitrary expression
that evaluates ${a === 1 ? b : c}.
`
console.log(literal);
```

Just remember that even though we can do something, doing something may not be the best idea. Specifically, we may be able to pass arbitrary expressions that will evaluate to something, but we should try to keep them as clean and simple as possible to make the code more readable.

Typed arrays

We will be discussing these at length in future chapters, but typed arrays are ways of representing arbitrary bytes in the system. This allows us to work with lower-level functionality, such as encoders and decoders, or even working on the byte streams of a `fetch` call directly instead of having to work with converting blobs to numbers or strings.

These usually start out with an `ArrayBuffer` and then we create a view over it. This can look like the following:

```
const arrBuf = new ArrayBuffer(16);
const uint8 = new Uint8Array(arrBuf);
uint8[0] = 255;
```

As we can see, we first create an array buffer. Think of this as a low-level instance. It just holds raw bytes. We then have to create a view over it. A lot of the time, we will be utilizing `Uint8Array` as we need to work with the arbitrary bytes, but we can utilize views all the way up to `BigInt`. These are usually utilized in low-level systems such as in 3D canvas code, WebAssembly, or raw streams from the server.

BigInt

`BigInt` is an arbitrarily long integer. Numbers in JavaScript are stored as 64-bit, floating-point doubles. This means that even if we only have a normal integer, we still only get 53 bits of precision. We can only store numbers inside variables up to the number 9 quadrillion. Anything bigger than this will usually cause the system to go into undefined behavior. To make up for this, we can now utilize the `BigInt` feature in JavaScript. This looks like the following:

```
const bigInt = 100n;
console.log('adding two big ints', 100n + 250n);
console.log('add a big int and a regular number', 100n + BigInt(250));
```

We will notice that *BigInts* are appended with an n. We also need to coerce regular numbers to *BigInts* if we want to utilize them in regular operations. Now that we have big integers, we can work with very large numbers, which can be of great use in 3D, financial, and scientific applications.

 Do not try to coerce *BigInts* back to regular numbers. There is some undefined behavior here and we may lose precision if we try to do this. The best approach is that if we need to use *BigInts*, stay in *BigInts*.

Internationalization

Finally, we come to internationalization. Before, we would need to internationalize such things as dates, number formats, and even currencies. We would use special lookups or converters that would do this for us. With the newer versions of ECMAScript, we have gained support for getting these new formats with the built-in `Intl` object. Some of the use cases can be seen as follows:

```
const amount = 1478.99;
console.log(new Intl.NumberFormat('en-UK', {style : 'currency', currency :
'EUR'}).format(amount));
console.log(new Intl.NumberFormat('de-DE', {style : 'currency', currency :
'EUR'}).format(amount));
const date = new Date(0);
console.log(new Intl.DateTimeFormat('en-UK').format(date));
console.log(new Intl.DateTimeFormat('de-DE').format(date));
```

With this, we can now internationalize our system depending on where someone may be located or what language they choose at the start of our application.

This will only perform conversions of the numbers to the stylings for that country code; it will not try to convert the actual values since options such as currency change within the course of the day. If we need to perform such conversions, we will need to use an API. On top of this, if we want to translate something, we will still need to have separate lookups for what we need to put in text since there is no direct translation between languages.

With these awesome features added in the ECMAScript standard, let's now move onto a way to encapsulate functions and data that go together. To do this, we will use classes and modules.

Understanding classes and modules

With the new ECMAScript standard, we got the new class syntax for having a form of **object-oriented programming** (**OOP**) and, later, we also got modules, a way of importing and exporting user-defined collections of functions and objects. Both of these systems have enabled us to remove certain hacks that we built into the system, and also remove certain libraries that were close to essential for modularizing our code bases.

First, we need to understand what type of language JavaScript is. JavaScript is a multi-paradigm language. This means that we can utilize many of the ideas that are out there for different programming styles and incorporate them into our code base. One style of programming that we have touched on in previous chapters is the functional style of programming.

In pure functional programming, we have pure functions, or functions that perform an action and have no side effects (do something outside what the function is supposed to do). When we write in this way, we can create generalized functions and put them together to create a chain of simple ideas that can work on complex ideas. We also treat functions as first-class citizens in the language. This means that functions can be assigned to variables and passed to other functions. We can also compose these functions, as we have seen in previous chapters. This is one way to think about a problem.

Another popular style of programming is object-oriented programming. This style states that a program can be described with a hierarchy of classes and objects that can be built and used together to create this complex idea. This idea can be seen in most of the popular languages that are out there. We build base classes that have some general functionality or some definitions that specific versions of them need to incorporate. We inherit from this base class and add our own specific functionality and then we create these objects. Once we put all of these objects together, we can work on the complex idea that we need to.

With JavaScript, we get both of these ideas, but the OOP design in JavaScript is a bit different. We have what is known as prototypal inheritance. What this means is that there is really no idea of these abstract ideas called *classes*. All we have in JavaScript are objects. We inherit an object's prototype that has methods and data on it that all objects with the same prototype share, but they are all instantiated instances.

When we talk about class syntax in JavaScript, we are talking about syntactic sugar for constructor functions and methods/data that we are adding to their prototype. Another way to think about this type of inheritance is to note that there are not abstract ideas in JavaScript, only concrete objects. If this seems a bit esoteric or confusing, the following code should clarify what these statements mean:

```
const Item = funciton() {
    this.a = 1;
    this.b = 'this';
    this.c = function() {
        console.log('this is going to be a new function each time');
    }
}
Item.prototype.d = function() {
    console.log('this is on the prototype so it will only be here
     once');
```

```
    }
    const item1 = new Item();
    const item2 = new Item();

    item1.c === item2.c; //false
    item1.d === item2.d; //true

    const item3 = new (Object.getPrototypeOf(item1)).constructor();
    item3.d === item2.d ;//true
    Object.getPrototypeOf(item1).constructor === Item; //true
```

We have shown a few things with this example. First, this is the older way of creating constructor functions. A constructor function is a function that sets up the scope and all of the functions that are directly available to an object when it gets instantiated. In this case, we have made a, b, and c as instance variables on an Item constructor. Second, we have added something to the item's prototype. When we declare something on the prototype of a constructor function, we are making that available to all instances of that constructor function.

From here, we declare two items that are based on the Item constructor. This means that they will both get separate instances of the a, b, and c variables, but they will share the function d. We can see this in action with the next two statements. This showcases that if we add something directly to the this scope of a constructor function, it will create a brand-new instance of that item, but if we put something on the prototype, the items will all share it.

Finally, we can see that item3 is a new Item, but we got to the constructor function in a roundabout way. Some browsers support the __proto__ property on items, but this function should be available in all browsers. We grab the prototype and we notice that there is a constructor function. This is the same exact function that we declared at the top, so we are able to utilize it to make a new item. We can see that it is also on the same prototype as the other items and that the constructor function on the prototype is the exact same thing as the item variable that we declared.

What all of this should showcase is the fact that JavaScript is purely made of objects. There are no abstract types such as true classes in other languages. If we utilize the new syntax, it is best to understand that all we are doing is utilizing syntactic sugar to do what we used to be able to do with the prototype. That said, the next example will showcase the exact same behavior, but one will be old-school prototype-based, and the other will utilize the new class syntax:

```
    class newItem {
        constructor() {
            this.c = function() {
```

```
            console.log('this is going to be a new function each time!');
        }
    }
    a = '1';
    b = 'this';
    d() {
        console.log('this is on the prototype so it will only be here
        once');
    }
}
const newItem1 = new newItem();
const newItem2 = new newItem();

newItem1.c === newItem2.c //false
newItem1.d === newItem2.d //true

newItem === Object.getPrototypeOf(newItem1).constructor; //true
```

As we can see with this example, we get some cleaner syntax while creating the same object as what we had before with the prototype version. The constructor function is the same thing as when we declared the Item as a function. We could pass in any parameters and do the setup in here. One interesting thing with classes is that we are able to create instance variables inside the class, just like when we declared them on this in the prototype example. We can also see that the declaration of d is put on the prototype. We will explore more aspects of the class syntax below, but take some time and play with both pieces of code. Understanding how JavaScript is prototype-based helps immensely when we are trying to write highly performant code.

 The public variables being inside the class is rather new (Chrome 72). If we do not have access to a newer browser, we will have to utilize Babel to transpile our code back down to a version that the browser will understand. We will also be taking a look at another feature that is only in Chrome and is experimental, but it should come to all browsers within the year.

Other notable features

JavaScript classes give us a bunch of nice features that make the code we write clean and concise, while also performing at or near the same speed as if we wrote directly to the prototype. One nice feature is the inclusion of static member variables and static member functions.

While there is not much of a difference, it does allow us to write functions that cannot be accessed by the member functions (they can still be accessed, but it is a lot harder) and it can provide a good tool for grouping utility functions to that specific class. An example of static functions and variables is shown here:

```
class newItem {
    static e() {
        console.log(this);
    }
    static f = 10;
}

newItem1.e() //TypeError
newItem.e() //give us the class
newItem.f //10
```

The two static definitions were added to the newItem class and then we showcase what is available. With the function e and the static variable f, we can see that they are not included on the objects we create from newItem, but we have access to them when we access newItem directly. On top of this, we can see that the this that is inside the static function points to the class. Static members and variables are great for creating utility functions or even for creating the singleton pattern in JavaScript.

If we want to create the same experience in the old style, it would look like the following:

```
Item.e = function() {
    console.log(this);
}
Item.f = 10;
```

As we can see, we have to put these definitions after the first definition of Item. This means that we have to be relatively careful in trying to group all of our code for the definition of our classes in the old style, whereas the class syntax allows us to put it all in a group.

On top of static variables and functions, we have the shorthand for writing the getters and setters for a variable in a class. This can be seen as follows:

```
get g() {
    return this._g;
}
set g(val) {
    if( typeof val !== 'string' ) {
        return;
    }
    this._g = val;
}
```

With this getter and setter, we are able to do various things inside these functions when someone or something tries to access this variable. In the same vein that we set up a proxy to event on a change, we can do something similar with the getter and setter. We can also set up logging inside here. This syntax is quite nice when we want to access something as just a property name instead of writing our something like `getG` and `setG`.

Finally, there are the new private variables that have come in Chrome 76. While this is still in the candidate recommendation phase, it is still going to be discussed since it will most likely come into play. A lot of the time, we want to expose as much information as possible. However, there are times when we want to utilize internal variables to hold state or just not generally be accessed outside of our object. In this vein, the JavaScript community has come up with the _ solution. Anything that has an _ is considered a private variable. But, a user can still get access to these variables and manipulate them. Even worse than this, a malicious user could find a vulnerability in these private variables and be able to manipulate the system in their favor. One technique of creating private variables in the old system is something that looked like the following:

```
const Public = (function() {
    let priv = 0;
    const Private = function() {}
    Private.prototype.add1 = function() {
        priv += 1;
    }
    Private.prototype.getVal = function() {
        return priv;
    }
    return Private;
})();
```

With this, no one has access to the `priv` variable except for the implementer. This gives us a public-facing system, without access to that private variable. However, there is still a catch with this system: if we create another `Public` object, we will still be affecting the same `priv` variable. There are other ways to make sure that we get new variables as we create new objects, but these are all workarounds to the system we are trying to make. Instead, we can now utilize the following syntax:

```
class Public {
    #h = 10;
    get h() {
        return this.#h;
    }
}
```

What that pound sign does is say that this is a private variable. If we try to get access to it from any one of our instances, it will come back undefined. This works great with the getter and setter interface as we will be able to control access to variables and even modify them if need be.

One final look into classes is the extend and super keywords. With extend, we are able to do just that with classes. Let's take our newItem class and extend its functionality. This could look like the following:

```
class extendedNewItem extends newItem {
    constructor() {
        super();
        console.log(this.c());
    }
    get super_h() {
        return super.h;
    }
    static e() {
        super.e();
        console.log('this came from our extended class');
    }
}
const extended = new extendedNewItem();
```

We have a few interesting behaviors happening in this example. First, if we run Object.getPrototypeOf on our extended object, we will see that the prototype is what we would expect, extendedNewItem. Now, if we get the prototype of that, we will see that it is newItem. We have created a prototype chain just like many of the built-in objects.

Second, we have the capability of getting to our parent's methods from inside our class with the use of super. This is essentially a reference to our parent's prototype. We cannot chain these if we want to keep going through all of the prototypes. We would have to utilize something like Object.getPrototypeOf. We can also see, by inspecting our extended object, that we got all of the member variables that were held in our parent's system.

This gives us the ability to compose our classes together and create base classes or abstract classes that give us some defined behavior and then we can create extended classes that give us specific behavior that we want. We will see more code later on that utilizes classes and many of the concepts that we have gone over here, but remember that classes are just syntactical sugar for the prototype system and a good understanding of that will go a long way into understanding how JavaScript works as a language.

There are many great things about that class interface with the JavaScript ecosystem and there appear to be some other great ideas potentially coming in the future, such as decorators. It is always a good idea to keep an eye on the **Mozilla Developer Network (MDN)** page to see what is new and what is possibly coming out in the future. We will now take a look at modules and how they work in our system of writing clean and fast code.

A good rule of thumb is to not extend any class more than one, maybe two levels deep. If we go any further, we can start to create a maintenance nightmare, on top of potential objects getting heavy with information that they don't need. Thinking ahead will always be the best bet when we are creating our systems, and trying to minimize the impact of our classes is one way of reducing memory use.

Modules

Before ECMAScript 2015, we had no concept of loading in code other than utilizing the script tag. We came up with many module concepts and libraries, such as **RequireJS** or **AMD**, but none of them were built into the language. With the advent of modules, we now had a way of creating highly modular code that could easily be packaged up and imported into other sections of our code. We also got scope lock on our systems where we used to have to utilize IIFEs to get this behavior.

First, before we can start to work with modules, we will need a static server to host all of our content. Even if we get Chrome to allow access to the local filesystem, the module system will get upset since it will not serve them as text/JavaScript. To get around this, we can install the node package, `node-static`. We are going to add this package to a static directory. We can run the following command: `npm install node-static`. Once this is finished downloading into the `static` directory, we can grab the `app.js` file from the `Chapter03` folder in our repository and run `node app.js`. This will start up the static server, along with serving them from the `files` directory inside our `static` directory. We can then place any files that we want to serve in there and be able to get at them from our code.

Now, we can write a basic module along the lines of the following and save it as `lib.js`:

```
export default function() {
    console.log('this is going to be our simple lib');
}
```

We can then import this module from an HTML file as follows:

```
<script type="module'>
    import lib from './lib.js';
</script>
```

With even this basic example, we can get an idea of how modules work in the browser. First, the type of script needs to be a module. This tells the browser that we are going to load in modules and that we are going to treat this body of code as if it were a module. This gives us several benefits. First, we are automatically put into strict mode when we are utilizing modules. Second, we are automatically scoped with modules. This means that the lib that we just imported is not available as a global. If we loaded in content as text/JavaScript and put variables on the global path, then we would automatically have them; that is why we usually have to utilize an IIFE. Finally, we get a nice syntax in which to load our JavaScript files. We could still utilize the old way of loading in a bunch of scripts, but we can also just import the ones that are module-based.

Next, we can see that the module itself uses the export and default keywords. The export means that we want this item to be available outside of this scope or file. We can now get to this item outside of our current file. The default means that if we load in the module without defining what we want, we will get this item automatically. This can be seen in the following example:

```
const exports = {
    this : 'that',
    that : 'this'
}

export { exports as Item };
```

First, we defined an object called exports. This is the object that we want to add as an exported item. Second, we added this item to an export declaration and we also renamed it. This is one nice thing about modules. On either the export or the import side, we can rename the items that we want to export. Now, in our HTML file, we would have a declaration such as the following:

```
import { Item } from './lib.js';
```

If we did not have the brackets around the declaration, we would be trying to bring in the default export. Since we have the curly brackets, it is going to look for an item called Item inside lib.js. If it finds it, then it will bring in the code that is associated with that.

Now, just as we renamed the exports from the export list, we can rename the import. Let's go ahead and change that to the following:

```
import { Item as _item } from './lib.js';
```

We can now utilize the item as we normally would, but as the variable _item instead of Item. This is great for name collisions. There are only so many variable names that we can come up with so, instead of changing the variables inside the separate libraries, we can just change them when they are loaded in.

A good styling convention is to declare all of our imports at the top. However, there are use cases where we may need to dynamically load our modules due to some type of user interaction or some other event. If this occurs, we can utilize dynamic imports to do this. These appear as follows:

```
document.querySelector('#loader').addEventListener('click', (ev) => {
    if(!('./lib2.js' in imported)) {
        import('./lib2.js')
        .then((module) => {
            imported['./lib2.js'] = module;
            module.default();
        });
    } else {
        imported['./lib2.js'].default();
    }
});
```

We have added a button that, when clicked, we try to load the module into our system. This is not the best way to cache the module in our system and most browsers will also do some caching for us, but this way is fairly straightforward and showcases the dynamic import system. The import function is based on promises, so we try to grab it and, if we succeed, we add it to an imported object. We then call the default method. We can get to any of the items that the module exports for us, but this is one of the easiest to get to.

Seeing how JavaScript has evolved has been amazing. All of these new features give us capabilities that we used to have to rely on from third parties. The same can be said regarding the changes to the DOM. We will now look at these changes.

Working with the DOM

The **Document Object Model (DOM)** has not always been the easiest technology to work with. We had old archaic APIs and, most of the time, they never lined up between browsers. But, within the last couple of years, we have gotten some nice APIs to do the following: grab elements with ease, build in-memory hierarchies for fast attachment, and templates with DOM shadowing. All of these have led to a rich environment for making changes to the underlying nodes and creating a number of rich frontends without the need for libraries such as jQuery. In the following sections, we will see how working with these new APIs has helped us.

Query selector

Before we had this API (or we were trying to be as cross-browser as we could), we relied on systems such as getElementById or getElementsByClassName. Each of these provided a way in which we could get DOM elements, as in the following example:

```
<p>This is a paragraph element</p>
<ul id="main">
    <li class="hidden">1</li>
    <li class="hidden">2</li>
    <li>3</li>
    <li class="hidden">4</li>
    <li>5</li>
</ul>
<script type="module">
    const main = document.getElementById('main');
    const hidden = document.getElementsByClassName('hidden');
</script>
```

One difference between this older API and the new querySelector and querySelectorAll is that the old API implements a collection of DOM nodes as an HTMLCollection and the newer API implements them as a NodeList. While this may not seem like a major difference, the NodeList API does give us a forEach already built into the system. Otherwise, we would have to change both of these collections to a regular array of DOM nodes. The preceding example, implemented in the new API, appears as follows:

```
const main = document.querySelector('#main');
const hidden = document.querySelectorAll('.hidden');
```

This becomes much nicer when we want to start adding other features to our selection process.

Let's say that we now have a few inputs and that we want to grab all inputs that are of the text type. How would this look inside the old API? We could attach a class to all of them if need be, but this would pollute our use of classes and is probably not the best way of handling this information.

The other way that we could get this data would be to utilize one of the old API methods and then check whether those elements have the input attribute set to `text`. This could look like the following:

```
const allTextInput = Array.from(document.getElementsByTagName('input'))
    .filter(item => item.getAttribute('type') === "text");
```

But we now have a certain level of verbosity that is not needed. Instead, we could grab them by utilizing CSS selectors, utilizing the Selector API as follows:

```
const alsoTextInput = doucment.querySelectorAll('input[type="text"]');
```

This means we should be able to get to any DOM node utilizing the CSS syntax, just like jQuery does. We can even start from another element so that we do not have to parse the entire DOM, like so:

```
const hidden = document.querySelector('#main').querySelectorAll('.hidden');
```

The other nice thing about the Selectors API is that it will throw an error if we do not utilize a correct CSS selector. This gives us the added benefit of the system running checks for us. While the new Selector API has been around, it has not been utilized much because of Internet Explorer needing to be included in the supported web browsers. It is highly suggested to start to utilize the new Selector API as it is less verbose and we are able to do a lot more with it than our old system.

 jQuery is a library that gives us a nicer API to utilize than the base system had. Most of the changes that jQuery supported have now become obsolete, with many of the new web APIs that we have been talking about taking over. For most new applications, they will no longer need to utilize jQuery.

Document fragments

We have seen these in previous chapters, but it is nice to touch upon them. Document fragments are reusable containers that we can create a DOM hierarchy in and attach all of those nodes at once. This leads to faster draw times and less repainting when utilized.

The following example showcases two ways of attaching a series of list elements utilizing straight-to-DOM addition and fragment addition:

```
const num = 10000;
const container = document.querySelector('#add');
for(let i = 0; i < num; i++) {
    const temp = document.createElement('li');
    temp.textContent = `item ${i}`;
    container.appendChild(temp);
}
while(container.firstChild) {
    container.removeChild(container.firstChild);
}
const fragment = document.createDocumentFragment();
for(let i = 0; i < num; i++) {
    const temp = document.createElement('li');
    temp.textContent = `item ${i}`;
    fragment.appendChild(temp);
}
container.appendChild(fragment);
```

While the time between these two is tiny, the number of repaints that take place is not. In our first example, the document is going to repaint each time we add an element directly to it, whereas our second example is only going to repaint the DOM once. This is the nice thing about document fragments; it makes adding to the DOM simple, while also only utilizing minimal repaints.

Shadow DOM

The shadow DOM is usually paired with templates and web components, but it can also be utilized by itself. The shadow DOM allows us to encapsulate our markup and styles for a specific section of our application. This is great if we want to have a certain styling for a piece of our page, but we do not want that to propagate to the rest of the page.

We can easily utilize the shadow DOM by utilizing its API, shown as follows:

```
const shadow = document.querySelector('#shadowHolder').attachShadow({mode : 'open'});
const style = document.createElement('style');
style.textContent = `<left out to shorten code snippet>`;
const frag = document.createDocumentFragment();
const header = document.createElement('h1');
const par = document.createElement('p');
header.textContent = 'this is a header';
par.textContent = 'Here is some text inside of a paragraph element. It is
```

```
going to get the styles we outlined above';

frag.appendChild(header);
frag.appendChild(par);
shadow.appendChild(style);
shadow.appendChild(frag);
```

First, we attach a shadow DOM to an element, in this case, our `shadowHolder` element. There is a mode option that allows us to say whether we can access the content through JavaScript outside of the shadow context, but it has been found that we can easily circumvent this, so it is recommended just to keep it open. Next, we create a few elements, one being a number of styling attributes. We then attach these to a document fragment and finally to the shadow root.

With all of that out of the way, we can take a look and notice that our shadow DOM gets affected by the styling attributes that were put inside with it instead of the ones that were put at the top of our main document. What happens if we put a style at the top of our document that our shadow styling does not have? It still does not get affected. With this, we are now able to create components that can be styled separately without the use of classes. This brings us to one of our final topics of the DOM.

Web components

The Web Component API allows us to create custom elements that have defined behaviors utilizing only the browser APIs. This is different to a framework such as Bootstrap or even Vue as we are able to utilize all of the technologies that are present in our browser.

 Chrome and Firefox have all of these APIs supported. Safari has most of them, and if this is a browser that we want to support, we will only be able to utilize some of the APIs. Edge does not have support for the Web Component APIs, but with it moving to a chromium base, we will see another browser able to utilize this technology.

Let's create a basic `tooltip` element. First, we need to extend the base `HTMLElement` in our class. We will then need to attach some properties to allow us to place the element and to give us the text that we need to use. Finally, we will need to register this component with our system to make sure it recognizes our custom element. The following code creates this custom element (modified from `https://developer.mozilla.org/en-US/docs/Web/Web_Components/Using_custom_elements`):

```
class Tooltip extends HTMLElement {
    constructor() {
        super();
```

```
        this.text = this.getAttribute('text');
        this.type = this.getAttribute('type');
        this.typeMap = new Map(Object.entries({
            'success' : "&#x2714",
            'error' : "&#x2716",
            'info' : "&#x2755",
            'default' : "&#x2709"
        }));

        this.shadow = this.attachShadow({mode : 'open'});
        const container = document.createElement('span');
        container.classList.add('wrapper');
        container.classList.add('hidden');
        const type = document.createElement('span');
        type.id = 'icon';
        const el = document.createElement('span');
        el.id = 'main';
        const style = document.createElement('style');
        el.textContent = this.text;
        type.innerHTML = this.getType(this.type);

        style.innerText = `<left out>`
        this.shadow.append(style);
        this.shadow.append(container);
        container.append(type);
        contianer.append(el);
    }
    update() {
        const x = this.getAttribute('x');
        const y = this.getAttribute('y');
        const type = this.getAttribute('type');
        const text = this.getAttribute('text');
        const show = this.getAttribute('show');
        const wrapper = this.shadow.querySelector('.wrapper');
        if( show === "true" ) {
            wrapper.classList.remove('hidden');
        } else {
            wrapper.classList.add('hidden');
        }
        this.shadow.querySelector('#icon').innerHTML = this.getType(type);
        this.shadow.querySelector('#main').innerText = text;
        wrapper.style.left = `${x}px`;
        wrapper.style.top = `${y}px`;
    }
    getType(type) {
        return type ?
            this.typeMap.has(type) ?
                this.typeMap.get(type) :
```

```
                    this.typeMap.get('default') :
            this.typeMap.get('default');
    }
    connectCallback() {
        this.update(this);
    }
    attributeChangedCallback(name, oldValue, newValue) {
        this.update(this);
    }
    static get observedAttributes() {
        return ['x', 'y', 'type', 'text', 'show'];
    }
}

customElements.define('our-tooltip', Tooltip);
```

First, we have a list of attributes that we are going to use to style and position our `tooltip`. They are called x, y, `type`, `text`, and `show`, respectively. Next, we create a map for some emoji-based text so that we can utilize icons without bringing in a full-fledged library for this. We then set up our reusable object inside a shadow container. We also put the shadow root on the object so we have easy access to it. The `update` method will fire on the first creation of our element and on any subsequent changes to our attributes. We can see this in the last three functions. `connectedCallback` will fire once we have been attached to the DOM. `attributeChangedCallback` will alert us to any attribute changes that have occurred. This is very similar to the Proxy API. The last piece lets our object know which attributes we specifically care about, in this case, x, y, `type`, `text`, and `show`. Finally, we register our custom component with the `customElements.define` method, giving it a name and the class that we want to run when one of these objects is created.

Now, if we create our `tooltip`, we can utilize these different properties to make a reusable system for `tooltip` or even alerts. The following code demonstrates this:

```
<our-tooltip show="true" x="100" y="100" icon="success" text="here is our
tooltip"></our-tooltip>
```

We should see a floating box with a checkmark and the text **Here is our tooltip**. We can make this `tooltip` a little bit easier to read by utilizing the templating system that also comes with the Web Component API.

Templates

Now, we have a nice reusable `tooltip` element, but we also have quite a bit of code along with our style tag that is made up entirely of a templated string. What would be best is if we could have this semantic markup put somewhere else and have the execution logic in our web component as it is now. This is where templates come into play. The `<template>` element will not be displayed on the page, but we can still grab it quite easily by giving it an ID. So, one way of refactoring our current code would be to do the following:

```
<template id="tooltip">
    <style>
        /* left out */
    </style>
    <span class="wrapper hidden" x="0" y="0" type="default" show="false">
        <span id="icon">&#2709</span>
        <span id="main">This is some default text</span>
    </span>
</template>
```

And our JavaScript class constructor should now look like this:

```
constructor() {
    super();
    this.type = this.getAttribute('type');
    this.typeMap = // same as before
    const template = document.querySelector('#tooltip').content;
    this.shadow = this.attachShadow({mode : 'open'});
    this.shadow.appendChild(template.cloneNode(true));
}
```

That is much easier to read and much easier to reason about. We now grab our template and get its content. We create a `shadow` object and append our template. We need to make sure to clone our template nodes otherwise we will share the same reference between all of the elements that we decide to create! One thing you will notice is that we cannot now control the text through an attribute. While it was interesting to see this behavior, we really want to leave that information up to the creator of our `tooltip`. We can do this through the `<slot>` element.

A slot gives us an area where we can put HTML in place of that location. We can utilize this to allow users of the `tooltip` to put in the markup they want for that slot. We could give them a template that looks like the following:

```
<span class="wrapper hidden" x="0" y="0" type="default" show="false">
    <span id="icon">&#2709</span>
    <span id="main"><slot name="main_text">This is default
text</slot></span>
</span>
```

And our implementation may appear as follows:

```
<our-tooltip show="true" x="100" y="100" type="success">
    <span slot="main_text">That was a successful operation!</span>
</our-tooltip>
```

As we can see, the use of the shadow DOM, along with web components and the template system in our browser, allows us to create rich elements without the need for external libraries such as Bootstrap or Foundation.

 We may still need these libraries to provide some base-level styling, but we should not need them to the extent we used to. The best-case scenario is that we can write all of our own components with styling and not need to utilize external libraries. But, seeing as how these systems are relatively new, if we are not able to control what our users use, we may be stuck polyfilling.

Understanding the Fetch API

Before the Fetch API, we had to utilize the `XMLHttpRequest` system. To create a request for server data, we had to write something like the following:

```
const oldReq = new XMLHttpRequest();
oldReq.addEventListener('load', function(ev) {
    document.querySelector('#content').innerHTML =
    JSON.stringify(ev.target.response);
});
oldReq.open('GET', 'http://localhost:8081/sample');
oldReq.setRequestHeader('Accept', 'application/json');
oldReq.responseType = 'json';
oldReq.send();
```

First, you will notice that the object type is called XMLHttpRequest. The reason is due to who invented it and the reason behind it. Microsoft had originally developed the technique for the Outlook web access product. Originally, they were transferring XML documents back and forth, and so they named the object for what it was built for. Once other browser vendors, mainly Mozilla, adopted it, they decided to keep the name even though its purpose had shifted from just sending XML documents to sending any type of response from a server to a client.

Second, we add an event listener to the object. Since this is a plain object and not promise-based, we add a listener the old fashioned way with the addEventListener method. This means we would also clean up the event listener once it has been utilized. Next, we open the request, passing in the method we want to send on and where we want to send it to. We can then set up a bunch of request headers (here specifically, we stipulate that we want application/JSON data and we set the responseType to json so that it will be converted properly by the browser). Finally, we send the request.

Once we achieve a response, our event will fire and we can retrieve the response from the event's target. Once we get into posting data, it can get even more cumbersome. This was the reason for things such as jQuery's $.ajax and such methods. It made working with the XMLHttpRequest object a lot easier. So what does this response look like in terms of the Fetch API? This exact same request can be seen as follows:

```
fetch('http://localhost:8081/sample')
.then((res) => res.json())
.then((res) => {
    document.querySelector('#content').innerHTML = JSON.stringify(res);
});
```

We can see that this is quite a bit easier to read and comprehend. First, we set up the URL that we want to hit. If we do not pass the action to the fetch call, it will automatically assume that we are creating a GET request. Next, we get the response and make sure that we get it in json. The responses will always come back as a *promise* (more about that in a bit) and so we want to convert it to the format that we want, in this case, json. From here, we get the final object that we are able to set to the innerHTML of our content. As we can see from this basic example of the two objects, the Fetch API has almost the exact same capabilities that we have with XMLHttpRequest, but it is in an easier-to-understand format and we can easily work with the API.

Promises

As we saw with the previous `fetch` example, we utilized something called a promise. A simple way to think of a promise is a value that we are going to want in the future, and what is returned to us is a contract that states *I will hand it to you later*. Promises were based on the concept of callbacks. If we look at an example of a callback that we could have wrapped around `XMLHttpRequest`, we can see how it functions as a promise:

```
const makeRequest = function(loc, success, failure) {
    const oldReq = new XMLHttpRequest();
    oldReq.addEventListener('load', function(ev) {
        if( ev.target.status === 200 ) {
            success(ev.target.response);
        } else {
            failure(ev.target.response);
        }
    }, { once : true });
    oldReq.open('GET', loc);
    oldReq.setRequestHeader('Accept', 'application/json');
    oldReq.responseType = 'json';
    oldReq.send();
}
```

With this, we get almost the same functionality that we have with a promise but utilizing callbacks or functions that we want to run when something happens. The problem with a callback system is something known as callback hell. This is the idea that highly asynchronous code will always have callbacks and this means that if we want to utilize it, we will have a wonderful tree view of callbacks. This would look like the following:

```
const fakeFetchRequest(url, (res) => {
    res.json((final) => {
        document.querySelector('#content').innerHTML =
        JSON.stringify(final);
    });
});
```

This fake version of `fetch` would be if the API for `fetch` were not promise-based. First, we would pass in our URL. We would also need to provide a callback for when our response comes back in. We would then need to pass that response to the `json` method that would also need a callback to turn the response data into `json`. Finally, we would have the result and would put it into our DOM.

As we can see, callbacks can lead to quite a few problems. Instead, we have the promise. A promise takes a single argument when it is created, a function that has two parameters—resolve and reject. With these, we can either give a success back to our caller through the `resolve` function, or we can error out with the `reject` function. This, in turn, will allow us to chain these promises together through `then` calls and the `catch` call, as we can see in our `fetch` example.

However, these can also lead to another problem. We can get a giant chain of promises that looks a bit better than callbacks, but not by much. We then get the `async/await` system. Instead of constantly chaining promises with `then`, we can use `await` to utilize the response. We can then turn our `fetch` call into something that looks like the following:

```
(async function() {
    const res = await fetch('http://localhost:8081/sample');
    const final = await res.json();
    document.querySelector('#content').innerHTML = JSON.stringify(final);
})();
```

The `async` descriptor before the function tells us that this is an `async` function. We cannot utilize `await` if we do not have this. Next, instead of chaining `then` functions together, we can just `await` the function. The result is what would have been wrapped in our `resolve` function. Now, we have something that reads quite well.

We do need to be careful with the `async/await` system. It does actually wait, so if we put this on the main thread or do not have this wrapped in something, it can block the main thread, causing us to lock up. Also, if we have a bunch of tasks that we want to run at the same time, instead of awaiting them one at a time (making our code sequential), we can utilize `Promise.all()`. This allows us to put a bunch of promises together and allows them all to run asynchronously. Once they all return, we can continue execution.

One nice thing about the `async/await` system is that it can actually be faster than using generic promises. Many browsers have added optimizations around these specific keywords and so we should try to use them at every opportunity we have.

 It has been stated before, but browser vendors are constantly making improvements to their implementations of the ECMAScript standard. This means that new technologies will be slow at first, but once they are in widespread use or they are agreed upon by all vendors, they will start to optimize and usually make them faster than their counterparts. When possible, utilize the newer technologies that browser vendors are giving us!

Back to fetch

So now that we have seen what a `fetch` request looks like, we should take a look at grabbing the underlying readable stream. The `fetch` system has been adding quite a few features, two of these being piping and streaming. This can be seen in a lot of recent web APIs and it can be observed that browser vendors have taken notice of how Node.js has gone about utilizing streams.

Streams, as stated in a previous chapter, are a way of handling chunks of data at a time. It also makes sure that we do not have to grab the entire payload at once, and instead, we can slowly build up the payload. This means that if we have to transform the data, we can do it on the fly as the blocks of data are coming in. It also means that we can work on data types that are not common, such as JSON and plain text.

We will write a basic example of a `TransformStream` that takes our input and does a simple ROT13 encoding to it (ROT13 is a very basic encoder that takes the thirteenth letter after the one that we get). We will be going into streams in much more detail later (these will be the Node.js version, but the concepts are relatively similar). The example looks something like the following:

```
class Rot13Transform {
    constructor() {
    }
    async transform(chunk, controller) {
        const _chunk = await chunk;
        const _newChunk = _chunk.map((item) => ((item - 65 + 13) % 26) +
          65);
        controller.enqueue(_newChunk);
        return;
    }
}

fetch('http://localhost:8081/rot')
.then(response => response.body)
.then(res => res.pipeThrough(new TransformStream(new Rot13Transform())))
.then(res => new Response(res))
.then(response => response.text())
.then(final => document.querySelector('#content').innerHTML = final)
.catch(err => console.error(err));
```

Let's break this example down into the actual `TransformStream` and then the code that utilizes it. First, we create a class that is going to house our rotation code. We then need a method called `transform` that takes two parameters, the chunk, and the controller. The chunk is the data that we are going to get.

Remember that this is not going to get the data all at once so if we needed to build objects or the like, we would need to create a possible holding location for previous data if the current chunk doesn't give us everything we want. In our case, we are simply running a rotation scheme on the underlying bytes so we don't need to have a temporary holder.

Next, the controller is the underlying system for both flow control and for stating that the data is either ready to be read from (a Readable or Transform stream) or written to (a Writable stream). We next await some data and put it in a temporary variable. We then run a simple map expression over each of the bytes and rotate them 13 to the right and then mod them by 26.

ASCII convention has all the uppercase characters starting at 65. This is the reason for some of the math involved here as we are trying to get the number between 0 and 26 first, do the operations, and then move it back into the normal ASCII range.

Once we have rotated our input, we enqueue it on the controller. This means that the data is ready to be read from another stream. Next, we can look at the series of promises that occur. First, we get our data. We then grab the underlying `ReadableStream` from the `fetch` request by grabbing the body of it. We then utilize a method called `pipeThrough`. The piping mechanism automatically handles flow control for us so it makes our lives easier when working with streams.

Flow control is vital to making streams work. It essentially tells other streams if we are backed up, don't send us any more data, or that we are good to keep receiving data. If we did not have this mechanism, we would constantly be having to keep our streams in check, which can be a real pain when we just want to focus on the logic that we want to incorporate.

We pipe the data into a new `TransformStream` that takes our rotation logic. This will now pipe all of the data from the response into our transforming code and make sure that it comes out transformed. We then wrap our `ReadableStream` in a new `Response` so we can work with it just like any other `Response` object from a `fetch` request. We then grab the data as normal text and put it in our DOM.

As we can see, this example showcases that we can do a lot of cool things with the streaming system. While the DOM API is still in flux, these concepts are similar to the streaming interface in Node.js. It also showcases how we could possibly write decoders for more complicated binary types that may come over the wire such as the smile format.

Stopping fetch requests

One action that we may want to do when making requests is to stop them. This could be for a multitude of reasons, such as:

- First, if we make a request in the background and we let a user update parameters for a POST request, we may want to stop the current request and let them make the new one.
- Second, a request could be taking too long and we want to make sure that we stop the request instead of hanging the application or getting it into an unknown state.
- Finally, we may have a caching mechanism that is set up and, once we are done caching a large amount of data, we want to use that. If this happens, we want to stop any pending requests and have it switch over to that source.

Any of these reasons are great for stopping a request and now we have an API that can do this. The AbortController system allows us to stop these requests. What happens is that AbortController has a signal property. We attach this signal to the fetch request and when we call the abort method, it tells the fetch request that we do not want it to keep going with the request. It is very simple and intuitive. The following is an example:

```
(async function() {
    const controller = new AbortController();
    const signal = controller.signal;
    document.querySelector('#stop').addEventListener('click', (ev) => {
        controller.abort();
    });
    try {
        const res = await fetch('http://localhost:8081/longload',
            {signal});
        const final = await res.text();
        document.querySelector('#content').innerHTML = final;
    } catch(e) {
        console.error('failed to download', e);
    }
})();
```

As we can see, we have set up an AbortController system and grabbed its signal property. We then set up a button that, when clicked, will run the abort method. Next, we see the typical fetch request, but inside the options, we pass the signal. Now, when we click the button, we will see that the request stops with a DOM error. We also see a bit of error handling in terms of async/await. aysnc/await can utilize basic try-catch statements to get to an error, just another way that the async/await API makes the code more readable than both the callback and the promise-based versions.

This is another API that is experimental and will most likely have changes in the future. But, we did have this same type of idea in XMLHttpRequest and it makes sense that the Fetch API will be getting it also. Just note that the MDN website is the best place to get up-to-date information on what browsers support and more documentation on any of the experimental APIs that we have discussed and will discuss in future chapters.

The fetch and promise system is a great way to get data from the server and to showcase the new way of handling asynchronous traffic. While we used to have to utilize callbacks and some nasty-looking objects, we now have a nice streamlined API that is quite easy to use. Even though parts of the API are in flux, just note that these systems are most likely going to be in place one way or another.

Summary

In this chapter, we have seen how much of the browser environment has changed over the past 5 years. With new APIs that have enhanced the way we code, through to the DOM APIs that have allowed us to write rich UIs with built-in controls, we are now able to become as vanilla as possible with our applications. This includes the use of fetching external data, along with the new asynchronous APIs such as promises and the async/await system.

In the next chapter, we will be looking at a library that focuses on outputting vanilla JavaScript and giving us a no runtime application environment. We will also be incorporating most of the modern APIs into the rest of the book when we talk about nodes and workers. Play around with these systems and get comfortable with them because we are just getting started.

4
Practical Example - A Look at Svelte and Being Vanilla

Since the past few chapters took a look at the modern web and the APIs available to us, we are now going to take a practical example of those same APIs in action. There has been quite a bit of development in web frameworks that create a kind of *runtime* associated with them. This *runtime* can be almost all attributed to a **Virtual DOM** (**VDOM**) and a state system. When these two things are interconnected, we are able to create rich and reactive frontend. Examples of these frameworks are React, Vue, and Angular.

But what happens if we got rid of the VDOM and runtime concept and somehow compiled all of this code down to vanilla JavaScript and web API calls? This is what the creators of the Svelte framework had in mind: to utilize what we have in the browser instead of creating our own version of the browser (this is an obvious oversimplification, but it does not stretch the truth too much). In this chapter, we will take a look a Svelte and how it achieves some of this magic, along with a few examples of applications written in this framework. This should give a good understanding of Svelte and the *runtime-less* frameworks that are out there and how they could potentially speed up our application runtime speed.

The topics covered in this chapter are as follows:

- A framework for pure speed
- Build the basics – a Todo application
- Getting fancier – basic weather application

Technical requirements

The following are required for this chapter:

- An editor or IDE such as **Visual Studio Code (VS Code)**
- A Node environment setup
- A good understanding of the DOM
- A web browser such as Chrome
- The code found at https://github.com/PacktPublishing/Hands-On-High-Performance-Web-Development-with-JavaScript/tree/master/Chapter04.

A framework for pure speed

The Svelte framework decided to shift the focus from a runtime-based system to a compiler-based system. This can be seen on their website, located at https://svelte.dev. On their front page, it even states the following:

> *Svelte compiles your code to tiny, framework-less vanilla JS – your app starts fast and stays fast.*

By moving the steps from the runtime to the initial compile, we are able to create applications that will download and run fast. But, before we can start looking at this compiler, we need to get it onto our machines. The following steps should enable us to start writing code for Svelte (taken directly from https://svelte.dev/blog/the-easiest-way-to-get-started):

```
> npx degit sveltejs/template todo
> cd todo
> npm install
> npm run dev
```

With these commands, we now have a running Svelte application located at localhost:5000. Let's take a look at what the package.json has inside of it that got us up and running so fast. First, we will notice that we have a bunch of Rollup-based dependencies. Rollup is a module bundler for JavaScript that also has a rich set of tools to do many other tasks. It is similar to webpack or Parcel, but it is the tool that Svelte has decided to rely on. We will look at Rollup in more depth in Chapter 12, *Building and Deploying a Full Web Application*. Just know that it is compiling and bundling our code for us.

It also seems that we got a `sirv` called (as can be seen in the `package.json` file). If we look up `sirv` inside `npm`, we will see that it is a static asset server, but, instead of looking for the files directly on the filesystem (which is quite an expensive operation), it caches the request headers and responses in memory for a certain period of time. This allows it to serve assets that may have already been served quickly, since it only has to look at its own memory instead of doing an I/O operation to look for the asset. The **command-line interface (CLI)** allows us to set up the server quite quickly.

Finally, we start our application in dev mode. If we look at the `scripts` section of the `package.json` file, we will see that it runs the following command: `run-p start:dev autobuild`. The `run-p` command says to run all subsequent commands in parallel. The `start:dev` command says to start our `sirv` server up in dev mode, and the `autobuild` command tells Rollup to compile and watch our code. This means that whenever we make changes to the files, it will automatically build for us. Let's quickly see this in action. Let's go into the `src` folder and make a change to the `App.svelte` file. Add the following:

```
//inside of the script tag
export let name;
export let counter;

function clicker() {
    counter += 1;
}

//add to the template
<span>We have been clicked {counter} times</span>
<button on:click={clicker}>Click me!</button>
```

We will notice that our web page has automatically updated, and we now have a reactive web page based on an event! This is really nice when we are in development mode since we don't have to keep triggering the compiler.

 The editor of choice in these examples is VS Code. If we head to the extensions section of VS Code, there is a nice plugin for Svelte. We can utilize this plugin for syntax highlighting and some alerts when we are doing something wrong. If the preferred editor does not have a Svelte plugin, try to at least get the HTML highlighting enabled for the editor.

Alright: this simple example already gives us plenty to look at. First, the `App.svelte` file gives us a similar syntax to Vue files. We have a section for JavaScript, a section for styling, and a section for our enhanced HTML. We have exported two variables, called `name` and `counter`. We also have a function that we are utilizing in the click handler of our button. We have also enabled a style for our `h1` element.

It looks like the curly braces add the one-way data binding that we expect from these reactive frameworks. It also looks like we attach events in a simple `on:<event>` binding, instead of utilizing the built-in `on<event>` system.

If we now head into the `main.js` file, we will see that we are importing the Svelte file that we were just looking at. We then create a new *app* (it should look familiar to other reactive frameworks) and we target the body of the document with our application. On top of this, we are setting up some properties, the `name` and `counter` variables that we exported before. We then export this as the default export for this file.

All of this should seem quite similar to the previous chapter, when we looked at the class and module system that is built into the browsers. Svelte has just piggybacked on these similar concepts to write their compiler. Now, we should take a look at the output of the compilation process. We will notice that we have a `bundle.css` and a `bundle.js` file. If we first take a look at the `bundle.css` file that was generated, we will see something like the following:

```
h1.svelte-i7qo5m{color:purple}
```

Essentially, Svelte is *mimicking* web components by putting them under a unique namespace, in this case, `svelte-i7qo5m`. This is quite straightforward, and those that have utilized other systems will notice that this is how a lot of frameworks create scoped stylesheets.

Now, if we go into the `bundle.js` file we will see quite a different story. First, we have an **Immediately Invoked Function Expression (IIFE)**, which is the live reload code. Next, we have another IIFE that is assigning our application to a global variable called `app`. The code inside then has a bunch of boilerplate code such as `noop`, `run`, and `blank_object`. We also can see that Svelte wraps many of the built-in methods, such as the DOM's `appendChild` and `createElement` APIs. This can be seen in the following code:

```
function append(target, node) {
    target.appendChild(node);
}
function insert(target, node, anchor) {
    target.insertBefore(node, anchor || null);
}
```

```
function detach(node) {
    node.parentNode.removeChild(node);
}
function element(name) {
    return document.createElement(name);
}
function text(data) {
    return document.createTextNode(data);
}
function space() {
    return text(' ');
}
```

They have even wrapped the addEventListener system in their own form so they can control callbacks and lifetime events. This can be seen with the following code:

```
function listen(node, event, handler, options) {
    node.addEventListener(event, handler, options);
    return () => node.removeEventListener(event, handler, options);
}
```

They then have a bunch of arrays that they are utilizing as queues for the various events. They loop through them and pop and run the events as they come up. This can is seen in the flush method that they have laid out. One interesting note is that they have seen_callbacks set. This is so that they stop infinite looping by counting methods/events that can cause an infinite loop. For example, component *A* gets an update that subsequently sends an update to component *B*, which then sends an update to component *A*. WeakSet may have been a better choice here, but they have opted to utilize the regular Set since it will be dumped once the flush method has finished.

One of the final functions that would be good to look at is the create_fragment method. We will notice that it returns an object that has a create function named c. As we can see, this creates the HTML elements that we had in our Svelte file. We will then see an m property, which is the mount function that adds our DOM elements to the actual document. The p property updates the properties that we have bound to this Svelte component (in this case, the name and counter properties). Finally, we have the d property, which relates to the destroy method and removes all the DOM elements and the DOM events.

Looking through this code, we can see that Svelte is utilizing a lot of the concepts that we would use if we were building a UI from scratch and utilizing the DOM API ourselves, but they have just wrapped it into a bunch of convenient wrappers and clever lines of code.

 A great way to understand a library is to read the source code or see what it outputs. By doing this, we can find where the magic usually lies. While this may not be beneficial right away, it can help us write for the framework or even utilize some of the tricks that we see in their code in our own code bases. One way of learning is to imitate others.

Out of all of this, we can see how Svelte states that there is no runtime. They are utilizing the basic elements that the DOM gives us in some nice convenient wrappers. They also give us a nice file format to write our code in. Even though this may seem like some basic code, we are able to write complex applications in this style.

The first application we will write is a simple Todo application. We will be adding some of our own ideas to it, but it will be a traditional Todo application at the start.

Build the basics – a Todo application

To start off our Todo application, let's go ahead and utilize the template that we already have. Now, in most Todo applications, we want to be able to do the following things:

- Add
- Remove/mark complete
- Update

So what we have is a basic CRUD application without any server operations. Let's go ahead and write the Svelte HTML that we would expect for this application:

```
<script>
    import { createEventDispatcher } from 'svelte';
    export let completed;
    export let num;
    export let description;

    const dispatch = createEventDispatcher();
</script>
<style>
    .completed {
        text-decoration: line-through;
    }
```

```
</style>
<li class:completed>
    Task {num}: {description}
    <input type="checkbox" bind:checked={completed} />
    <button on:click="{() => dispatch('remove', null)}">Remove</button>
</li>
```

We have split our Todo application into a Todo component and the general application. The Todo element will hold all of our logic for the completion and deletion of the element. As we can see from the preceding example, we are doing the following things:

- We expose the number this task is and the description.
- We have a completed property that is hidden from the main application.
- We have a class for styling a completed item.
- The list element with the completion variable is bound to the complete class.
- The num and description properties are tied to information.
- A checkbox is added for when we complete an item.
- And there's a button that will tell our application what we want to be removed.

That is quite a bit to digest, but when we put it all together, we will see that this holds most of the logic for an individual Todo item. Now, we need to add all of the logic for our application. It should look something like the following:

```
<script>
    import Todo from './Todo.svelte';

    let newTodoText = '';
    const Todos = new Set();

    function addTodo() {
        const todo = new Todo({
            target: document.querySelector('#main'),
            props: {
                num : Todos.size,
                description : newTodoText
            }
        });
        newTodoText = '';
        todo.$on('remove', () => {
            Todos.delete(todo);
            todo.$destroy();
        });
        Todos.add(todo);
    }
</script>
```

```
<style></style>
<h1>Todo Application!</h1>
<ul id="main">
</ul>
<button on:click={addTodo}>Add Todo</button>
<input type="text" bind:value={newTodoText} />
```

We first import the `Todo` that we created before. We then have `newTodoText` as a property bound to our input text. Then, we create a set to store all of our `Todos`. Next, we create an `addTodo` method that will be bound to the `click` event of our **Add Todo** button. This will create a new `Todo`, binding the element to our unordered list and setting the properties to our set size and input text respectively. We reset the `Todo` text, and add a remove listener to destroy the `Todo` and also remove it from our set. Finally, we add it to our set.

We now have a basic Todo application! All of this logic should be fairly straightforward. Let's add some additional features as we had in a previous chapter. We will add the following things to our Todo application to make it a bit more robust and useful:

- Have due dates associated with each `Todo`
- Keep a count of all the `Todos`
- Create filters that will filter based on overdue, completed, and all
- Transitions based on the filters and the addition of each `Todo`

First, let's add a due date to our Todo application. We will add a new exported field inside our `Todo.svelte` file called `dueDate`, and we will also add it to our template like the following:

```
//inside of script tag
export let dueDate;

//part of the template
<li class:completed>
    Task {num}: {description} - Due on {dueDate}
    <input type="checkbox" bind:checked={completed} />
    <button on:click="{() => dispatch('remove', null)}">Remove</button>
</li>
```

Then, inside of our `App.svelte` file, we will add a date control and make sure that when we add our `Todo` to the list, we also make sure that we put this field back in. This should look like the following:

```
//inside of the script tag
let newTodoDate = null;
function addTodo() {
    const todo = new Todo({
```

```
        target: document.querySelector('#main'),
        props: {
            num : Todos.size + 1,
            dueDate : newTodoDate,
            description : newTodoText
        }
    });
    newTodoText = '';
    newTodoDate = null;
    todo.$on('remove', () => {
        Todos.delete(todo);
        todo.$destroy();
    });
    Todos.add(todo);
}

//part of the template
<input type="date" bind:value={newTodoDate} />
```

We now have a fully functioning due date system. Next, we will add the number of current `Todos` to our application. This is as simple as binding some text in a span to the size of our set, as shown in the following code:

```
//inside of script tag
let currSize = 0;
function addTodo() {
    const todo = new Todo({
        // code removed for readability
    });
    todo.$on('remove', () => {
        Todos.delete(todo);
        currSize = Todos.size;
        todo.$destroy();
    });
    Todos.add(todo);
    currSize = Todos.size;
}

//part of the template
<h1>Todo Application! <span> Current number of Todos:
{currSize}</span></h1>
```

Alright, now we want to be able to do something with all of the dates and completed states. Let's add some filters so we can remove `Todos` that do not fit our criteria. We will be adding the completed and overdue filters. We are going to make these checkboxes since an item can be both overdue and completed at the same time:

```
//inside of script tag
let completed = false;
let overdue = false;

//part of the template
<label><input type="checkbox" bind:checked={completed}
    on:change={handleFilter}/>Completed</label>
<label><input type="checkbox" bind:checked={overdue}
    on:change={handleFilter}/>Overdue</label>
```

Our handle filter logic should look something like the following:

```
function handleHide(item) {
    const currDate = Date.now();
    if( completed && overdue ) {
        item.hidden = !item.completed || new Date(item.dueDate).getTime() <
currDate;
        return;
    }
    if( completed ) {
        item.hidden = !item.completed;
        return;
    }
    if( overdue ) {
        item.hidden = new Date(item.dueDate).getTime() < currDate;
        return;
    }
    item.hidden = false;
}

function handleFilter() {
    for(const item of Todos) {
        handleHide(item);
    }
}
```

We also need to make sure that we have the same hide logic for any new `Todo` items:

```
const todo = new Todo({
    target: document.querySelector('#main'),
    props: {
        num : Todos.size + 1,
        dueDate : newTodoDate,
```

```
                description : newTodoText
            }
    });
    handleHide(todo);
```

Finally, our `Todo.svelte` component should look like the following:

```svelte
<svelte:options accessors={true} />
<script>
    import { createEventDispatcher } from 'svelte';
    export let num;
    export let description;
    export let dueDate;
    export let hidden = false;
    export let completed = false;

    const dispatch = createEventDispatcher();
</script>
<style>
    .completed {
        text-decoration: line-through;
    }
    .hidden {
        display : none;
    }
</style>
<li class:completed class:hidden>
    Task {num}: {description} - Due on {dueDate}
    <input type="checkbox" bind:checked={completed} />
    <button on:click="{() => dispatch('remove', null)}">Remove</button>
</li>
```

Most of this should look familiar, except for the top portion. There are special tags that we can add to Svelte files that allow us access to certain properties, such as the following:

- `<svelte:window>` gives us access to the window events.
- `<svelte:body>` gives us access to the body events.
- `<svelte:head>` gives us access to the head of the document.
- `<svelte:component>` gives us access to ourselves as a DOM element.
- `<svelete:self>` allows us to contain ourselves (for recursive structures such as trees).
- `<svelte:options>` allows us to add compiler options to our component.

In this case, we want our parent component to be able to access our properties through getters/setters, so we set the `accessors` option to `true`. This is how we are able to change our hidden property inside of the `App.svelte` file and allows us to get properties that are on each `Todo`.

Finally, let's add in some fade in and out transitions. Svelte comes with some nice animations when we add/remove elements. The one that we are going to use is the `fade` animation. So, our `Todo.svelte` file will now have the following added:

```
//inside of script tag
import { fade } form 'svelte/transition';

//part of template
{#if !hidden}
    <li in:fade out:fade class:completed>
        Task {num}: {description} - Due on {dueDate}
        <input type="checkbox" bind:checked={completed} />
        <button on:click="{() => dispatch('remove', null)}">Remove</button>
    </li>
{/if}
```

The special syntax is for conditional DOM addition/subtraction. The same way we can add/remove children with the DOM API, Svelte is doing the same. Next, we can see that we added the `in:fade` and `out:fade` directives to the list elements. Now, when the element is added or removed from the DOM, it will fade in and out.

We now have a fairly functional Todo application. We have filtering logic, `Todos` that are tied to due dates, and even a bit of animation. The next step is to clean up the code a bit. We can do this with the stores built into Svelte.

Stores are a way of sharing state without having to do some of the trickery that we have had to use in our application (we opened up the accessor system when we probably should not have). The shared state between our `Todos` and our main application is the overdue and completed filters. Each `Todo` should most likely be in control of this property, but we are currently utilizing the accessor option and all of the filtering is done in our main application. With a writable store, we no longer have to do that.

First, we write a `stores.js` file like the following:

```
import { writable } from 'svelte/store';

export const overdue = writable(false);
export const completed = writable(false);
```

Next, we update our `App.svelte` file to not target the `hidden` property in the `Todos`, and we bind the `checked` properties of our checkbox inputs to the stores like the following:

```
//inside of script tag
import { completed, overdue } from './stores.js';

//part of the template
<label><input type="checkbox" bind:checked={$completed} />Completed</label>
<label><input type="checkbox" bind:checked={$overdue} />Overdue</label>
```

The dollar sign in front of our stores means that these are stores and not variables in our scripts. It allows us to update and subscribe to the stores without having to unsubscribe from them on destroy. Finally, we can update our `Todo.svelte` file to look like the following:

```
<script>
    import { overdue, completed } from './stores.js';
    import { createEventDispatcher, onDestroy } from 'svelte';
    import { fade } from 'svelte/transition';
    export let num;
    export let description;
    export let dueDate;
    let _completed = false;

    const dispatch = createEventDispatcher();
</script>
<style>
    .completed {
        text-decoration: line-through;
    }
</style>
{#if
    !(
        ($completed && !_completed) ||
        ($overdue && new Date(dueDate).getTime() >= Date.now())
    )
}
    <li in:fade out:fade class:_completed>
        Task {num}: {description} - Due on {dueDate}
        <input type="checkbox" bind:checked={_completed} />
        <button on:click="{() => dispatch('remove', null)}">Remove</button>
    </li>
{/if}
```

We have added the overdue and completed stores to our system. You may have noticed that we got rid of the compiler option at the top of the file. We then link our `#if` condition to these stores. We have now put the responsibility of hiding the `Todos` based on filters on the `Todos` themselves while also removing quite a bit of code. It should start to become obvious that there are many ways that we can build applications in Svelte and maintain quite a bit of control over our application.

Before moving onto the next application, go ahead and look at the bundled JavaScript and CSS along with adding new features to the application. Next, we are going to look at building a weather application and getting data from a server for this information.

Getting fancier – a basic weather application

It should be quite obvious that Svelte has built up its compiler to work with most of the modern ECMAScript standards. One area where they do not provide any sort of wrapper is for fetching data. A good way to add this and see the effects is to build a basic weather application.

A weather application, at its core, needs to be able to take in a zip code or city and spit out information about the current weather for that region. We can also get an outlook for the weather based on this location. Finally, we can also save these choices in the browser, so we can use them when we come back to the application.

For our weather data, we are going to pull from `https://openweathermap.org/api`. Here, the free service will allow us to get the current weather. On top of this, we will need an input system that will accept the following:

- The city/country
- The zip code (if no country is given, we will assume US since that is the default for the API)

When we enter the correct value, we will store it in `LocalStorage`. Later in the chapter, we will take a more in-depth look at the `LocalStorage` API, but just note that it is a key-value storage mechanism in the browser. When we go to enter a value for the input, we will get a drop-down of all of our previous searches. We will also add the ability to remove any one of these results from the list.

First, we need to get an API key. To do so, follow these steps:

1. Go to `https://openweathermap.org/api` and follow the instructions to get an API key.
2. Once we have created an account and verify it, we will be able to add API keys.
3. After login, there should be a tab that says **API keys**. If we go to that, we should be greeted with a **no api keys** message.
4. We can create a key and add a name to it if we want (we can just call it `default`).
5. With this key, we are now able to start calling their server.

Let's go ahead and set up a test call. The following code should work:

```
let api_key = "<your_api_key>";
fetch(`https://api.openweathermap.org/data/2.5/weather?q=London&appid=${api
_key}`)
    .then((res) => res.json())
    .then((final) => console.log(final));
```

If we put this into a code snippet, we should get back a JSON object with a bunch of data inside of it. Now we can move onto utilizing Svelte with this API to create a nice weather application.

Let's set up our application in the same way we set up our Todo application. Run the following commands:

```
> cd ..
> npx degit sveltejs/template weather
> cd weather
> npm install
> npm run dev
```

Now that we have started the environment, let's create a boilerplate application with some basic styling. In the `global.css` file, add the following lines to the body:

```
display: flex;
flex-direction : column;
align-items : center;
```

This will make sure our elements are both column-based and that they will start from the center and grow out. This will give us a nice look for our application. Next, we are going to create two Svelte components, a `WeatherInput` and a `WeatherOutput` component. Next, we are going to focus on the input.

We will need to have the following items so we can get the correct input from our users:

- Input for the zip code or the city
- Input for the country code
- A Submit button

We are also going to add some conditional logic to our application. Instead of trying to parse the input, we are going to conditionally render a text or number input based on a checkbox to the left of our input. With these ideas, our `WeatherInput.svelte` file should look like the following:

```
<script>
    import { zipcode } from './stores.js';
    const api_key = '<your_api_key>'

    let city = null;
    let zip = null;
    let country_code = null;

    const submitData = function() {
        fetch(`https://api.openweathermap.org/data/2.5/weather?q=${zipcode
         ? zip : city},${country_code}&appid=${api_key}`)
            .then(res => res.json())
            .then(final => console.log(final));
    }
</script>
<style>
    input:valid {
        border: 1px solid #333;
    }
    input:invalid {
        border: 1px solid #c71e19;
    }
</style>
<div>
    <input type="checkbox" bind:checked={$zipcode} />
    {#if zipcode}
        <input type="number" bind:value={zip} minLength="6" maxLength="10"
         require />
    {:else}
        <input type="text" bind:value={city} required />
    {/if}
    <input type="text" bind:value={country_code} minLength="2"
     maxLength="2" required />
    <button on:click={submitData}>Check</button>
</div>
```

With this, we have the basic template for our input. First, we create a `zipcode` store to conditionally display a number or text input. Then, we create a couple of local variables that we will bind to our input values. The `submitData` function will submit everything once we are ready to get some type of response. Currently, we are just logging the output to the developer console.

For styling, we just added some basic styling for valid versus invalid inputs. Our template gives us a checkbox to turn on the `zipcode` feature or to turn it off. We then conditionally show the `zipcode` or the city textbox. Each of these textboxes has the built-in validation added to it. Next, we added another text field to get a country code from our users. Finally, we added a button that will go out and check for the data.

 The brackets are heavily utilized in Svelte. One feature of input validation is regex based. The field is called a pattern. If we try to utilize brackets in here, it will cause the Svelte compiler to fail. Just be aware of this.

Before we get to the output, let's go ahead and add some labels to our input to make it easier for users to use. The following should do it:

```
//in the style tag
input {
    margin-left: 10px;
}
label {
    display: inline-block;
}
#cc input {
    width: 3em;
}
```

For every `input` element, we have wrapped them in a `label` like so:

```
<label id="cc">Country Code<input type="text" bind:value={country_code}
minLength="2" maxLength="2" required /></label>
```

With this, we have the basic user interface for our `input` element. Now, we need to have the `fetch` call actually output to something that can be available to our `WeatherOutput` element once we have made it. Instead of just passing this data out as props, let's create a custom store that implements a `gather` method. Inside of `stores.js`, we should have something that looks like the following:

```
function createWeather() {
    const { subscribe, update } = writable({});
    const api_key = '<your_api_key>';
```

```
return {
    subscribe,
    gather: (cc, _z, zip=null, city=null) => {
        fetch(`https://api.openweathermap.org/data/2.5/weather?=${_z ?
        zip : city},${cc}&appid=${api_key})
            .then(res => res.json())
            .then(final => update(() => { return {...final} }));
    }
}
}
```

We have now moved the logic of getting the data into a store and we can now subscribe to this store to update ourselves. This will mean that we can make the WeatherOutput component subscribe to this for some basic output. The following code should be put into WeatherOtuput.svelte:

```
<script>
    import { weather } from './stores.js';
</script>
<style>
</style>
<p>{JSON.stringify($weather)}</p>
```

All we are doing for now is putting the output of our weather into a paragraph element and stringifying it so we can read the output without looking at the console. We also need to update our App.svelte file and import the WeatherOutput component like so:

```
//inside the script tag
import WeatherOutput from './WeatherOutput.svelte'

//part of the template
<WeatherOutput></WeatherOutput>
```

If we now test our application, we should get some ugly-looking JSON, but we have now tied our two components through the store! Now, all we need to do is pretty up the output, and we have a fully functioning weather application! Change the styling and the template inside of WeatherOutput.svelte to the following:

```
<div>
    {#if $weather.error}
        <p>There was an error getting your data!</p>
    {:else if $weather.data}
        <dl>
            <dt>Conditions</dt>
            <dd>{$weather.weather}</dd>
            <dt>Temperature</dt>
            <dd>{$weather.temperature.current}</dd>
```

```
            <dd>{$weather.temperature.min}</dd>
            <dd>{$weather.temperature.max}</dd>
            <dt>Humidity</dt>
            <dd>{$weather.humidity}</dd>
            <dt>Sunrise</dt>
            <dd>{$weather.sunrise}</dd>
            <dt>Sunset</dt>
            <dd>{$weather.sunset}</dd>
            <dt>Windspeed</dt>
            <dd>{$weather.windspeed}</dd>
            <dt>Direction</dt>
            <dd>{$weather.direction}</dd>
        </dl>
    {:else}
        <p>No city or zipcode has been submitted!</p>
    {/if}
</div>
```

Finally, we should add a new control so our users can pick metric or imperial units for the output. Add the following to the `WeatherInput.svelte`:

```
<label>Metric?<input type="checkbox" bind:checked={$metric}</label>
```

We will also use a new `metric` store to the `stores.js` file that defaults to `false`. With all of this, we should have now have a functioning weather application! The only piece that we have left is to add the `LocalStorage` capabilities.

There are two types of storage that do similar things. They are `LocalStorage` and `SessionStorage`. The main difference is how long they will stay cached. `LocalStorage` stays until the user deletes the cache or the application developer decides to delete it. `SessionStorage` stays in the cache for the lifetime of the page. Once the user decides to leave the page, `SessionStorage` will clear out. Leaving the page means closing the tab or navigating away; it does not mean reloading the page or Chrome crashing and the user recovering the page. It is up to the designer which one to use.

Utilizing `LocalStorage` is quite easy. The object is held on the window in our case (if we were in a worker, it would be held on the global object). One thing to keep in mind is that when we utilize `LocalStorage`, it converts all values to strings, so we will need to convert complex objects if we want to store them.

To change our application, let's create a new component specifically for our drop-down. Let's call it `Dropdown`. First, create a `Dropdown.svelte` file. Next, add the following code to the file:

```
<script>
    import { weather } from './stores.js';
    import { onDestroy, onMount } from 'svelte';

    export let type = "text";
    export let name = "DEFAULT";
    export let value = null;
    export let required = true;
    export let minLength = 0;
    export let maxLength = 100000;
    let active = false;
    let inputs = [];
    let el;

    const unsubscribe = weather.subscribe(() => {
        if(!inputs.includes(value) ) {
            inputs = [...inputs, value];
            localStorage.setItem(name, inputs);
        }
        value = '';
    });
    const active = function() {
        active = true;
    }
    const deactivate = function(ev) {
        if(!ev.path.includes(el) )
            active = false;
    }
    const add = function(ev) {
        value = ev.target.innerText;
        active = false;
    }
    const remove = function(ev) {
        const text = ev.target.parentNode.querySelector('span').innerText;
        const data = localStorage.getItem(name).split(',');
        data.splice(data.indexOf(text));
        inputs = [...data];
        localStorage.setItem(name, inputs);
    }
    onMount(() => {
        const data = localStorage.getItem(name);
        if( data === "" ) { inputs = []; }
        else { inputs = [...data.split(',')]; }
    });
```

```
        onDestroy(() => {
            unsubscribe();
        });
</script>
<style>
    input:valid {
        border 1px solid #333;
    }
    input:invalid {
        border 1px solid #c71e19;
    }
    div {
        position : relative;
    }
    ul {
        position : absolute;
        top : 100%;
        list-style-type : none;
        background : white;
        display : none;
    }
    li {
        cursor : hand;
        border-bottom : 1px solid black;
    }
    ul.active {
        display : inline-block;
    }
</style>
<svelte:window on:mousedown={deactivate} />
<div>
    {#if type === "text"}
        <input on:focus={activate} type="text" bind:value={value}
         {minLength} {maxLength} {required} />
    {:else}
        <input on:focus={activate} type="number" bind:value={value}
         {minLength} {maxLength} {required} />
    {/if}
    <ul class:active bind:this={el}>
        {#each inputs as input }
            <li><span on:click={add}>{input}</span> <button
             on:click={remove}>&times;</button></li>
        {/each}
    </ul>
</div>
```

This is quite a bit of code, so let's break down what we have just done. First, we are taking our inputs and changing them to a `dropdown` component. We are also internalizing a lot of the state for this component. We open up various fields for the user to be able to customize the fields themselves. The main field that we need to make sure that we set is `name`. This is what we are using for the `LocalStorage` key to store our searches.

Next, we subscribe to the `weather` store. We do not use the actual data, but we do get the event so we can add the selection to the store if it is unique (a set could be used here instead of an array). We add some basic logic if we want to activate the drop-down if we are focused or if we have clicked outside of our drop-down. We also add some logic to the click event of the list element (we actually add it to the children of the list element) for putting the text into the drop-down or removing from our `LocalStorage`. Finally, we add behavior to the `onMount` and the `onDestroy` of our component. `onMount` will pull from `localStorage` and add this to our inputs list. The `onDestroy` just removes our subscription so we do not have a memory leak.

The rest of the styling and the templating should look familiar, except for the `bind:this` in the unordered list system. This allows us to bind a variable to the element itself. This allows us to deactivate our drop-down list if the element is not inside of the list of elements in the event path.

With this, make the following updates to the `WeatherInput.svelte`:

```
//inside the script tag
import Dropdown from './Dropdown.svelte';

//part of the template
{#if $zipcode}
    <label>Zip<Dropdown name="zip" type="number" bind:value={zip}
      minLength="6" maxLength="10"></Dropdown></label>
{:else}
    <label>City<Dropdown name="city" bind:value={city}></Dropdown></label>
{/if}
<label>Country Code<Dropdown name="cc" bind:value={country_code}
  minLength="2" maxLength="2"></Dropdown></label>
```

We have now created a semi-reusable `dropdown` component (we do rely on the weather store, so it really only works with our application) and have created something that looks like a single component.

Summary

Svelte is an interesting framework in which we compile our code to Vanilla JavaScript. It utilizes modern ideas such as modules, templates, and scoped styling. We are also able to create reusable components in a simple manner. While there are even more optimizations that we could make to the applications that we have built, we can see how fast they truly are. While Svelte may not become a mainstream choice for application development, it is a great framework to see many of the concepts we have explored in previous chapters.

Next, we will take a break from the browser and take a look at how we can utilize JavaScript on the server utilizing Node.js. Many of the ideas that we have seen here will be applied there. We will also see new ways of coding our applications and how we can use one language across the entire web ecosystem.

Switching Contexts - No DOM, Different Vanilla

5

As we turn our attention away from the browser, we'll move on to a context that most backend programmers will be familiar with. Node.js provides us with a familiar language, known as JavaScript, that can be used in a system context. While Node.js is known for being a language that servers can be written in, it can be used for most capabilities that other languages are known for. If we wanted to create a **command-line interface** (**CLI**) tool, for example, we have the ability to do that.

Node.js also gives us a similar programming context that we have seen in the browser. We get an event loop that allows us to have asynchronous **input and output** (**I/O**). How this is achieved is through the libuv library. Later in this chapter, we will explain this library and how it helps to give us the common event loop that we are used to. First, we will look at getting Node.js up and running, along with writing some simple programs that we can run.

In this chapter, we will cover the following topics:

- Getting Node.js
- Understanding the DOM-less world
- Debugging and inspecting code

Let's get started.

Technical requirements

This chapter requires the following technical requirements:

- An editor or IDE such as VS Code
- This chapter's code, which can be found at `https://github.com/PacktPublishing/Hands-On-High-Performance-Web-Development-with-JavaScript/tree/master/Chapter05`.

Getting Node.js

Previous chapters have asked for a Node.js runtime. In this chapter, we will take a look at how we can get this installed on our system. If we head over to `https://Node.js.org/en/`, we will be able to download either the **Long-Term Support** (**LTS**) version or the current version. For this book, it is recommended to get the current version as the module support is better.

For Windows, all we need to do is download and run the executable. For OS X and Linux, this should also be simple. For Linux users especially, there may be a version in the repository manager for a specific distribution, but this version may be old or line up with the LTS version. Remember: we want to be running the latest version of Node.js.

Once we have it installed, we should be able to invoke the `node` command from any command line (Linux users may have to invoke the `Node.js` command since some repositories already had a node package inside of their repository). Once invoked, we should be greeted with a **Read Evaluate Print Loop** (**REPL**) tool. This gives us the ability to test out some code before we actually write it into a file. Run the following fragments of code:

```
1 + 2 //3
typeof("this") //'string'
const x = 'what' //undefined
x //'what'
x = 'this' //TypeError: Assignment to a constant variable
const fun = function() { console.log(x); } //undefined
fun() //'what' then undefined
fun = 'something' //TypeError: Assignment to a constant variable
```

From these examples, it should be obvious that we are working in a similar environment to the one we are used to in the browser. We have access to most of the data manipulation and functional concepts that we had in the browser.

Many of the libraries/APIs that we do not have access to are ones that are specific to the browser, such as the DOM APIs. We also don't have access to any of the browser external resource access libraries, such as `Fetch` or `XMLHttpRequest`. We have lower-level versions of them that we will talk about later, but it should be noted that, in some ways, it isn't as simple as calling the fetch API.

Go ahead and play with the REPL system. If we want to come out of it, we just need to use *Ctrl + C* twice on Windows (Linux should be the same; for OS X, we need to use *command + C*). Now, to run a script, all we need to do is put some code in a JavaScript file and call `node <filename>`. This should run our script in immediate mode. This can be seen in the following `example.js` file:

```
const x = 'what';
console.log('this is the value of x', x); //'this is the value of x what'
const obj = {
    what : 'that',
    huh : 'this',
    eh : 'yeah'
}
console.log(obj); // { what : 'that', huh : 'this', eh : 'yeah' }
```

To get access to the various built-in libraries that Node.js gives us, we can utilize two different methods. First, we can use the old `require` system. The following script shows this capability:

```
const os = require('os');

console.log(os.arch()); //prints out x64 on 64-bit OS
console.log(os.cpus()); //prints out information on our CPU
```

This is the current way of bringing in built-in/user-built modules. It was the style that the Node team decided on since there was no common way of bringing in modules. We had systems such as RequireJS or CommonJS, and Node.js decided on the CommonJS style of bringing in modules. However, as we have learned, there is also a standardized way of bringing modules into the browser. The same is true for the Node.js platform.

 The module system is currently in its experimental phase, but if need be, use a system such as RollupJS to change the code into a system version that is universally recognized, such as the **Universal Module Dependency (UDM)** system.

This system should look very familiar. The following script shows the previous example but in the module import system:

```
import os from 'os';

console.log(os.arch());
console.log(os.cpus());
```

We will also need to have a `package.json` file that has `"type" : "module"` in its manifest.

Overview of the package.json file

The `package.json` file holds all of the information about the package we are trying to build. It even gives us the ability to tie it into our version control system, and we can even tie it into our build system. Let's go over this now.

First, a `package.json` file should have the following fields filled out:

- `name`: This is the name of the package.
- `version`: This is the current version of our software package.
- `type`: This should either be `module` or `commonjs`. This will allow us to distinguish between legacy systems and the new ECMAScript module system.
- `license`: This is how we want to license our module. Most of the time, just go ahead and put the MIT license. However, if we do want to lock it down more, we could always use the GPL or LGPL license.
- `author`: This is an object with the `name`, `email`, and `url` fields. This gives attribution to the software and helps people to know who built it.
- `main`: This is the main entry point of the module. This will allow others to use our module and require/import it. It will also let the system know where to look for our starting point of the module.

There are many additional fields that can be used, as follows:

- `man`: This allows the `man` command to find the file that we wish to serve for our documentation.
- `description`: This allows us to provide more information about our module and what it does. If the description is longer than two to three sentences, it is recommended to have an accompanying `README` file.
- `repository`: This allows others to find the repository and contribute to it or submit bug reports/feature requests.

- `config`: This is an object that can be used by the scripts that we define in the scripts section of our `package.json` file. Scripts will be discussed in more detail soon.
- `dependencies`: This is a list of modules that our module depends on. This can range from modules that live in the public `npm` registry, private repositories, Git repositories, tarballs, and even local file paths for local development.
- `devDependencies`: This is a list of dependencies that are needed for the development of this package.
- `peerDependencies`: This is a list of dependencies that our package may need if someone utilizes a piece of the system. This allows our users to download the core system, and if they want to utilize other pieces, they can download the peer dependencies that these other subsystems need.
- `os`: This is a list of OSes that we run on. This can also be the negative version of this, such as `!darwin`, meaning that this system will run on all OSes other than OS X.
- `engines`: The versions of Node.js that we run on. We will want to use this when we utilize a feature (such as ECMAScript modules) that has been introduced in a recent version. We may also want to utilize this feature if we're using modules that have been deprecated and want to lock the Node.js version to an older one.

There are a few more fields that are located in the `package.json` file, but these are the most common ones.

One specific section of the `package.json` file that we want to look at is the scripts section. If we go to the website of `npm`, about the scripts section, it states the following:

> *The* `scripts` *property is a dictionary containing script commands that are run at various times in the life cycle of your package. The key is the life cycle event, and the value is the command to run at that point.*

If we go to the more details section, we will see that there are life cycle hooks that we can use so that we have various scripts running through the bundling and distribution process.

 It should be noted that this information is specific to **Node Package Manager (npm)**. While learning about Node.js, we will come across `npm` quite a bit, so learning about Node.js has also meant learning about `npm`.

Some of the specific points that we are interested in are the **prepare** and **install** sections of the packaging life cycle. Let's see what these sections cover:

- **Prepare** will run the script before the package is packed into a tarball and published to the remote repository. It's a great way to run compilers and bundlers to get our package ready for deployment.
- **Install** will run the script after the package has been installed. This is great when we pull a package and want to run something such as node-gyp or something that our package may need that's specific to the OS.

Another great thing about the scripts section is that we can put any arbitrary strings here and run npm run <script>. Whatever we decide to use as the value will be evaluated when we run the command. Let's add the following to our package.json file:

```
"config" : {
    "port" : 8080,
    "name" : "example",
    "testdata" : {
        "thing" : 5,
        "other" : 10
    }
},
"scripts" : {
    "example-script" : "node main.js"
}
```

This will give us the ability to grab configuration data. On top of this, we have added a script that can be run with the npm run example-script command. If we create a main.js file and add the following fields to it, we should get the following output:

```
console.log(process.env.npm_package_config_port); //8080
console.log(process.env.npm_package_config_name); //'example'
console.log(process.env.npm_package_config_testdata); //undefined
```

This shows that we can put primitive values inside the configuration, but we can't try to access something that is a complex object. We can do the following to get to the properties of the testdata object:

```
console.log(process.env.npm_package_config_testdata_thing) //5
console.log(process.env.npm_package_config_testdata_other) //10
```

Now that we've gained some insight into the Node.js and npm ecosystems, let's take a look at how Node.js is put together and some of the key modules that we will be utilizing in the following chapters.

Understanding the DOM-less world

As we stated in the introduction, Node.js came out of the idea that if we are writing code in the browser, then we should be able to run it on the server. Here, we have a single language for both contexts and we don't have to context switch when we work on either section.

Node.js can function in this way with a mixture of two libraries. These libraries are V8, which we should already be familiar with, and libuv, which we aren't currently familiar with. The libuv library gives us asynchronous I/O. Every OS has a different way of handling this I/O, so libuv gives us a nice C wrapper around all of these instances.

The libuv library queues up requests for I/O onto a stack of requests. Then, it farms them out to a certain amount of threads (Node.js utilizes four by default). Once the responses come back from these threads, libuv will put them on the response stack and alert V8 that the responses are ready to be consumed. Once V8 gets around to this alert, it will pull the value off and utilize it for its response to the request that we made. This is how the Node.js runtime is able to have asynchronous I/O and still maintain a single thread of execution (at least, that's how it looks to the user).

With this basic understanding, we should be able to start writing some basic scripts that handle various I/O operations and utilize one of the ideas that made Node.js special: the streaming system.

A first look at streams

As we saw in the DOM, streams give us the ability to control the flow of data and be able to process data in a way that creates a nonblocking system. We can see this by creating a simple stream. Let's go ahead and utilize one of the built-in streams that comes with Node.js, `readFileStream`. Let's write the following script:

```
import fs from 'fs';
import { PassThrough } from 'stream'

const str = fs.createReadStream('./example.txt');
const pt = new PassThrough();
str.pipe(pt);
pt.on('data', (chunk) => {
    console.log(chunk);
});
```

Here, we have imported the `fs` library and the `PassThrough` stream from the `stream` library. Then, we created a read stream for the `example.txt` file, as well as a `PassThrough` stream.

A `PassThrough` stream allows us to process the data without having to explicitly create a stream ourselves. We read in the data and piped it to our `PassThrough` stream.

From here, we are able to get a handle to the data event, which gives us a chunk of data. On top of this, we have made sure to put our data event listener after the `pipe` method. By doing this, we have made sure that no `data` events run before we have attached our listener.

Let's create the following `example.txt` file:

```
This is some data
it should be processed by our system
it should be coming in chunks that our system can handle
most likely this will all come in one chunk
```

Now, if we run the `node --experimental-modules read_file_stream.js` command, we will see that it prints out a `Buffer`. All of the data processing is in binary chunks that are wrapped in `Buffer` objects unless we explicitly set it to something such as object mode. If we change the console log command to print out the following, we should get output in plain text:

```
console.log(chunk.toString('utf8'));
```

Let's create a program that counts the number of times the word `the` is used in the text. We can do this with our `PassThrough` stream, like so:

```
import fs from 'fs';
import { PassThrough } from 'stream';

let numberOfThe = 0;
const chars = Buffer.from('the');
let currPos = 0;
const str = fs.createReadStream('./example.txt');
const pt = new PassThrough();
str.pipe(pt);
pt.on('data', (chunk) => {
    for(let i = 0; i < chunk.byteLength; i++) {
        const char = chunk[i];
        if( char === chars[currPos] ) {
            if( currPos === chars.byteLength - 1 ) // we are at the end so
              reset
                numberOfThe += 1;
                currPos = 0;
            } else {
                currPos += 1;
            }
        }
```

```
        } else {
            currPos += 1;
        }
    }
});
pt.on('end', () => {
    console.log('the number of THE in the text is: ', numberOfThe);
});
```

We need to keep a count of the number of times we see the word `the`. We also are going to create a byte buffer of the `the` string. We will also need to keep track of our current position. By doing this, whenever we get data, we can run through it and test each byte. If the byte matches the current position that we are holding, then we need to do another check. If it equals our character byte count for the word `the`, then we update the number of `the` and reset our current position. Otherwise, we set our current position to the next index. If we don't get a match, we need to reset our current position; otherwise, we will get any combination of the characters *t*, *h*, and *e*.

This is an interesting example of how to utilize a `PassThrough` stream, but let's go ahead and create our own write `Transform` stream. We are going to apply the same operation that we did before, but we are going to build a custom stream. As stated in the documentation, we must write the `_transform` function and, optionally, implement the `_flush` function. We are going to implement both the `_transform` and `_flush` functions. We are also going to utilize the new class syntax instead of utilizing the old prototype-based system. One thing to keep in mind when building our own custom streams is to run the `super(options)` method before we do anything else in our stream. This will allow the user to pass various stream options that they have access to without us needing to do anything.

With all of this in mind, we should get something that looks like the following:

```
import { Transform } from 'stream';

class GetThe extends Transform {
    #currPos = 0;
    #numberOfThe = 0;

    static chars = Buffer.from('the');
    constructor(options) {
        super(options);
    }
    _transform(chunk, encoding, callback) {
        for(let i = 0; i < chunk.byteLength; i++) {
            const char = chunk[i];
            if( char === GetThe.chars[this.#currPos]) {
```

```
                    if( this.#currPos === GetThe.chars.byteLength - 1 ) {
                        this.#numberOfThe += 1;
                        this.#currPos = 0;
                    } else {
                        this.#currPos += 1;
                    }
                } else {
                    this.#currPos = 0;
                }
            }
            callback();
        }
        _flush(callback) {
            callback(null, this.#numberOfThe.toString());
        }
    }

    export default GetThe;
```

First, we import the `Transform` stream from the `stream` base library. We extend it and create a couple of private variables, that is, the current position in the `the` buffer and the current count of `the` in our stream. We also create a static variable for the buffer that we are comparing it to. Then, we have our constructor. This is where we pass the options to the `Transform` stream's constructor.

Next, we implement the `_transform` method in the same way that we implemented the `data` event on the `PassThrough` stream. The only new piece should be the call to the callback at the end. This lets our stream know that we are ready to process more data. If we need to error out, we can pass that as the first argument. We can also pass a second parameter, as shown in the `_flush` function. This allows us to pass the processed data to whoever may be listening. In our case, we only want to pass the number of `the` that we found in the text. We can also only pass a `Buffer`, `String`, or `Uint8Array`, so we decide to pass the string version of our number (we could have used a `Buffer` and this would have probably been the better choice). Finally, we export this from our module.

Inside of our `read_file_stream` file, we will import this module with the following command:

```
import GetThe from './custom_transform.js';
```

Then, we can utilize it with the following code:

```
const gt = new GetThe();
gt.on('data', (data) => {
    console.log('the number of THE produced by the custom stream is: ',
    data.toString('utf8'));
```

```
});
const str2 = fs.createReadStream('./example.txt');
str2.pipe(gt);
```

By doing this, we have wrapped all of that logic into a separate module and a reusable stream instead of just doing this in the `data` event of `PassThrough`. We also have the ability to chain our stream implementation to another stream (in this case, there would probably be no point unless we were going to pass it to a socket).

This was a short introduction to the stream interface and provided an overview of what we will be discussing at length in later chapters. Next, we will take a look at some modules that come with Node.js and how they can help us to write server applications.

A high-level look at modules

There are three I/O modules that allow our applications to work with the filesystem and access the outside world. These are as follows:

- `fs`
- `net`
- `http`

These three modules will likely be the main modules that a user will utilize when developing Node.js applications. Let's take a look at each of them individually.

fs module

First, let's create a basic example of accessing the filesystem and opening a file, adding some text to it, closing the file, and then appending some more text to it. This would look similar to the following:

```
import { promises } from 'fs';

(async() => {
    await promises.writeFile('example2.txt', "Here is some text\n");
    const fd = await promises.open('example2.txt', 'a');
    await fd.appendFile("Here is some more text\n");
    await fd.close();
    console.log(await promises.readFile('example2.txt', 'utf8'));
})();
```

First, we are grabbing the promise-based version of the library. Most of the built-in modules have a promise-based version, which can lead to nice-looking code, especially compared to the callback system. Next, we write to a file and give it some text. The `writeFile` method allows us to write to a file and create the file if it doesn't exist. After this, we open up `FileHandle` for our file.

 Node.js took the POSIX style of I/O. This means that everything is treated like a file. In this case, everything is assigned a **file descriptor** (**fd**). This looks like a number to us in languages such as C++. After, we can pass this number to a variety of file functions that are available to us. Node.js, in the promises API, decided to switch to a `FileHandle` object, which is what we get instead of this file descriptor. It leads to cleaner code and a layer of abstraction over the system that is sometimes needed.

The `a` that we can see as the second argument states how we are going to use the file. In this case, we are going to append to the file. If we opened it with `r`, this means that we want to read from it, while if we opened it with `w`, this means that we want to overwrite whatever is already there.

 Having an understanding of a Unix system can go a long way to understanding how Node.js works and how all of this corresponds to the programs that we are trying to write.

Then, we append some text to the file and close it. Finally, we console log whatever is in the file and state that we want to read it in as UTF-8 text instead of in binary.

There are many more APIs associated with the filesystem, and it is recommended to go through the promise documentation to see what capabilities we have, but they all boil down to us having access to the filesystem and being able to read/write/append to various files and directories. Now, let's move on to the `net` module.

net module

The `net` module gives us access to lower-level socket systems and even to local **InterProcess Communication** (**IPC**) schemes that we can use. IPC schemes are communication strategies that allow us to talk between processes. Processes don't share memory, which means that we have to communicate through other means. In Node.js, this usually means three different strategies, and they all depend on how quickly and how tightly coupled we want the systems to be. These three strategies are as follows:

- Unnamed pipes
- Named pipes/local domain sockets
- TCP/UDP sockets

First, we have unnamed pipes. These are one-way communication systems that are not seen on the filesystem and are shared between a `parent` and a `child` process. This means that a `parent` process would spawn a `child` process and `parent` would pass the *location* of one end of the pipe to `child`. By doing this, they would be able to communicate over this channel. An example of this is as follows:

```
import { fork } from 'child_process';

const child = fork('child.js');
child.on('message', (msg) => {
    switch(msg) {
        case 'CONNECT': {
            console.log('our child is connected to us. Tell it to dispose
             of itself');
            child.send('DISCONNECT');
            break;
        }
        case 'DISCONNECT': {
            console.log('our child is disposing of itself. Time for us to
             do the same');
            process.exit();
            break;
        }
    }
});
```

Our `child` file will look as follows:

```
process.on('message', (msg) => {
    switch(msg) {
        case 'DISCONNECT': {
            process.exit();
            break;
```

```
        }
    }
});
process.send('CONNECT');
```

We grab the fork method from the `child_process` module (this allows us to spawn new processes). Then, we fork a new `child` off of the `child` JavaScript file and are given a handler to that `child` process. As part of the fork process, Node.js automatically creates an unnamed pipe for us so that we can talk between the two processes. Then, we listen for events on the `child` process and do various things based on the message that we receive.

On the `child` side, we can automatically listen for events from whoever spawned us and we can send messages through our process interface (this is global in each Node.js file that is started). As shown in the following code, we are able to talk between two separate processes. If we wanted to actually see this, we would have to add a timeout to our `parent` process so that it doesn't send the `DISCONNECT` message for 15 seconds, like so:

```
setTimeout(() => {
    child.send('DISCONNECT');
}, 15000);
```

Now, if we bring up a task manager, we will see that two Node.js processes have been started. One of these is `parent` while the other one is `child`. We are talking over an unnamed pipe, so they are considered tightly coupled because they are the only ones that share it. This is great for systems that we want to have a `parent`/`child` relationship and do not expect to have either of them spawned in a different way.

Instead of creating this tight link between the two processes, we can use something called a named pipe (these are known as Unix domain sockets on OS X and Linux). It works similarly to an unnamed pipe, but we are able to connect two unrelated processes. To achieve this type of connection, we can utilize the `net` module. It provides a low-level API that can be used to create, connect, and listen to these connections. We also get a low-level socket connection, so it behaves similarly to the `http(s)` modules.

To start up a connection, we can do the following:

```
import net from 'net';
import path from 'path';
import os from 'os';

const pipeName = (os.platform() === 'win32' ?
    path.join('\\\\?\\pipe', process.cwd(), 'temp') :
    path.join(process.cwd(), 'temp');
const server = net.createServer().listen(pipeName);
server.on('connection', (socket) => {
```

```
        console.log('a socket has joined the party!');
        socket.write('DISCONNECT');
        socket.on('close', () => {
            console.log('socket has been closed!');
        });
    });
});
```

Here, we import the net, path, and os modules. The path module helps to create and resolve filesystem paths without us having to write path expressions specifically for an OS. The os module, as we saw previously, can give us information about the OS that we are currently on. When we create the pipe name, Windows needs to be at \\?\pipe\<something>. On another OS, it can just be a regular path. Something else to note is that any other OS besides Windows will not clean the pipe after we have finished using it. This means that we will need to make sure we delete the file before we exit the program.

In our case, we create a pipe name based off of the platform. In any case, we make sure that it is in our current working directory (process.cwd()) and that it is called temp. From here, we can create a server and listen for connections on this file. When someone connects, we receive a Socket object. This is a full Duplex stream, which means that we can read and write from it. We are also able to pipe information to and from it. In our case, we want to log to the console that socket joined and then send a DISCONNECT message. Once we get the close event, we just log that socket closed down.

For our client code, we should have something similar to the following:

```
import net from 'net';
import path from 'path';
import os from 'os';

const pipeName = (os.platform() === 'win32') ?
    path.join('\\\\?\\pipe', process.cwd(), 'temp') :
    path.join(process.cwd(), 'temp');
const socket = new net.Socket().connect(pipeName);
socket.on('connect', () => {
    console.log('we have connected');
});
socket.on('data', (data) => {
    if( data.toString('utf8') === 'DISCONNECT' ) {
        socket.destroy();
    }
});
```

This code is fairly similar, except we create a `Socket` object directly and try to connect to the same pipe name. Once we're connected, we log this. When we get data, we check whether it is equal to our `DISCONNECT` message, and if it is, we get rid of the socket.

What's nice about the IPC mechanism is that we can pass messages between different programs written in different languages. The only thing that they need to have in common is some form of common *language*. There are many systems out there that can do this. Although this isn't the focus of this book, note that if we needed to hook into another program, we could do this fairly easily with the `net` module.

http module

The final module we are going to take a high-level look at is the `http` module. This module allows us to create `http` servers with ease. The following is a simple example of an `http` server:

```
import http from 'http';

const server = http.createServer((req, res) => {
    res.writeHead(200, { 'Content-Type' : 'application/json'});
    res.end(JSON.stringify({here : 'is', some : 'data'}));
});
server.listen(8000, '127.0.0.1');
```

If we head to `localhost:8000` in our browser, we should see the JSON object in our browser. If we wanted to get even fancier, we could send back some basic HTML, such as the following:

```
const server = https.createServer((req, res) => {
    res.writeHead(200, { 'Content-Type' : 'text/html' });
    res.end(`
        <html>
            <head></head>
            <body>
                <h1>Hello!</h1>
                <p>This is from our server!</p>
            </body>
        </html>
    `);
});
```

Instead of setting our content type to `application/json`, we set it to `text/html` so that the browser knows how to interpret this request. Then, we end the response with our basic HTML. How would we be able to respond to the server if our HTML requests a CSS file?

We would need to interpret the request and be able to send some CSS. We could do this with something like the following:

```
const server = http.createServer((req, res) => {
    if( req.method === 'GET' &&
        req.url === '/main.css' ) {
        res.writeHead(200, { 'Content-Type' : 'text/css' });
        res.end(`
            h1 {
                color : green;
            }
            p {
                color : purple;
            }
        `);
    } else {
        res.writeHead(200, { 'Content-Type' : 'text/html' });
        // same as above
    }
});
```

We are able to pull various pieces of information from the request that we receive. In this case, all we care about is whether this was a GET request and that it is asking for the `main.css` resource. If it is, we return the CSS; otherwise, we just return our HTML. It should be noted that this code should look somewhat familiar to web server frameworks such as Express. Express adds a bunch of helper methods and ways to protect our server, but it should be noted that we can write simple servers with fewer dependencies and only by utilizing the modules that are internal to Node.js.

We can also use the `http` module to fetch data from various resources. If we use the `get` method built into the `http` module or even the more generic request method, we can get resources from various other servers. The following code illustrates this:

```
import https from 'https';

https.get('https://en.wikipedia.org/wiki/Surprise_(emotion)', (res) => {
    if( res.statusCode === 200 ) {
        res.on('data', (data) => {
            console.log(data.toString('utf8'));
        });
        res.on('end', () => {
            console.log('no more information');
```

```
        });
    } else {
        console.error('bad error code!', res.statusCode);
    }
});
```

First, we can see that we have to utilize the `https` module. Since this web page is located on a server that is utilizing **Secure Socket Layer** (**SSL**) certificates, we have to use the secure connection method. Then, we simply call the `get` method, passing in the URL that we want, and read the data from the response. If, for some reason, we do not get a 200 response (an okay message), we error out.

These three modules should showcase that we have quite a bit of power inside of the Node.js ecosystem and should spark some curiosity in how we can use Node.js, without any dependencies, to make useful systems. In the next section, we will take a look at how we can debug our Node.js code in a command-line debugger, along with the code inspection system that we are used to using with Chrome.

Debugging and inspecting code

One area that new Node.js developers struggle with is debugging code. Instead of having the inspector, we have a system where the first crash will dump some information to our screen and instantly kick us to the command-line. This can be seen with the following code:

```
const thing = 'this';
console.log(thing);
thing = 10;
```

Here, we can see that we are trying to reassign a constant, so Node.js is going to throw an error similar to the following one:

```
TypeError: Assignment to constant variable.
    at Object.<anonymous> (C:\Code\Ch5\bad_code.js:3:7)
    at Module._compile (internal/modules/cjs/loader.js:774:30)
    at Object.Module._extensions..js
(internal/modules/cjs/loader.js:785:10)
    at Module.load (internal/modules/cjs/loader.js:641:32)
    at Function.Module._load (internal/modules/cjs/loader.js:556:12)
    at Function.Module.runMain (internal/modules/cjs/loader.js:837:10)
    at internal/main/run_main_module.js:17:11
```

While this can be scary, it also shows us where the error is. The first line in this stack trace tells us it is at *line 3, character 7*.

A stack trace is a way for a system to provide the developer with information about which functions were calling what. In our case, `Object.<anonymous>` was called by `Module.__compile`, and so on. This can help when a good chunk of the stack is ours and the error actually occurs farther up.

With this information, we know how to correct the issue, but what do we do if we want to break on a specific statement or a specific line? This is where the inspector system comes into play. Here, we can utilize statements that are similar to the ones we saw in the web version of our code. If we insert a debug statement in the middle of our code, our command line will stop at that point.

Let's create some rudimentary code to showcase this. The following code should give us plenty to showcase the use of the inspector:

```
const fun = function() {
    const item = 10;
    for(let i = 0; i < item; i++) {
        const tempObj = {};
        tempObj[i] = "what " + i;
    }
    return function() {
        console.log('we will have access to other things');
        const alternative = 'what';
        debugger;
        return item;
    }
}

console.log('this is some code');
const x = 'what';
debugger;
fun()();
```

This code will allow us to play around with various parts of the inspector. If we run the `npm inspect bad_code.js` command, we should break on the call to `fun`. We are greeted with a Terminal interface that states we are in debug mode. Now that we have stopped execution here, we can set up a watcher. This allows us to capture various variables and expressions and see what their results are on the next break. Here, we set up a watcher on the x variable by executing `watch('x')` in the debugger. From here, if we type `next`, we will move to the next line. If we do this a couple of times, we will notice that once we pass the assignment of our variable, the watcher will change the x variable from undefined to 10.

This can be especially helpful when we need to debug a stateful system that is sharing state among quite a few objects. It can also be helpful when we are trying to see what we have access to. Let's set up a few more watchers so that we can see what their values are when our next debug statement is hit. Set up watchers on the following variables: `item`, `tempObj`, and `alternative`. Now, type `cont`. This will move us to our next debugger statement. Let's see what's printed out by our watchers. When we move to the next point, we will see that `tempObj` and `x` are not defined, but that we have access to `item` and `alternative`.

This is what we expect, seeing how we are scoped inside the outer `fun` function. There's much more we can do with this version of the inspector, but we can also hook up to the inspector that we are used to.

Now, if we use the following command to run our code, we will be able to attach the debug tools to our script:

```
> node --inspect bad_code.js
```

With this, we will get an address that we can connect to. Let's do just that. We will also need to have some long-running code; otherwise, the script will exit and we will have nothing to listen to. Let's move back to the `named_pipe.js` example. Run `node --inspect --experimental-modules named_pipe.js`.

We should get something that looks like the following:

```
Debugger listening on ws://127.0.0.1:9229/6abd394d-
d5e0-4bba-8b28-69069d2cb800
```

If we head to the following address in our Chrome browser, we should be greeted with a familiar sight:

```
chrome-
devtools://devtools/bundled/js_app.html?experiments=true&v8only=true&ws=<ur
l>
```

Now, we have the full power of the inspector from Chrome for our Node.js code. Here, we can see that if we connect to our named pipe server with our `named_pipe_child.js` file, we will be greeted with the console logs in the debugger. Now, if we add debugger statements, we should get breakpoints inside of the inspector. If we add a debug statement right when a socket connects to us, when we connect with our child socket, we will be able to run through our code the same way we can in the browser! This is a great way to debug and step through our code.

We are also able to memory profile. If we head to the **Memory** tab and create a heap snapshot, we will get a nice dump of our memory. It should look quite familiar to what we have seen already.

With all of this under our belt, we can move onto more complex topics surrounding Node.js.

Summary

With the advent of Node.js, we are able to have a programming language that we can utilize on both the client and server. While the APIs that are given to us in Node.js may not look familiar, we can create powerful server applications with them.

In this chapter, we covered the basics of streaming and some of the APIs that allow us to create these powerful server applications. We also took a look at the tools that allow us to debug with and without a GUI.

With all of this under our belt, in the next chapter, we will take a deeper dive into the mechanisms we can use to pass data between threads and processes.

6
Message Passing - Learning about the Different Types

In the previous chapter, we looked at Node.js and the base environment we need to create server-side applications. Now, we will look at how we can use the communication techniques we looked at previously to write scalable systems. Message passing is a great way for applications to be decoupled yet still work together. This means that we can create modules that work independently from each other, either through processes or threads, and still achieve a common goal.

In this chapter, we will cover the following topics:

- Local communication using the net module
- Utilizing the network
- A quick glance at HTTP/3

We will also take a look at the future of client/server communication while looking at the HTTP/3 standard that is being developed. Then, we will look at the implementation of the QUIC protocol, a protocol developed by Google that HTTP/3 takes some of its ideas from.

Let's get started!

Technical requirements

For this chapter, you'll need the following technical requirements:

- An IDE or code editor (VS Code is preferred)
- A running Node.js environment
- OpenSSL or the ability to install Cygwin
- This chapter's code, which can be found at `https://github.com/PacktPublishing/Hands-On-High-Performance-Web-Development-with-JavaScript/tree/master/Chapter06`.

Local communication using the net module

While many applications can run on a single thread and utilize the event loop to run, when we are writing server applications we will want to try and utilize all of the cores that we have available to us. We can do this through the use of **processes** or **threads**. In most cases, we are going to want to use threads since they are lighter and faster to start.

We can find out whether we need a process or a thread based on whether we need to have the subsystem still running if the main system dies. If we don't care, we should utilize a thread, but if we need to have that subsystem still running even after the main process dies, we should utilize a decoupled process. This is only one way of thinking about when to use a process or a thread, but it is a good indicator.

In both the browser and Node.js, we have web workers that take the place of threads in traditional systems. While they have many of the same concepts as the threads of other languages, they are unable to share state (in our case, this is preferred).

There's a way to share state between workers. This can be done through `SharedArrayBuffer`. While we can utilize this to share state, we want to highlight that the event system and IPC are almost always fast enough to move state and coordinate between different pieces. Also, we don't have to deal with concepts such as locks.

To start up a worker, we need to call `new Worker(<script here>)`. Let's go over this concept:

1. Create a file called `Main_Worker.js` and add the following code to it:

```
import { Worker } from 'worker_threads';

const data = {what: 'this', huh: 'yeah'};
const worker = new Worker('./worker.js');
worker.postMessage(data);
worker.on('message', (data) => {
    worker.terminate();
});
worker.on('exit', (code) => {
    console.log('our worker stopped with the following code: ',
     code);
});
```

2. Create a file called `worker.js` and add the following code to it:

```
import { parentPort } from 'worker_threads'

parentPort.on('message', (msg) => {
    console.log('we received a message from our parent: ', msg);
    parentPort.postMessage({RECEIVED: true});
});
```

As we can see, this system is similar to the one in the browser. First, we import the worker from the `worker_threads` module. Then, we start it up. The thread will start, which means we post messages to it and listen for events, similar to the way we were able to with processes in the previous chapter.

Inside of the `worker.js` file, we import the `parentPort` message channels from the `worker_threads` module. We listen and pass messages the same way as the parent does. Once we receive a message, we state that we received the message. The parent then terminates us and we print out that we have been terminated.

Now, this form of message passing is perfectly fine if we want to tightly couple all of our subsystems together. But what if we want different threads to have different jobs? We could have one that just caches data for us. Another one could potentially make requests for us. Finally, our main thread (the starting process) can move all of this data and take in data from the command line.

To do all of this, we could simply use the built-in system. Alternatively, we could utilize the mechanism that we looked at in the previous chapter. Not only does this give us a highly scalable system, but it also allows us to change these various subsystems from threads into processes if we need to. This also allows us to write these separate subsystems in another language, if needed. Let's go over this now:

1. Let's go ahead and make this system. We are going to create four files: main.js, cache.js, send.js, and package.json. Our package.json file should look something like this:

```
{
    "name" : "Chapter6_Local",
    "version" : "0.0.1",
    "type" : "module",
    "main" : "main.js"
}
```

2. Next, add the following code to the cache.js file:

```
import net from 'net';
import pipeName from './helper.js';

let count = 0;
let cacheTable = new Map();
// these correspond to !!!BEGIN!!!, !!!END!!!, !!!GET!!!, and
// !!!DELETE!!! respectively
const begin, end, get, del; //shortened for readability they will
use the Buffer.from() methods
let currData = [];

const socket = new net.Socket().connect(pipeName());
socket.on('data', (data) => {
    if( data.toString('utf8') === 'WHOIS' ) {
        return socket.write('cache');
    }
    if( data.includes(get) ) {
        const loc =
parseInt(data.slice(get.byteLength).toString('utf8'));
        const d = cacheTable.get(loc);
        if( typeof d !== 'undefined' ) {
            socket.write(begin.toString('utf8') + d +
             end.toString('utf8'));
        }
    }
    if( data.includes(del) ) {
        if( data.byteLength === del.byteLength ) {
            cacheTable.clear();
```

```
        } else {
            const loc =
parseInt(data.slice(del.byteLength).toString('utf8'));
            cacheTable.delete(loc);
        }
    }
    if( data.includes(begin) ) {
currData.push(data.slice(begin.byteLength).toString('utf8'));
    }
    if( currData.length ) {
        currData.push(data.toString('utf8'));
    }
    if( data.includes(end) ) {
        currData.push(data.slice(0, data.byteLength -
         end.byteLength).toString('utf8'));
        cacheTable.set(count, currData.join(''));
        currData = [];
    }
});
```

 This is definitely not a foolproof mechanism for handling streaming data. !!!BEGIN!!! and other command messages could be chunked and we would never see them. While we are keeping this simple, remember that production-level streaming needs to handle all of these types of issues.

The `cache` submodule checks for different headers on the message. Depending on each type, we will do that type of action. This can be thought of as a simple way to do remote procedure calls. The following list describes what we do, depending on each event:

- !!!BEGIN!!!: We need to start listening for more data on the line since this means we are going to store the data.
- !!!END!!!: Once we see this message, we can put all of this data together and store it, based on our count in the cache.
- !!!GET!!!: We are going to try to get the file stored at the numbered location that's supplied to us by the server.
- !!!DELETE!!!: If the length of the message is as long as this string, this means we want to delete everything from the cache. Otherwise, we will try to delete the data at the location specified later in the message.

3. Add the following code to the `send.js` file:

```
import net from 'net'
import https from 'https'
import pipeName from './helpers.js'
```

```
const socket = new net.Socket().connect(pipeName());
socket.on('data', (data) => {
    if( data.toString('utf8') === 'WHOIS' ) {
        return socket.write('send');
    }
    const all = [];
    https.get(data.toString('utf8'), (res) => {
        res.on('data', (data) => {
            all.push(data.toString('utf8'));
        });
        res.on('end', () => {
            socket.write('!!!BEGIN!!!');
            socket.write(all.join(''));
            socket.write('!!!END!!!');
        });
    }).on('error', (err) => {
        socket.write('!!!FALSE!!!');
    });
    console.log('we received data from the main application',
     data.toString('utf8'));
});
```

For each of the submodules that we have, we handle specific commands that may come across the wire. As shown by the send submodule, we handle anything on the wire other than the WHOIS command, which tells the main application who is connected to it. We try to grab the file from the specified address and write it back to the main application so that it's stored in the cache.

We also added our own *protocol* to send the data. While this system is not foolproof and we should add some type of locking (such as a Boolean, so that we don't try to take in any more data before fully sending out the current data), it does showcase how we can send data across our system. In Chapter 7, *Streams - Understanding Streams and Non-Blocking I/O*, we will look at a similar concept, but we will utilize streams so that we don't use so much memory per thread.

 As we can see, we're only importing the https module. This means that we are only allowed to make requests to addresses that are served over HTTPS. If we wanted to support HTTP, we would have to import the http module and then check the address that the user types in. In our case, we made it as simple as possible.

When we want to send data, we send the !!!BEGIN!!! message to let the receiver know that we are about to send data that will not fit into a single frame. Then, we end our message with the !!!END!!! message.

If we can't read the endpoint that we are trying to grab or our connection times out (both of these will drop into the error condition), we will send a !!!FALSE!!! message to let the receiver know that we are unable to fully transmit the data.

This concept of wrapping our data in *frames* is used in almost all data transmission systems. Without framing, we would have to send a header that says how large the data transmission is. However that would mean we need to know the size of the content before we send it. Framing gives us the option of not sending the length of messages, so we can process infinitely large messages.

Framing or even boxing the data is done everywhere. If we were to look at how packets are created, for example, the concept still applies. Understanding this concept is key to understanding lower levels of the communication stack. Another concept that is good to know about is that not all of this data is sent at once. It is sent in pieces. The amount that can be sent at one time is usually set at the operating system level. One of the only properties that we can set is the highWaterMark property on streams. This property allows us to say how much data we will hold in memory before we stop reading/writing.

The cache application acts similar to the send submodule, except it responds to more commands. If we get a get command, we can try and grab that item from the cache and send it back to the main module; otherwise, we just send back null. If we get a delete command, we will delete the entire cache if we get no other arguments; otherwise, we delete the item at that specific location. Finally, if we get the beginning or ending wrappers, we will process the data and cache it.

Currently, we infinitely increase our cache. We could easily add a concept of a certain time threshold that is allowed for data to stay in the cache (**Time To Live** or **TTL**) or only hold a certain number of records, usually by utilizing a **Least Recently Used** (**LRU**) destroy system. We will look at how to implement caching strategies in Chapter 9, *Practical Example - Building a Static Server*. Just note that these concepts are quite ubiquitous with caches and caching strategies.

Heading back into the code, create main.js and add the following code:

4. Create placeholders for our state variables. These correspond to the various states that our messages could be in and the data that is passing through the socket:

```
// import required modules and methods
const table = new Map();
let currData = [];
```

```
// These three items correspond to the buffers for:  !!!FALSE!!!,
// !!!BEGIN!!!, and !!!END!!! respectively
const failure, begin, end;
const methodTable = new WeakMap();
```

5. Create the method to handle data that comes in through our cache:

```
const cacheHandler = function(data) {
    if( data.includes(begin) || currData.length ) {
        currData.push(data.toString('utf8'));
    }
    if( data.includes(end) ) {
        currData.push(data.toString('utf8'));
        const final = currData.join('');
        console.log(final.substring(begin.byteLength,
         final.byteLength - end.byteLength));
        currData = [];
    }
}
```

6. Next, add the method that will handle the messages from our send worker:

```
const sendHandler = function(data) {
    if( data.equals(failure) ) { //failure }
    if( data.includes(begin) ) {
     currData.push(data.toString('utf8')); }
    if( currData.length ) { currData.push(data.toString('utf8')); }
    if( data.includes(end) ) {
        table.get('cache').write(currData.join(''));
        currData = [];
    }
}
```

7. Create two final helper methods. These will test the number of workers we have to know when we are ready to start and the other will add the method handlers to each worker socket:

```
const testConnections = function() {
    return table.size === 2;
}
const setupHandler = function() {
    table.forEach((value, key) => {
        value.on('data', methodTable.get(value.bind(value));
    });
}
```

8. The final large method will handle all of the messages that we receive via the command-line:

```javascript
const startCLIMode = function() {
    process.stdin.on('data', function(data) {
        const d = data.toString('utf8');
        const instruction = d.trim().split(/\s/ig);
        switch(instruction[0]) {
            case 'delete': {
table.get('cache').write(`!!!DELETE!!!${instruction[1] || ''}`);
                break; }
            case 'get': {
                if( typeof instruction[1] === 'undefined' ) {
                    return console.log('get needs a number
                      associated with it!');
                }
table.get('cache').write(`!!!GET!!!${instruction[1]}`);
                break; }
            case 'grab': {
                table.get('send').write(instruction[1]);
                break; }
            case 'stop': {
                table.forEach((value, key) => value.end());
                process.exit();
                break; }
        }});
}
```

9. Finally, create the server and start the workers:

```javascript
const server = net.createServer().listen(pipeName());
server.on('connection', (socket) => {
    socket.once('data', (data) => {
        const type = data.toString('utf8');
        table.set(type, socket);
        if( testConnections() ) {
            setupHandlers();
            startCLIMode();
        }
    });
    socket.once('close', () => {
        table.delete(type);
    });
    socket.write('WHOIS');
});

const cache = new Worker('./cache.js');
const send = new Worker('./send.js');
```

Certain parts of the main file have been removed to shorten the amount of code in this book. The full example can be found in this book's GitHub repository.

Here, we have a bunch of helpers that will handle messages from the cache and send subsystems. We also map the socket to our handler. The utilization of a `WeakMap` means that we don't need to clean up if these subsystems ever crash or are somehow removed. We also map the name of the subsystem to the socket so that we can easily send messages to the correct subsystem. Finally, we create a server and handle the incoming connections. In our case, we only want to check for two subsystems. Once we can see two, we start our program.

There are some flaws in the way we wrap our messages, and testing the number of connections to see whether we are ready is also not the best way to handle our program. However, this does allow us to create a somewhat complex application so that we can quickly test the ideas that can be seen here. With this application, we are now able to cache various files from a remote resource and grab them when we want them. This is a system that is similar to how some static servers work.

By looking at the preceding application, it is easy to see how we can utilize local connections to create a message-passing system with only the core Node.js system. What is also interesting is that we can replace the `listen` method's argument from a pipe name with a port number and we would be able to turn this application from utilizing named pipes/Unix domain sockets to utilizing TCP sockets.

Before we had these worker threads inside of Node.js, we had to separate everything out with processes. In the beginning, we only had the fork system. This made some systems quite complex when we started creating more processes. To help us with this concept, the `cluster` module was created. With the `cluster` module, it's easier to manage processes in a master/slave architecture.

Understanding the cluster module

While the `cluster` module may not be used as much as it was in the past, since we have worker threads inside of Node.js, one concept still makes it powerful. We are able to share server connections between the various worker threads that are in our application. Our main process will use a strategy so that we only send requests to one of the slave processes. This allows us to handle quite a few simultaneous connections that are all running on the exact same address and port.

With this concept, let's implement the preceding program but by utilizing the `cluster` module. Now, we will ensure the send and cache subsystems are tied to the main process. Our child processes will be tied to handling requests that come over our server. One thing to remember is that if the parent process dies, our child processes will also die. If we don't want this behavior, when we call the fork inside our main process, we can pass the `detached : true` option. This will allow the worker threads to still run. This is usually not a behavior that we want when we are using the `cluster` module, but it is good to know that it's available.

 We have split up the following program into more manageable chunks. To see the full program, head over to the code repository for this chapter.

Now, we should be able to write a program that's similar to our IPC program. Let's take a look:

1. First, we will import all of the Node modules that are needed to implement our previous example in `cluster` mode:

```
import cluster from 'cluster';
import https from 'https';
import http from 'http';
import { URL } from 'url';
```

2. Next, we set up the constants that we can use across our processes:

```
const numWorkers = 2;
const CACHE = 0;
const SEND = 1;
const server = '127.0.0.1';
const port = 3000;
```

3. After, we add an `if/else` check to see whether we are the master process or whether we are a slave process. The same file is used for both types of processes, so we need a way to distinguish between the two:

```
if( cluster.isMaster ) {
    // do master work
} else {
    // handle incoming connections
}
```

4. Now, write the master code. This will go into the first block of the `if/else` statement. Our master node needs to spin the slave nodes up, as well as initialize our cache:

```
let count = 1; //where our current record is at. We start at 1
const cache = new Map();
for(let i = 0; i < numWorkers; i++ ) {
    const worker = cluster.fork();
    worker.on('message', (msg) => {
        // handle incoming cache request
    });
}
```

5. Add some code that will handle each of the requests, just like we did in the previous example. Remember that if we stop our main process, it will destroy all of the slave processes. If we receive the STOP command, we will just kill the main process:

```
// inside of the worker message handler
switch(msg.cmd) {
    case 'STOP': {
        process.exit();
        break;
    }
    case 'DELETE': {
        if( msg.opt != 'all' ) {
            cache.delete(parseInt(msg.opt);
        } else {
            cache.clear();
        }
        worker.send({cmd : 'GOOD' });
        break;
    }
    case 'GET': {
        worker.send(cache.get(parseInt(msg.opt)));
        break;
    }
    case 'GRAB': {
        // grab the information
        break;
    }
}
```

6. Write the GRAB case statement. To do this, utilize the `https` module to make the request for the resource:

```
// inside the GRAB case statement
const buf = [];
https.get(msg.opt, (res) => {
    res.on('data', (data) => {
        buf.push(data.toString('utf8'));
    });
    res.on('end', () => {
        const final = buf.join('');
        cache.set(count, final);
        count += 1;
        worker.send({cmd : 'GOOD' });
    });
});
```

Now, we will write the slave code. All of this will be held in the `else` block. Remember that we can share the same server location and port between the slaves. We will also handle all incoming requests through the search parameters of the URL being passed to us. This is why we imported the URL class from the `url` module. Let's get started:

1. Start the slave code by starting an HTTP server. Remember that they will all share the same location and port:

```
// inside of the else block
http.Server((req, res) => {
    const search = new URL(`${location}${req.url}`).searchParams;
    const command = search.get('command');
    const params = search.get('options');
    // handle the command
    handleCommand(res, command, params);
}).listen(port);
```

2. Now, we can handle the command that's been passed to us. This will be similar to our previous example, except we will talk to the master process through **Inter-Process Communication (IPC)** and handle the requests through the HTTP/2 server. Only the `get` command is shown here; the rest can be found in this chapter's GitHub repository:

```
const handleCommand = function(res, command, params=null) {
    switch(command) {
        case 'get': {
            process.send({cmd: 'GET', opt : params});
            process.once('message', (msg) => {
                res.writeHead(200, { 'Content-Type' : 'text/plain'
```

```
        });
                            res.end(msg);
                    });
                    break;
            }
        }
    }
```

Here, we can see that both of the workers create an `HTTP` server. While they are both creating separate objects, they are sharing the underlying port. This is completely hidden from us, but this is done with the `cluster` module. If we tried doing something similar to this with our own version while utilizing the `child_process` fork method, we would get an error stating `EADDRINUSE`.

If we request the data that we stored in HTML format, we'll see it come back as pure text. This is in relation to the `writeHead` method. We are telling the browser that we are writing `text/plain`. The browser takes this information and utilizes it to see how it needs to parse the data. Since it gets told that the data is plain, it will just display it on the screen. If we change that to `text/html` when we get HTML data, it will parse it and try to render it.

With these two methods, we are able to write programs that can fully utilize all of the cores on our system while still being able to work together. The first architecture gives us a nice decoupled system and is how most applications should be written, but the `cluster` module gives us a nice way to handle servers. By mixing these two methods, we can create a high throughput server. While building these client/server applications can be easy in Node.js, there are some things to watch out for.

Common pitfalls for new developers

While utilizing the Unix domain sockets/Windows named pipes are great, there are a couple of differences between the two systems. Node.js tries to hide these details so that we can focus on the applications that we want to write, but they still show up. Two of the most common causes that can trip up new developers are as follows:

- Windows named pipes will automatically be destroyed when the application quits. Unix domain sockets will not. This means that when we exit our application, we should try to utilize the `fs` module and unlink the file through the `unlink` or `unlinkSync` methods. We should also check to see whether it exists when we start up, just in case we don't exit gracefully.

- Windows' framing of data can be larger than the Unix domain sockets. This means an application can appear to work on Windows but will fail on Unix systems. This is why we created the framing system that we did. It is good to keep this in mind, especially when we might want to use external libraries to handle parts of building the IPC systems. Some of these systems do not keep this idea in mind, and bugs can easily creep up because of this.

Node.js aims to be completely cross-operating system compatible, but these systems always have slight quirks when it comes to actually operating across systems. If we want to make sure that it works, just like we have to do if we can't guarantee what browser our end users will use, then we need to test it on all of our systems.

While developing server applications that span a single computer is common, we still need to hook all of these applications up. When we are no longer able to utilize a single computer, we will need to talk over the network. We'll take a look at these protocols next.

Utilizing the network

While building applications that can talk among themselves on the same machine can be cool, eventually, we'll need to talk to external systems. Most of these systems will be browsers in our case, but they may be other servers. Since we can't use named pipes/Unix domain sockets over these channels, we need to use various protocols of a network.

 Technically, we could still use the preceding two concepts across servers by utilizing shared drives/filesystem sharing, but this isn't a good idea. We've already shown that we can change the `listen` method from pointing to a file to pointing to a port. In the worst case, we can use a shared filesystem, but it is nowhere near optimal and it should be converted into utilizing one of the protocols we'll cover here.

The protocols that we will focus on are the two low-level protocols known as **Transmission Control Protocol** (TCP) and **User Datagram Protocol** (UDP). We will also take a look at the higher-level protocol of the web: **Hyper Text Transfer Protocol version 2** (HTTP/2). With these protocols, we will be able to create highly available applications that can be accessed over a network.

TCP/UDP

TCP and UDP are the two low-level network protocols that we have access to in Node.js. Either of these allows us to send and receive messages, but they differ in a couple of key areas. First, TCP needs to have a receiver and sender for the connection. Because of this, we can't just broadcast on a channel and not care whether anybody is listening.

Second, on top of TCP needing the handshake process, it also gives us guaranteed transmission. This means that we know when we send data that it should get to the other end (obviously, there are ways for this to fail, but we aren't going to look at that). Finally, TCP guarantees the order of delivery. If we send data on a channel to a receiver, it will get the data in the order that we sent it. Because of these reasons, we utilize TCP when we need to guarantee delivery and ordering.

 TCP actually doesn't necessarily need to send the data in order. Everything is sent in packets. They can actually go to different servers and the routing logic can mean that later packets arrive at the receiver earlier than later ones. However, our receiver's network card reorders them for us so that it looks like we are getting them sequentially. There are many other cool aspects that go into TCP, including the transmission of data, that are outside the scope of this book, but anyone can look up networking and look at more of these concepts and how they are implemented.

This being said, TCP seems like something that we would always want to use. Why wouldn't we use something that guarantees delivery? Also, we don't necessarily need to broadcast if we can just loop through all of the current connections and send the data to everyone. However, because of all of these guarantees, this makes TCP heavier and slower. This isn't good for systems that we need to send data as fast as possible over. For this type of data transmission, we can utilize UDP. UDP gives us something called stateless transmission. Stateless transmission means we can send data on a channel and it will blast the data out and forget it. We don't need to connect to an address; instead, we can just send the data (as long as no one else is bound to that address and port). We can even set up a multicast system where anyone can listen to that address and it might pick up the data.

Some areas where this type of transmission is wanted/needed are as follows:

- Send buy/sell orders for a stock exchange. Since the data moves fast, we only care about the latest information. Due to this, if we don't receive some of the buy/sell orders, it doesn't really matter.

- Player position data for video games. We can only update the game so fast. We can also interpolate or *infer* where a player is on the screen if we already know which direction they were moving and the speed that they were going at. Because of this, we can receive a player position at any rate and figure out where they should be (this is sometimes known as the tick rate of the server).
- Telecommunication data does not necessarily care if we send all of the data as long as we sent most of it. We don't need to guarantee delivery of the full video/audio signal since we can still give a great picture with most of the data.

These are just a couple of the areas where UDP comes in handy. With an understanding of both these systems, we will take a look at them by building a highly simplified and impractical stock application. The behavior will be as follows:

1. The server will post new stock symbols and the amount of stock that is available. Then, it will blast the information on a known port to everyone over UDP.
2. The server will store all of the information related to a client's positions. This way, there is no way for a client to be able to manipulate how many shares they may have.
3. A client will send a buy or sell order to the server. The server will figure out whether it can handle the request. All of this traffic will be over TCP since we need to guarantee that we know the server received our message.
4. The server will respond with an error or a success message, telling the client that their book has updated.
5. The server will blast that a buy or sell happened for stock over the UDP channel.

This application looks as follows:

```
import dgram from 'dgram';
import { Socket } from 'net';
const multicastAddress = '239.192.0.0';
const sendMessageBadOutput = 'message needs to be formatted as follows:
BUY|SELL <SYMBOL> <NUMBER>';
const recvClient = dgram.createSocket({type : 'udp4', reuseAddr: true });
//1.
const sendClient = new Socket().connect(3000, "127.0.0.1");
// receiving client code seen below
process.stdin.setEncoding('utf8');
process.stdin.on('data', (msg) => {
    const input = msg.split(' ');
    if( input.length !== 3 ) {
        console.log(sendMessageBadOutput);
        return;
    }
    const num = parseInt(input[2]);
```

```
        if( num.toString() === 'NaN' ) {
            console.log(sendMessageBadOutput);
            return;
        }
        sendClient.write(msg);
    });
    sendClient.on('data', (data) => {
        console.log(data.toString('utf8'));
    });
```

Most of the preceding program should be familiar, except for the new module that we are utilizing: the dgram module. This module allows us to send data while utilizing UDP.

Here, we are creating a socket that is utilizing UDP4 (UDP over IPv4, or what we normally know as IP addresses). We also state that we are reusing the address and port. We're doing this so that we can test this locally. We wouldn't want this in any other scenario:

```
    recvClient.on('connect', () => {
        console.log('client is connected to the server');
    });
    recvClient.on('message', (msg) => {
        console.log('client received message', msg.toString('utf8'));
    });
    recvClient.bind(3000, () => {
        recvClient.addMembership(multicastAddress);
    });
```

We bind to port 3000 since that is where the server is going to send data. Then, we state that we want to add ourselves to the multicast address. For multicasting to work, the server needs to send data over a multicast address. These addresses are usually specific addresses that the OS has set up. Each OS can decide what addresses to use, but the one we have chosen should work on any OS.

Once we receive a message, we print it out. Again, this should look familiar. Node.js is based around events and streams and they are usually named the same thing for consistency.

The other pieces of this program handle user input and then send data over the TCP channel that we opened up when we created a new socket (this should look similar to our IPC program from before, except we pass a port and an IP address).

The server for this application is a bit more involved since it holds all of the logic of the stock application. We will break this down into several steps:

1. Create a file called `main.js` and import the `dgram` and `net` modules into it:

```
import dgram from 'dgram';
import net from 'net';
```

2. Add some constants for our multicast address, the error message for bad input, and the `Maps` for our stock tickers and clients:

```
const multicastAddress = '239.192.0.0';
const badListingNumMessage = 'to list a new ticker the following
format needs to be followed <SYMBOL>
<NUMBER>';
const symbolTable = new Map();
const clientTable = new Map();
```

3. Next, we create two servers. The first is used to listen for UDP messages, while the second is used to receive TCP messages. We will utilize the TCP server to process client requests. TCP is reliable, while UDP isn't:

```
const server = dgram.createSocket({type : 'udp4', reuseAddr :
true}).bind(3000);
const recvServer = net.createServer().listen(3000, '127.0.0.1');
```

4. Then, we need to set up a listener on the TCP server for any connections. Once we have a client connection, we will set them up with a temporary table so that we can store their portfolio:

```
recvServer.on('connection', (socket) => {
    const temp = new Map();
    clientTable.set(socket, temp);
});
```

5. Now, set up a data listener for the client. When we receive data, we will parse the message according to the following format, SELL/BUY <Ticker> <Number>:

```
// inside of the connection callback for recvServer
socket.on('data', (msg) => {
    const input = msg.toString('utf8').split(' ');
    const buyOrSell = input[0];
    const tickerSymbol = input[1];
    const num = parseInt(input[2]);
});
```

6. Based on this parsing, we check to see whether the client can perform the action. If they can, we will change their portfolio and send them a message stating the change was successful:

```
// inside the socket 'data' handler
const numHeld = symbolTable.get(input[1]);
if( buyOrSell === "BUY" && (num <= 0 || numHeld - num <= 0) ) {
    socket.write("ERROR!");
    return;
}
const clientBook = clientTable.get(socket);
const clientAmount = clientBook.get(tickerSymbol);
if( buyOrSell === "SELL" && clientAmount - num < 0 ) {
    socket.write("ERROR!");
    return;
}
if( buyOrSell === "BUY" ) {
    clientBook.set(tickerSymbol, clientAmount + num);
    symbolTable.set(tickerSymbol, numHeld - num);
} else if( buyOrSell === "SELL" ) {
    clientBook.set(tickerSymbol, clientAmount - num);
    symbolTable.set(tickerSymbol, numHeld + num);
}
socket.write(`successfully processed request. You now hold
${clientBook.get(tickerSymbol)}` of ${tickerSymbol}`);
```

7. Once we have told the client that we have processed their request, we can write to all of the clients through the UDP server:

```
// after the socket.write from above
const msg = Buffer.from(`${tickerSymbol}
${symbolTable.get(tickerSymbol)}`);
server.send(msg, 0, msg.byteLength, 3000, multicastAddress);
```

8. Finally, we need to process new stock tickers from the server through our standard input. Once we have processed the request, we send the data out on the UDP server so that every client knows about the new stock:

```
process.stdin.setEncoding('utf8');
process.stdin.on('data', (data) => {
    const input = data.split(' ');
    const num = parseInt(input[1]);
    symbolTable.set(input[0], num);
    for(const client of clientTable) {
        client[1].set(input[0], 0);
    }
```

```
        server.send(Buffer.from(data), 0, data.length, 3000,
    multicastAddress);
    });
```

Almost all of the error logic has been removed for clarity, but you can find it in this book's GitHub repository. As shown in the preceding example, it is very simple to utilize all of the interfaces for sending data to various other points, be it other parts of our application or remote clients that are listening for data. They all use almost the exact same interface and only differ in slight implementation details. Just remember that if there needs to be a guarantee of delivery, TCP should be used; otherwise, UDP isn't a bad choice.

Next, we will look at the HTTP/2 standard and how the server system is a bit different in Node.js compared to the net, dgram, and http/https modules.

HTTP/2

While it was introduced in 2015, the adoption of the technology is slow. HTTP/2 builds on the HTTP/1.1 protocol to allow for various features that caused issues for the previous system. This gives us the ability to use a single TCP connection to receive different requests. This wasn't possible with HTTP/1.1 and it caused an issue called head of line blocking. This meant that we could only really handle so many TCP connections and that if we had a long-running TCP connection, it could block all of the requests after it.

HTTP/2 also gave us the ability to push server-side resources. This means that if a server knows that a resource is going to be needed by a browser, such as a CSS file, it could push it to the server before it was needed. Finally, HTTP/2 gave us built-in streaming capabilities. This means we're able to use a connection and send data down as a stream instead of needing to send it all at once.

There are other benefits that HTTP/2 gives us, but these are the main ones. While the http and https modules will probably still be used for some time to come, the http2 module in Node.js should be used for any new applications.

The http2 module in Node.js differs from the http and https modules in a few ways. While it doesn't follow the standards that many of the other IPC/networking modules give us, it does give us some nice ways to send data over HTTP/2. One of these allows us to stream files directly from the filesystem instead of needing to create a pipe for the file and send it to the sender. An example of some of these differences can be seen in the following code:

```
import http2 from 'http2';
import fs from 'fs';
const server = http2.createSecureServer({
```

```
        key : fs.readFileSync('server.key.pem'),
        cert : fs.readFileSync('server.crt.pem')
    });
    server.on('error', (err) => console.error(err));
    server.on('stream', (stream, headers) => {
        stream.respond({
            'content-type': 'text/plain',
            ':status' : 200
        });
        stream.end('Hello from Http2 server');
    });
    server.listen(8081, '127.0.0.1');
```

First, notice that the server needs a private key and a public certificate. These are used to make sure that the connection that is set up is secure, meaning that no one can see what's being sent. For us to be able to do this, we need a tool such as openssl to create these keys and certificates. With Windows 10 and other Unix operating systems, we get this for free. Otherwise, we need to download Cygwin (http://www.cygwin.com/). With openssl, we can run the following command:

```
> openssl req -x509 -newkey rsa:4096 -keyout server.key.pem -out
server.crt.pem -days 365
```

This command generates the necessary private key and public certificate for the server and clients to communicate securely. We won't go into the details of how this is implemented here, but information on how this can be achieved with SSL/TLS can be found at: https://www.cloudflare.com/learning/ssl/transport-layer-security-tls/.

With our certificate and key generated, we can read them in so that our server can start running. We will also notice that instead of responding to a message event or a request event, we respond to the stream event. HTTP/2 utilizes streams instead of trying to send all of the data at once. While Node.js wrapped the requests and responses in streams for us, this is not how it may be handled at the OS layer. HTTP/2 utilizes streaming right away. This is the reason why the event is called a stream.

Next, instead of calling the writeHead method, we are just responding to the stream. When we want to send information, we utilize the respond method and send the headers this way. We will also notice that some of the headers are prefixed with a colon. This is specific to the http2 module and if problems are found when sending specific headers, putting a colon in front may solve the issue.

Other than what we've talked about here, this should look quite similar to a normal HTTP(s) server that we write in Node.js. There are some other benefits that we get with the `http2` module, however, and one of them is responding with a file instead of having to read in that file and send it that way. This can be seen in the following code:

```
import http2 from 'http2';
import fs from 'fs';
import path from 'path';

const basePath = process.env.npm_package_config_static; //1.
const supportedTypes = new Set(['.ico', '.html', '.css', '.js']);
const server = http2.createSecureServer({
    key : fs.readFileSync(process.env.npm_package_config_key),
    cert : fs.readFileSync(process.env.npm_package_config_cert),
    allowHTTP1 : true //2.
});
server.on('error', (err) => console.error(err));
server.on('stream', (stream, header) => {
    const fileLoc = header[':path'];
    const extension = path.extname(fileLoc); //3.
    if(!supportedTypes.has(extension)) {
        stream.respond({
            ':status' : 400,
            'content-type' : 'application/json'
        });
        stream.end(JSON.stringify({
            error : 'unsupported data type!',
            extension
        }));
        return;
    }
    stream.respondWithFile( //4.
        path.join(process.cwd(), basePath, fileLoc),
        {
            ':status' : 200,
            'content-type' :
                extension === ".html" ?
                'text/html' :
                extension === ".css" ?
                'text/css' :
                'text/javascript'
        },
        {
            onError : (err) => { //5.
                if( err.code === 'ENOENT') {
                    stream.respond({ ':status' : 404 });
                } else {
```

```
                    stream.respond({ ':status' : 500 });
            }
            stream.end();
        }
    }
  )
});
server.listen(80, '127.0.0.1');
```

The program numbers are key points of interest, and they work as follows:

1. We are reading information from the `package.json` file, just like we did in the previous chapter. We are also running this through the `npm run <script>` command. Check out the previous chapter to see how to do this and how we can use configuration data from the `package.json` file in our programs.

2. We have set a specific configuration option for our server. If the client that connects to us can't use HTTP/2, then we will automatically convert everything back into the negotiated protocol, for example, HTTP/1.1.

3. We grab the extension from the URL. This way, we can see whether we support that file type and send the appropriate file; otherwise, we will pass back a 400 error message and state that it was a bad request.

4. This method allows us to pass a path in. Then, the core system will handle sending the file for us. All we need to do is make sure that we set the content type correctly so that the browser can interpret the data for us.

5. If there is an error at any point, such as the file not existing, we will respond with the correct status, such as a 404 or a 500 error.

While what we've presented here is just a small fraction of the `http2` module, this showcases how the `http2` module is different and how we can set one up quite quickly. If need be, refer back to `https://Node.js.org/dist/latest-v12.x/docs/api/http2.html` to see how the `http2` module is different from `http` and all of the capabilities that come with it. Now, we will take a look at the future state of the web and take a look at HTTP/3 in Node.js.

A quick glance at HTTP/3

While what we have talked about is the present state of communicating among processes, threads, and other computers, there is a new way for information to be passed around. The new standard is called HTTP/3 and it differs from the previous two iterations significantly.

The QUIC protocol

Quick UDP Internet Connections (**QUIC**) was introduced by Google in 2012. It is a protocol similar to the TCP, **Transport Layer Security** (**TLS**), and HTTP/2 protocols, but it is all transmitted over UDP. This means that a lot of the overhead that is built into TCP has been removed and replaced with a new method of sending data. On top of this, since TLS is built into the protocol, it means that the overhead of adding security to an already defined protocol has been removed.

QUIC is currently used by Google for things such as YouTube. While QUIC never gained mass appeal, it helped spawn the group that would create the HTTP/3 standard committee and helped guide the committee to utilize UDP as the base layer for the protocol. It also showcased how security can be built into the protocol and has lead HTTP/3 to have it built into it.

 Other companies have started to implement the QUIC protocol while HTTP/3 is being developed. One notable inclusion to this list is Cloudflare. Their blogpost on implementing QUIC can be found here: `https://blog.cloudflare.com/the-road-to-quic/`.

While HTTP/3 has not been added to Node.js, there are some packages that implement the QUIC protocol.

A look at node-quic

While QUIC is not the easiest to work with right now and the only official implementation is written in the Chromium source, there have been other implementations that allow us to play around with this protocol. The `node-quic` module has been deprecated in favor of the QUIC implementation that is trying to be built into Node.js directly, but we can still use it to see how we might utilize QUIC or even HTTP/3 in the future.

First, we need to install the module by running the `npm install node-quic` command. With this, we are able to write a simple client-server application. The client should look something like the following:

```
import quic from 'node-quic'

const port = 3000;
const address = '127.0.0.1';
process.stdin.setEncoding('utf8');
process.stdin.on('data', (data) => {
    quic.send(port, address, data.trim())
        .onData((data) => {
```

```
            console.log('we received the following back: ', data);
       });
});
```

We will notice that sending data is similar to how we would do so in the UDP system; that is, we can send data without actually needing to bind to the port and address. Other than this, the system runs similarly to how other applications would run when written with the `http` or `http2` module. One interesting thing to note here is that data is automatically converted into a string for us when we receive it from the `quic` stream.

A server for the previous client would look as follows:

```
import quic from 'node-quic'

const port = 3000;
const address = '127.0.0.1';
quic.listen(port, address)
    .then(() => {})
    .onError((err) => console.error(err))
    .onData((data, stream, buffer) => {
        console.log('we received data:', data);
        if( data === 'quit' ) {
            console.log('we are going to stop listening for data');
            quic.stopListening();
        } else {
            stream.write("Thank you for the data!");
        }
    });
```

Again, it should look familiar to the other applications that we have written. One of the major differences here is that this module was written with promises in mind. Other than this, the data we receive is a string, so we turn ourselves off if we receive `quit` by running the `stopListening` method. Otherwise, we write the data we want to send to the steam, similar to what we do with the HTTP/2 protocol.

 To stay on top of the implementation status for HTTP/3, it is recommended that you check out the following link and check it periodically: `https://quicwg.org/`.

As we can see, it is quite simple to utilize the QUIC protocol with this module. This may also be useful for internal applications. Just note that neither the QUC protocol nor the HTTP/3 standard has been fully finished and probably won't be for a few more years. This doesn't mean that you shouldn't utilize them—it just means that things can change quite quickly while the standard is in flux.

Summary

Sending data between different systems, be it threads, processes, or even other computers, is what we do as developers. There are many tools we can use to do this, and we have looked at most of them. Just remember that while one option can appear to make an application simple, that doesn't always mean it is the best choice. When it comes to breaking our systems up, we usually want to assign a specific job to a unit and use some form of IPC, such as named pipes, to communicate. If we need to move that task to another computer, we can always switch it out for TCP.

With these IPC and web protocols under our belt, we will be able to tackle most problems with ease in Node.js and to write both the client-side and server-side code when it comes to web applications. However, Node.js isn't just built for web applications. We can pretty much do anything that other languages can and even have most of the tools that these other languages have. This chapter should have helped to clarify that and helped solidify how Node.js can be built into an already developed application ecosystem.

With all of this in mind, we will be looking at streaming and how we can implement our own streams in Node.js.

7

Streams - Understanding Streams and Non-Blocking I/O

We have touched on almost all of the subjects that help us write highly performant code for the server with JavaScript. The two last topics that should be discussed are streams and data formats. While these two topics can go hand in hand (since most data formats are implemented through read/write streams), we will focus on streaming in this chapter.

Streaming gives us the capability to write systems that can process data without taking up a lot of working memory and without blocking the event queue. For those that have been reading this book sequentially, this may sound familiar to the concept of generators, and this is correct. We will focus on the four different types of streams that Node.js provides and that we can extend easily. From there, we will look at how we can combine streams and generators to process data with the built-in generator concepts.

The following topics are covered in this chapter:

- Streaming basics
- Readable streams
- Writable streams
- Duplex streams
- Transform streams
- Aside – generators and streams

Technical requirements

The following are prerequisites for this chapter:

- A code editor or IDE, preferably VS Code
- An operating system that can run Node.js
- The code found at `https://github.com/PacktPublishing/Hands-On-High-Performance-Web-Development-with-JavaScript/tree/master/Chapter07`.

Getting started with streams

Streaming is the act of working on an infinite dataset. This does not mean that it is, but it means that we have the possibility of having an unlimited data source. If we think in the traditional context of processing data, we usually run through three main steps:

1. Open/get access to a data source.
2. Process the data source once it is fully loaded in.
3. Spit out computed data to another location.

We can think of this as the basics of **input and output (I/O)**. Most of our concepts of I/O involve batch processing or working on all or almost all of the data. This means that we know the limits of that data ahead of time. We can make sure that we have enough memory, storage space, computing power, and so on, to deal with the process. Once we are done with the process, we kill the program or queue up the next batch of data.

A simple example of this is seen as follows, where we count the number of lines that the file has:

```
import { readFileSync } from 'fs'
const count = readFileSync('./input.txt', {encoding : 'utf8'})
 .split(/\n|\r\n/g).length;
console.log('number of lines in our file is: ', count);
```

We bring in the `readFileSync` method from the `fs` module and then read in the `input.txt` file. From here, we split on `\n` or `\r\n`, which gives us an array of all the lines of the file. From there, we get the length and put it on our standard output channel. This seems quite simple and seems to work quite well. For small- to medium-length files, this works great, but what happens when the file becomes abnormally large? Let's go ahead and see. Head over to `https://loremipsum.io` and give it an input of 100 paragraphs. Copy this and paste it a few times into the `input.txt` file. Now, when we run this program, we can see in our task manager a spike in memory usage.

We are loading a roughly 3 MB file into memory, counting the number of newlines, and then printing this out. This should still be quite fast, but we are now starting to utilize a good chunk of memory. Let's do something a bit more complex with this file. We will count the number of times the word `lorem` appears in the text. We can do that with the following code:

```
import { readFileSync } from 'fs'
const file = readFileSync('./input.txt', {encoding : 'utf8'});
const re = /\slorem\s/gi;
const matches = file.match(re);

console.log('the number of matches is: ', matches.length);
```

Again, this should process quite quickly, but there should be some lag in how it processes. While the use of a regular expression here could give us some false positives, it does showcase that we are batch processing on this file. In many cases, when we are working in a high-speed environment, we are working with files that can be close to or above 1 GB. When we get into these types of files, we do not want to load them all into memory. This is where streaming comes into play.

 Many systems that are considered big data are working with terabytes of data. While there are some in-memory applications that will store large amounts of data in memory, a good chunk of this type of data processing uses a mix of both streaming with files and using in-memory data sources to work with the data.

Let's take our first example. We are reading from a file and trying to count the number of lines in the file. Well, instead of thinking about the number of lines as a whole, we can look for the character that denotes a newline. The character(s) we are looking for in our regular expression are the use of a newline character ($\n$) or the carriage return plus the newline ($\r\n$) character. With this in mind, we should be able to build a streaming application that can read the file and count the number of lines without loading the file completely into memory.

 This example presents the API for utilizing a stream. We will go over what each Stream API gives us and how we can utilize it for our purposes. For now, take the code examples and run them to see how these types of applications work.

This can be seen in the following code snippet:

```
import { createReadStream } from 'fs';

const newLine = 0x0A;
const readStream = createReadStream('./input.txt');
let counter = 1;
readStream.on('data', (chunk) => {
    for(const byte of chunk) {
        if( newLine === byte ) counter += 1;
    }
}).on('end', () => {
    console.log('number of line in our file is: ', counter);
});
```

We grab a `Readable` stream from the `fs` module and create one. We also create a constant for the newline character represented in HEX format. We then listen for the data event so we can process data as it comes in. Then, we process each byte to see whether it is the same as the newline character. If it is, then we have a newline, otherwise we just keep searching. We do not need to explicitly look for the carriage return since we know it should be followed by a newline character.

While this will be slower than loading the entire file into memory, it does save us quite a bit of memory when we are processing the data. Another great thing about this method is that these are all events. With our full processing example, we are taking up the entire event loop until we are done processing. With the stream, we have events for when the data comes in. This means that we can have multiple streams running at the same time on the same thread without having to worry too much about blocking (as long as we are not spending too much time on the processing of the data chunk).

With the previous example, we can see how we could write the counterexample in streaming form. Just to drive the point home, let's go ahead and do just that. It should look something like the following:

```
const stream = createReadStream('./input.txt');
const buf = Buffer.from('lorem');
let found = 0;
let count = 0;
stream.on('data', (chunk) => {
    for(const byte of chunk) {
        if( byte === buf[found] ) {
            found += 1;
        } else {
            found = 0;
        }
        if( found === buf.byteLength ) {
```

```
            count += 1;
            found = 0;
        }
    }
}).on('end', () => {
    console.log('the number of matches is: ', count)
});
```

First, we create a read `stream` as we did before. Next, we create a `Buffer` form of the keyword that we are looking for (working on the raw bytes can be faster than trying to convert the stream into text, even if the API allows us to do that). Next, we maintain a `found` count and an `actual` count. The `found` count will let us know whether we have found the word; the other count keeps track of how many instances of `lorem` we have found. Next, we process each byte when a chunk comes in on the data event. If we find that the next byte is not the character we are looking for, we automatically return the `found` count to 0 (we did not find this particular string of text). After this check, we will see whether we have the full byte length found. If we do, we can increase the count and move `found` back to 0. We keep the `found` counter outside the data event because we receive the data in chunks. Since it is chunked, one part of `lorem` could come at the end of one chunk and the other piece of `lorem` could come at the beginning of the next chunk. Once the stream ends, we output the count.

Now, if we run both versions, we will find that the first actually catches more `lorem`. We added the case insensitive flag for regular expressions. If we turn this off by removing the trailing `i` and we remove the need for the character sequence to be by itself (the `\s` surrounding our character sequence), we will see that we get the same result. This example showcases how writing streams can be a bit more complicated than the batch processing version, but it usually leads to lower memory use and sometimes faster code.

While utilizing built-in streams such as the streams inside of the `zlib` and `fs` modules will get us quite far, we will see how we can be the producers of our own custom streams. We will take each one and write an extended stream type that will handle the data framing that we were doing in the previous chapter.

 For those that have forgotten or skipped to this chapter, we were framing all of our messages over a socket with the `!!!BEGIN!!!` and `!!!END!!!` tags to let us know when the full data had been streamed to us.

Building a custom Readable stream

A `Readable` stream does exactly what it states, it reads from a streaming source. It outputs data based on some criteria. Our example of this is a take on the simple example that is shown in the Node.js documentation.

We are going to take our example of counting the number of `lorem` in the text file, but we are going to output the location in the file that we found `lorem`:

1. Import the `Readable` class and the `createReadStream` method from their respective modules:

```
import { Readable } from 'stream'
import { createReadStream } from 'fs'
```

2. Create a class that extends the `Readable` class and set up some private variables to track the internal state:

```
class LoremFinder extends Readable {
    #lorem = Buffer.from('lorem');
    #found = 0;
    #totalCount = 0;
    #startByteLoc = -1;
    #file = null;
}
```

3. Add a constructor that initializes our `#file` variable to a `Readable` stream:

```
// inside our LoremFinder class
constructor(opts) {
    super(opts);
    if(!opts.stream ) {
        throw new Error("This stream needs a stream to be
        provided!");
    }
    this.#file = opts.stream;
    this.#file.on('data', this.#data.bind(this)); // will add #data
     method next
    this.#file.on('end', () => this.push(null));
}
```

4. Based on the constructor, we are going to utilize a `#data` private variable that will be a function. We will utilize it to read from our `#file` stream and to check for the locations of `lorem`:

```
// inside of the LoremFinder class
#data = function(chunk) {
    for(let i = 0; i < chunk.byteLength; i++) {
        const byte = chunk[i];
        if( byte === this.#lorem[this.#found] ) {
            if(!this.#found ) {
                this.#startByteLoc = this.#totalCount + i;
            }
            this.#found += 1;
        } else {
            this.#found = 0;
        }
        if( this.#found === this.#lorem.byteLength ) {
            const buf = Buffer.alloc(4);
            buf.writeUInt32BE(this.#startByteLoc);
            this.push(buf);
            this.#found = 0;
        }
    }
    this.#totalCount += chunk.byteLength;
}
```

We run through each byte and check whether we currently have the byte we are looking for in the `lorem` word. If we do and it is the l of the word, then we set our location `#startByteLoc` variable. If we find the entire word, we output `#startByteLoc`, otherwise, we reset our lookup variable and keep looping. Once we have finished looping, we add to our `#totalCount` the number of bytes we read and wait for our `#data` function to get called again. To end our stream and let others know that we have fully consumed the resource, we output a `null` value.

5. The final piece we add is the _read method.

This will get called either through the `Readable.read` method or through hooking a data event up. This is how we can make sure that a *primitive* stream such as `FileStream` is consumed:

```
// inside of the LoremFinder class
_read(size) {
    this.#file.resume();
}
```

6. Now we can add some test code to make sure that this stream is working properly:

```
const locs = new Set();
const loremFinder = new LoremFinder({
    stream : createReadStream('./input.txt')
});
loremFinder.on('data', (chunk) => {
    const num = chunk.readUInt32BE();
    locs.add(num);
});
loremFinder.on('end', () => {
    console.log('here are all of the locations:');
    for(const val of locs) {
        console.log('location: ', val);
    }
    console.log('number of lorems found is', locs.size);
});
```

With all of these concepts, we can see how we are able to consume primitive streams and be able to wrap them with a superset stream. Now that we have this stream, we could always use the pipe interface and pipe it into a `Writable` stream. Let's write the indices out to a file. To do this, we can do something as simple as `loremFinder.pipe(writeable)`.

If we open the file, we will see that it is just a bunch of random data. The reason for this is that we encoded all of the indices into 32-bit buffers. If we wanted to see them, we could rewrite our stream implementation just a little bit. This modification could look like this: `this.push(this.#startByteLoc.toString() + "\r\n");`.

With this modification, we can now look at the `output.txt` file and see all of the indices. It should start to become apparent how powerful it is writing streams and being able to just pipe one to the next, on top of how readable the code can become if we just keep piping them through various stages.

Understanding the Readable stream interface

The `Readable` stream has a few properties that we have available to us. All of them are explained in the Node.js documentation, but the main ones that we are interested in are `highWaterMark` and `objectMode`.

`highWaterMark` allows us to state how much data the internal buffer should hold before the stream will state that it can no longer take any data. One problem with our implementation is that we do not handle pauses. A stream can pause if this `highWaterMark` is reached. While we may not be worried about it most of the time, it can cause problems and is usually where stream implementors will run into issues. By setting a higher `highWaterMark`, we can prevent these problems. Another way of handling this would be to check the outcome of running `this.push`. If it comes back `true`, then we are able to write more data to the stream, otherwise, we should pause the stream and then resume when we get the signal from the other stream. The default `highWaterMark` for streams is around 16 KB.

`objectMode` allows us to build streams that are not `Buffer` based. This is great when we want to run through a list of objects. Instead of utilizing a `for` loop or even a `map` function, we could set up a piping system that moves objects through the stream and performs some type of operation on it. We are also not limited to plain old objects, but to almost any data type other than the `Buffer`. One thing to note about `objectMode` is it changes what the `highWaterMark` counts. Instead of it counting how much data to store in the internal buffer, it counts the number of objects that it will store until it pauses the stream. This defaults to `16`, but we can always change it if need be.

With these two properties explained, we should discuss the various internal methods that are available to us. For each stream type, there is a method that we *need* to implement and there are methods that we *can* implement.

For the `Readable` stream, we only need to implement the `_read` method. This method gives us a `size` argument, which is the number of bytes to read from our underlying data source. We do not always need to heed this number, but it is available to us if we want to implement our stream with it.

Other than the `_read` method, we need to utilize the `push` method. This is what pushes data onto our internal buffer and helps emit the data event as we have seen previously. As we stated before, the `push` method returns a Boolean. If this value is `true`, we can continue using `push`, otherwise, we should stop pushing data until our `_read` implementation gets called again.

As stated previously, when first implementing a `Readable` stream, the return value can be ignored. However, if we notice that data is not flowing or data is getting lost, the usual culprit is that the `push` method returned `false` and we continued to try pushing data on our stream. Once this happens, we should implement pausing by stopping the use of the `push` method until `_read` gets called again.

Two other pieces of the readable interface are the `_destroy` method and how to make our stream error out if something comes through that we are not able to handle. The `_destroy` method should be implemented if there are any low-level resources that we need to let go of.

This can be file handles opened with the `fs.open` command or sockets created with the `net` module. If an error occurred, we should also use that so we can emit an error event.

To handle errors that may come up with our streams, we should emit our error through the `this.emit` system. If we throw an error, as per the documentation, it can lead to unexpected results. By emitting an error, we let the user of our stream deal with the error and handle it as they see fit.

Implementing the Readable stream

From what we have learned here, let's implement the framing system that we talked about earlier. From our previous example, it should be obvious how we might handle this. We will hold the underlying resource, in this case, a socket. From there, we will find the `!!!BEGIN!!!` buffer and let it pass. We will then start to store the data that is held. Once we reach the `!!!END!!!` buffer, we will push out the data chunk.

We are holding on to quite a bit of data in this case, but it showcases how we might handle framing. The duplex stream will showcase how we might handle a simple protocol. The example is seen as follows:

1. Import the `Readable` stream and create a class called `ReadMessagePassStream`:

   ```
   import { Readable } from 'stream';

   class ReadMessagePassStream extends Readable {
   }
   ```

2. Add some private variables to hold our internal state for the stream:

   ```
   // inside of the ReadMessagePassStream class
   #socket = null;
   #bufBegin = Buffer.from("!!!START!!!");
   #bufEnd = Buffer.from("!!!END!!!");
   #internalBuffer = [];
   #size = 0;
   ```

3. Create a `#data` method like the one before. We will now be looking for the beginning and end frame buffers that we set up before, `#bufBegin` and `#bufEnd`:

```
#data = function(chunk) {
    let i = -1
    if((i = chunk.indexOf(this.#bufBegin)) !== -1) {
        const tempBuf = chunk.slice(i + this.#bufBegin.byteLength);
        this.#size += tempBuf.byteLength;
        this.#internalBuffer.push(tempBuf);
    }
    else if((i = chunk.indexOf(this.#bufEnd)) !== -1) {
        const tempBuf = chunk.slice(0, i);
        this.#size += tempBuf.byteLength;
        this.#internalBuffer.push(tempBuf);
        const final = Buffer.concat(this.#internalBuffer);
        this.#internalBuffer = [];
        if(!this.push(final)) {
            this.#socket.pause();
        }
    } else {
        this.#size += chunk.byteLength;
        this.#internalBuffer.push(chunk);
    }
}
```

4. Create the constructor for the class to initialize our private variables:

```
constructor(options) {
    if( options.objectMode ) {
        options.objectMode = false //we don't want it on
    }
    super(options);
    if(!options.socket ) {
        throw "Need a socket to attach to!"
    }
    this.#socket = options.socket;
    this.#socket.on('data', this.#data.bind(this));
    this.#socket.on('end', () => this.push(null));
}
```

One new piece of information is the `objectMode` property, which can be passed into our stream. This allows our streams to read objects instead of raw buffers. In our case, we do not want this to happen; we want to work with the raw data.

5. Add the `_read` method to make sure that our stream will start up:

```
// inside the ReadMessagePassStream
_read(size) {
    this.#socket.resume();
}
```

With this code, we now have a way of handling a socket without having to listen to the data event in our main code; it is now wrapped in this `Readable` stream. On top of this, we now have the capability of piping this stream into another. The following test harness code shows this:

```
import { createWriteStream } from 'fs';

const socket = createConnection(3333);
const write = createWriteStream('./output.txt');
const messageStream = new ReadMessagePassStream({ socket });
messageStream.pipe(write);
```

We have a server being hosted on localhost at port `3333`. We create a `write` stream and pipe any data from our `ReadMessagePassStream` to that file. If we hook this up to the server in the test harness, we will notice that an output file is created and holds only the data that we sent over it, not the framing code.

 The framing technique that we are utilizing is not always going to work. Just as it has been shown in the `lorem` example that our data can get chunked at any point, we could have our `!!!START!!!` and `!!!END!!!` end up on one of the chunk boundaries. If this happened, our streams would fail. There is additional code that we would need to handle these cases, but these examples should provide all the necessary ideas to implement the streaming code.

Next, we will take a look at the `Writable` stream interface.

Building a Writable stream

A `Writable` stream is one that we write data to and it can pipe into a `Readable`, `Duplex`, or `Transform` stream. We can use these streams to write data in a chunked manner so a consuming stream can process the data in chunks instead of all at once. The API for a writable stream is quite similar to that of a `Readable` stream except for the methods that are available to us.

Understanding the Writable stream interface

A writable stream gives us nearly the same options that are available to a `Readable` stream so we will not go into that. Instead, we will take a look at the four methods that are available to us—one that we *must* implement and the rest that we *can* implement:

- The _write method allows us to perform any type of transformations or data manipulations that we need to and provides us with the ability to use a callback. This callback is what signals that the write stream is able to take in more data.

 While not inherently true, it is what pops data off the internal buffer if there is any. However, for our purposes, it is best to think of the callback as a way to process more data.

  We can utilize this to wrap a more primitive stream and add our own data before or after the main data chunk. We will see this with the practical counterpart to our `Readable` stream.

- The _final method allows us to perform any actions that we need to before the writable stream closes. This could be a cleanup of resources or sending out any data that we may have been holding on to. We will usually not implement this method unless we are holding on to something such as a file descriptor.
- The _destroy method is the same as the `Readable` stream and should be treated similar to the _final method, except we can potentially get errors on this method.
- The _writev method gives us the capability of handling multiple chunks at the same time. We can implement this if we have some sort of ordering system for the chunks or we do not care what order the chunks come in. While this may not be apparent now, we will implement this method when we implement the duplex stream next. The use cases can be somewhat limited, but it still can be beneficial.

Implementing the Writable stream

The following `Writable` stream implementation showcases our framing method and how we can use it to put the `!!!START!!!` and `!!!END!!!` frames on our data. While simplistic, it does showcase the power of framing and building more complex streams around the primitive ones:

1. Import the `Writable` class from the stream module and create the shell for `WriteMessagePassStream`. Set this as the default export for this file:

    ```
    import { Writable } from 'stream';

    export default class WriteMessagePassStream extends Writable {
    }
    ```

2. Add the private state variables and the constructor. Make sure not to allow `objectMode` through since we want to work on the raw data:

    ```
    // inside the WriteMessagePassStream
    #socket = null;
    #writing = false;
    constructor(options) {
      if( options.objectMode ) {
          options.objectMode = false;
      }
      if(!options.socket ) {
          throw new Error("A socket is required to construct this
            stream!");
      }
      super(options);
      this.#socket = options.socket;
    }
    ```

3. Add the `_write` method to our class. It will be explained as follows:

    ```
    _write(chunk, encoding, callback) {
        if(!this.#writing ) {
            this.#writing = true;
            this.#socket.write("!!!START!!!");
        }
        let i = -1;
        let prevI = 0;
        let numCount = 0;
        while((i = chunk.indexOf([0x00], i)) !== -1) {
            const buf = chunk.slice(prevI, i);
            this.#socket.write(buf);
            this.#socket.write("!!!END!!!");
    ```

```
        if( i !== chunk.byteLength - 1 ) {
            this.#socket.write("!!!START!!!");
        } else {
            return callback();
        }
        numCount += 1;
    }
    if(!numCount ) {
        this.#socket.write(chunk);
    }
    return callback();
}
```

With this code, we can see some similar points to how we handled the readable side. Some notable exceptions include the following items:

- We implement the _write method. We are ignoring, again, the encoding parameter of this function, but we should check this in case we get an encoding that we are not expecting. The chunk is the data that is being written, and the callback is what we call when we are finished processing the write for this chunk.
- Since we are wrapping a socket and we do not want to kill it once we are done sending the data, we need to send some type of stop signal to our stream. In our case, we are using the simple 0x00 byte. In a more robust implementation, we would utilize something else, but this should work for now.
- No matter what, we either use the framing or we just write to the underlying socket.
- We call the callback once we are finished with our processing. In our case, if we have the writing flag set, this means we are still in a frame and we want to return early, otherwise, we want to put our stream into writing mode and write out the !!!START!!! and then the chunk. Again, if we never use the callback, our stream will be infinitely paused. The callback is what tells the internal mechanism to pull more data from the internal buffer for us to consume.

With this code, we can now look at the test harness and how we are utilizing it to create a server and handle incoming Readable streams that implement our framing context:

```
import { createServer } from 'net'
import WrappedWritableStream from '../writable/main.js'
const server = createServer((con) => {
 console.log('client connected. sending test data');
 const wrapped = new WrappedWritableStream({ socket : con });
 for(let i = 0; i < 100000; i++) {
 wrapped.write(`data${i}\r\n`);
 }
```

```
wrapped.write(Buffer.from([0x00]));
wrapped.end();
console.log('finished sending test data');
});
server.listen(3333);
```

We create a server and listen in on port `3333` for localhost. Whenever we receive a connection, we wrap it with our `Writable` stream. We then send down a bunch of test data and, once that is finished, we write out the `0x00` signal to tell our stream this frame is done, and we then call the `end` method to say we are finished with this socket. If we added another test run after our first, we can see how our framing system works. Let's go ahead and do just that. Add the following code after `wrapped.write(Buffer.from([0x00]))`:

```
for(let i = 0; i < 100000; i++) {
    wrapped.write(`more_data${i}\r\n`);
}
wrapped.write(Buffer.from([0x00]));
```

 If we ever hit the `highWaterMark` of our stream, the write stream will pause until the read stream has started to consume from it.

If we now run the test harness with our `Readable` stream from before, we will see that we are processing all of this data and writing out to our file without any of the framing passing through. With these two stream implementations, we are now able to pipe data across a socket with a custom framing option. We would now be able to use this system to implement our data-passing system from the previous chapter. However, we will instead implement a `Duplex` stream that will improve on this system and allow us to work with multiple writable chunks, which is what we will see in the next section.

Implementing a Duplex stream

A duplex stream is just that, one that works both ways. It combines a `Readable` and `Writable` stream into a single interface. With this type of stream, we can now just pipe from the socket into our custom stream instead of wrapping the stream like we have been (even though we will still implement it as a wrapped stream).

There is not much more to talk about with `Duplex` streams other than one fact that trips up newcomers to the stream type. There are two separate buffers: one for `Readable` and one for `Writable`. We need to make sure to treat them as separate instances. This means whatever we use for the _read method in terms of variables, should not be used for the _write and _writev method implementations, otherwise, we could run into bad bugs.

As stated before, the following code implements a `Duplex` stream along with a counting mechanism so, that way, we can utilize the _writev method. As mentioned in the *Understanding the Writable stream interface* section, the _writev method allows us to work on multiple chunks of data at a time:

1. Import the `Duplex` class from the `stream` module and add the shell for our `MessageTranslator` class. Export this class:

    ```
    import { Duplex } from 'stream';

    export default class MessageTranslator extends Duplex {
    }
    ```

2. Add all the internal state variables. Each of them will be explained in the following:

    ```
    // inside the MessageTranslator class
    #socket = null;
    #internalWriteBuf = new Map();
    #internalReadHoldBuf = [];
    #internalPacketNum = 0;
    #readSize = 0;
    #writeCounter = 0;
    ```

3. Add the constructor for our class. We will handle the data event for our `#socket` inside of this constructor instead of creating another method as we have in the past:

    ```
    // inside the MessageTranslator class
    constructor(opts) {
        if(!opts.socket ) {
            throw new Error("MessageTranslator stream needs a
              socket!");
        }
        super(opts);
        this.#socket = opts.socket;
        // we are assuming a single message for each chunk
        this.#socket.on('data', (chunk) => {
            if(!this.#readSize ) {
                this.#internalPacketNum = chunk.readInt32BE();
    ```

```
        this.#readSize = chunk.readInt32BE(4);
        this.#internalReadHoldBuf.push(chunk.slice(8));
        this.#readSize -= chunk.byteLength - 8
    } else {
        this.#internalReadHoldBuf.push(chunk);
        this.#readSize -= chunk.byteLength;
    }
    // reached end of message
    if(!this.#readSize ) {
        this.push(Buffer.concat(this.#internalReadHoldBuf));
        this.#internalReadHoldBuf = [];
    }
    });
}
```

We will automatically assume we have a single message per chunk. This makes the processing much easier. When we do get data, we will read in the packet number, which should be the first four bytes of data. We then read in the size of the message, which is the next 4 bytes of data. Finally, we push the rest of the data into our internal buffer. Once we have finished reading the entire message, we will put all the internal chunks together and push them out. Finally, we will reset our internal buffer.

4. Add the _writev and _write methods to our class. Remember that the _writev method is utilized for multiple chunks, so we will have to loop through them and write each one out:

```
// inside the MessageTranslator class
_writev(chunks, cb) {
    for(const chunk of chunks) {
        this.#processChunkHelper(chunk); //shown next
    }
    this.#writeHelper(cb); //shown next
}
_write(chunk, encoding, cb) {
    this.#processChunkHelper(chunk); //shown next
    this.#writeHelper(cb); //shown next
}
```

5. Add helper methods to process the chunks and to actually write them out. We will utilize the number –1 as a 4-byte message to state we are done with this message:

```
// inside the MessageTranslator class
#processChunkHelper = function(chunk) {
    if(chunk.readInt32BE() === -1) {
```

```
            this.#internalWriteBuf.get(this.#writeCounter).done = true;
            this.#writeCounter += 1;
            this.#internalWriteBuf.set(this.#writeCounter, {buf : [],
              done : false});
        } else {
            if(!this.#internalWriteBuf.has(this.#writeCounter)) {
                this.#internalWriteBuf.set(this.#writeCounter, {buf :
                  [], done : false}); }
                this.#internalWriteBuf.get(this.#writeCounter)
                  .buf.push(chunk);
            }
        }
    }
    #writeHelper = function(cb) {
        const writeOut = [];
        for(const [key, val] of this.#internalWriteBuf) {
            if( val.done ) {
                const cBuf = Buffer.allocUnsafe(4);
                const valBuf = Buffer.concat(val.buf);
                const sizeBuf = Buffer.allocUnsafe(4);
                cBuf.writeInt32BE(valBuf.readInt32BE());
                sizeBuf.writeInt32BE(valBuf.byteLength - 4);
                writeOut.push(Buffer.concat([cBuf, sizeBuf,
                  valBuf.slice(4)]));
                val.buf = [];
            }
        }
        if( writeOut.length ) {
            this.#socket.write(Buffer.concat(writeOut));
        }
        cb();
    }
```

Our #processChunkHelper method checks to see whether we hit the magical -1 4-byte message to say we have finished writing our message. If we do not, we keep adding to our internal buffer (the array). Once we have reached the end, we will put all of the data together and then move onto the next packet of data.

Our #writeHelper method will loop through all of those packets and check to see whether any of them are finished. If they are, it will get the packet number, the size of the buffer, the data itself, and concatenate it all together. Once it has done this, it will reset the internal buffer to make sure we are not leaking memory. We will write all of this data to the socket and then call our callback to state that we are done writing.

6. Finish up the `Duplex` stream by implementing our `_read` method as we have before. The `_final` method should just call the callback since there is no processing left:

```
// inside the MessageTranslator class
_read() {
    this.#socket.resume();
}
_final(cb) {
    cb(); // nothing to do since it all should be consumed at this
          // point
}
```

 `_writev` should really be used when order does not matter and we are just processing the data and possibly turning it into something else. This could be a hashing algorithm or something similar to that. In almost all cases, the `_write` method should be used.

While this implementation has quite a few flaws (one being that we do not look for possible other packets if we reach the –1 number), it does showcase how we can build a `Duplex` stream and also another way of handling messages. It is not recommended to come up with our own schemes of moving data across a socket (as we will see in the next chapter), but if there is a new specification that comes out, we could always write for it utilizing the `Duplex` socket.

If we test this implementation with our test harness, we should get a file called `output.txt` that has the duplex plus the number message written 100,000 times, plus a trailing end-of-line character. Again, a `Duplex` stream is just a separate `Readable` and `Writable` stream put together and should be used when implementing a data transmission protocol.

The final stream that we will take a look at is the `Transform` stream.

Implementing a Transform stream

Out of the four streams, this may be the most useful and possibly the most used stream out of the group. A `Transform` stream hooks up the readable and writable portions of a stream and allows us to manipulate the data that comes across it. This may sound similar to a `Duplex`. Well, a `Transform` stream is a special type of `Duplex` stream!

Built-in implementations of `Transform` streams include any of the streams implemented in the `zlib` module. The basic idea is that we are not just trying to pass information from one end to the other; we are trying to manipulate that data and turn it into something else. That is what the `zlib` streams give us. They compress and decompress the data. `Transform` streams change the data into another form. This also means that we can make a transform stream be a one-way transformation; whatever is output from the transform stream cannot be undone. We will create one of these `Transform` streams here, specifically creating a hash of a string.

First, let's go through the interface for a `Transform` stream.

Understanding the Transform stream interface

We have access to two methods that we almost always want to implement, no matter what. One gives us access to the underlying chunk of data and allows us to perform the transformation on it. We implement this one with the `_transform` method. It takes three arguments: the chunk of data that we are working on, the encoding, and a callback to let the underlying system know that we are ready to process more information.

One special thing about the callback function that differs from the `_write` callback for a `Writable` stream is that we can pass data to it to emit data on the readable side of the `Transform` stream, or we can pass nothing to it to signal that we want to process more data. This allows us to only send out data events when we want to instead of almost always needing to pass them out.

The other method is the `_flush` method. This allows us to finish any processing of any data that we may still be holding. Or, it will allow us to output once all of the data that has been sent into the stream. This is what we will implement with our string hashing function.

Implementing a Transform stream

Our `Transform` stream is going to take in string data and keep running a hashing algorithm. Once it has finished, it will output the final hash that was calculated. A hashing function is one where we take some form of input and output a unique piece of data. This unique piece of data (in our case, a number) should not be vulnerable to collisions. Collisions is the concept that two values that differ from each other could come to the exact same hash value. In our case, we are converting the string to a 32-bit integer in JavaScript so we have a low chance of collision, but not an impossible chance of it.

The example is as follows:

```
// implemented in stream form from
//
https://stackoverflow.com/questions/7616461/generate-a-hash-from-string-in-
javascript
export default class StreamHashCreator extends Transform {
    #currHash = 0;
    constructor(options={}) {
        if( options.objectMode ) {
            throw new Error("This stream does not support object mode!");
        }
        options.decodeStrings = true;
        super(options);
    }
    _transform(chunk, encoding, callback) {
        if( Buffer.isBuffer(chunk) ) {
            const str = chunk.toString('utf8');
            for(let i = 0; i < str.length; i++) {
                const char = str.charCodeAt(i);
                this.#currHash = ((this.#currHash << 5) - this.#currHash )
                + char;
                this.#currHash |= 0;
            }
        }
        callback();
    }
    _flush(callback) {
        const buf = Buffer.alloc(4);
        buf.writeInt32BE(this.#currHash);
        this.push(buf);
        callback(null);
    }
}
```

Each function of the previous stream is explained below:

1. The only thing that we need to persist until the stream is destroyed is the current hash code. This will allow the hash function to keep track of what we have already passed into it and work off of the data after each write.

2. We do a check here to see whether the chunk we received is a `Buffer`. Since we made sure to turn the option of `decodeStrings` on, this means that we should always get buffers, but it still helps to check.

3. While the contents of the hash function can be seen at the URL provided, the only major thing that we need to worry about is that we call our callback, just like we had to do when we were implementing our `Writable` stream.

4. Once we are ready to produce data, we utilize the `push` method, just like we did with the `Readable` stream. Remember, `Transform` streams are just special `Duplex` streams that allow us to manipulate the data that is being input and change it into something for the output. We can also change the last two lines of code to just do `callback(null, buf)`; this is just the shorthand of what we've seen previously.

Now, if we run some test cases on the previous code, we will see that we do get a unique hash code for each unique string that we enter, but we get the same hash code when we input the exact same thing. This means that our hashing function is good and we can hook it up to a streaming application.

Using generators with streams

Everything that we have seen up to this point showcases how we can utilize all of the built-in systems in Node.js to create streaming applications. However, for those that have been following sequentially in the book, we have discussed generators. Those that have been keen to think about them would notice a strong correlation between streams and generators. This is actually the case! We can utilize generators to hook into the Streaming API.

With this concept, we could build generators that can both work in the browser and inside of Node.js without that much overhead. We have even seen in a Chapter 6, *Message Passing – Learning about the Different Types,*how we can get at the underlying stream for the Fetch API. Now, we can write a generator that can work with both of these subsystems.

For now, let's just look at an example of an `async` generator and how we can hook them into the Node.js streaming system. The example will be to see how we can have a generator as the input for a `Readable` stream:

1. We are going to set up a `Readable` stream to read out the 26 lowercase characters of the English alphabet. We can do this fairly easily by writing the following generator:

```
function* handleData() {
    let _char = 97;
    while(_char < 123 ) { //char code of 'z'
        yield String.fromCharCode(_char++);
    }
}
```

2. While the character code is below `123`, we keep sending data. We can then wrap this in a `Readable` stream, like so:

```
const readable = Readable.from(handleData());
readable.on('data', (chunk) => {
    console.log(chunk);
});
```

If we now run this code, we will see the characters *a* through *z* appear in our console. The `Readable` stream knows that it is the end because a generator produces an object with two keys. The `value` field gives us the value from the `yield` expression and the `done` tells us if the generator has finished running.

This lets the readable interface know when to send out `data` events (through us yielding a value) and when to close the stream (through the `done` key being set to `true`). We could also pipe the output of our readable system into that of the writable to chain the process. This can easily be seen with the following code:

```
(async() => {
    const readable2 = Readable.from(grabData());
    const tempFile = createWriteStream('./temp.txt');
    readable2.pipe(tempFile);
    await once(tempFile, 'finish');
    console.log('all done');
})();
```

 Implementing streams through generators and `async/await` may seem like a good idea, but we should only utilize this if we are trying to put an already `async/await` piece of code with a stream. Always try to go for readability; utilizing the generator or `async/await` method will most likely lead to something unreadable.

With the previous example, we have combined the readable from a generator and we have utilized the piping mechanism to send it to a file. With `async/await` and generators becoming constructs in the JavaScript language, it won't be long before we have streaming as a first-class concept.

Summary

Streaming is one of the pillars of writing highly performant Node.js code. It allows us to not block the main thread, while still being able to process data. The Streaming API allows us to write different types of streams for our purposes. While most of these streams will be in the form of transform streams, it is nice to see how we could implement the other three.

The final topic we will look at in the next chapter is data formats. Handling different data formats besides JSON will allow us to interface with many big data providers and be able to handle the data formats that they like to use. We will see how they utilize streaming to implement all of their format specifications.

8
Data Formats - Looking at Different Data Types Other Than JSON

We have almost finished our discussion on server-side JavaScript. One topic that seems to fly under the radar, but does come up quite a bit when interfacing with other systems or even making things faster, is transmitting data in different formats. One of the most common, if not the most common, formats is JSON. JSON is quite easily one of the easiest data formats to interface with, especially in JavaScript.

In JavaScript, we do not have to worry about JSON objects that do not match a class. If we were utilizing a strongly typed language such as Java (or TypeScript for those that are using it), we would have to worry about the following things:

- Creating a class that mimics the format of the JSON object.
- Creating a map structure that keeps nesting based on how many nested objects there are.
- Creating on-the-fly classes based on the JSON that we get.

None of these are necessarily hard, but it can add to speed and complexity when we are interfacing with systems that are written in these languages. With other data formats, we may get some major speed benefits; not only from possibly smaller data transfers, but also from the other languages being able to parse the objects more easily. There are even more benefits when we move to a schema-based data format, such as versioning, which can make backward compatibility easier.

With all of this in mind, let's go ahead and take a look at JSON and see some of the benefits, but also the losses that we get with utilizing it. On top of this, we will take a look at a new custom format that we will create for our services to transfer data at a hopefully smaller size. After this, we will take a look at a schema-less data format such as JSON and, finally, take a look at a schema-based format.

This chapter might be lighter than almost all of the other chapters, but it is one that will prove useful when developing enterprise applications or interfacing with them.

The topics covered in this chapter are as follows:

- Using JSON
- Encoding in JSON
- Decoding in JSON
- A look at data formats

 In TypeScript, we could just use the any type if we wanted to, but that would partially defeat the purpose of TypeScript. While we will not be looking at TypeScript in this book, it is good to know that it is out there, and it is easy to see how developers may run into it when developing backend applications.

Technical requirements

The following tools are needed to complete this chapter:

- An editor or IDE, preferably VS Code
- An operating system that supports Node.js
- The code found at `https://github.com/PacktPublishing/Hands-On-High-Performance-Web-Development-with-JavaScript/tree/master/Chapter08`.

Using JSON

As stated previously, JSON provides an easy-to-use and easy-to-operate interface for sending and receiving messages between services. For those that do not know, JSON stands for **JavaScript Object Notation,** which is one of the reasons that it interfaces with JavaScript so well. It mimics a lot of the behavior that JavaScript's objects do, except for some fundamental types (things such as functions). This also makes it quite easy to parse. We could use something such as the built-in `JSON.parse` function to turn stringified versions of JSON into objects, or `JSON.stringify` to turn one of our objects into its over-the-wire format.

So what are some of the disadvantages when utilizing JSON? We first have the problem that the format can get very verbose when sending data over the wire. Consider an array of objects that have the following format:

```
{
    "name" : "Bob",
    "birth" : "01/02/1993",
    "address" : {
        "zipcode" : 11111,
        "street" : "avenue of av.",
        "streetnumber" : 123,
        "state" : "CA",
        "country" : "US"
    },
    "contact" : {
        "primary" : "111-222-3333",
        "secondary" : "444-555-6666",
        "email" : "bob@example.com"
    }
}
```

This is probably a common sight for those that have worked with contact forms or customer information. Now, while we should involve paging of some kind for a website, we still might grab 100 or even 500 of these at a time. This could easily lead to a huge wire transfer cost. We can simulate this with the following code:

```
const send = new Array(100);
send.fill(json);
console.log('size of over the wire buffer is: ',
  Buffer.from(JSON.stringify(send)).byteLength);
```

By using this method, we get the byte length of the buffer that would come out of stringifying `100` entries for the data that we are sending. We will see that it comes out to around 22 KB worth of data. If we up this to `500`, we can deduce that it would be around 110 KB worth of data. While this may not seem like a lot of data, we could see this type of data being sent to a smartphone, where we want to limit the amount of data that we transfer in order that we do not drain the battery.

 We have not heavily discussed cellular phones and our applications, especially on the frontend, but it is something we need to increasingly be conscious of since we are becoming more and more of a remote business world. Many users, even if there is not a mobile version of the application, will still try to utilize it. One personal anecdote is utilizing email services that are meant for desktop applications because of some functionality that was not available in the mobile version of the application. We always need to be conscious of the amount of data we are transferring, but mobile has made that idea become a primary objective.

One way around this is to utilize some type of compression/decompression format. One fairly well-known format is `gzip`. This format is quite fast, has no loss in data quality (some compression formats have this, such as JPEG), and is ubiquitous with web pages.

Let's go ahead and `gzip` this data by utilizing the `zlib` module in Node.js. The following code showcases an easy-to-use `gzip` method inside of `zlib`, and showcases the size difference between the original and the gzipped version:

```
gzipSync(Buffer.from(JSON.stringify(send))).byteLength
```

We will now see that the gzipped version is only 301 bytes and, for the 500-length array, we see a gzipped version of around 645 bytes. That is quite a saving! However, there are a couple of points to remember here. First, we are using the exact same object for each item in the array. Compression algorithms are based on patterns, so seeing the exact same object over and over again is giving us a false sense of the original to the compressed form. This does not mean that this is not indicative of the size differences between uncompressed versus compressed data, but it is something to keep in mind when testing out various formats. Based on various sites, a compression ratio of 4-10 times the original is what we would see (this means if the original was 1 MB, we would see a compression size of anywhere from 250 KB to 100 KB).

Instead of utilizing JSON, we can create a format ourselves that should represent the data in a much more compact way. First, we are going to only support three item types: a whole number, a floating number, and strings. Second, we will store all of the keys in the header of the message.

A schema can be best described as the definition of the data that is coming through. This means that we will know how to interpret the data that is coming through and not have to look for special encoding symbols to tell us when the end of the payload is (even though our format will use an end-of-body signal).

Our schema is going to look something like the following:

1. We will use wrapper bytes for both the header and body of the message. The header will be denoted with the `0x10` byte and the body with the `0x11` byte.

2. We will support the following types and their conversions will look similar to the following:

   - Whole number: `0x01` followed by a 32-bit integer
   - Floating-point number: `0x02` followed by a 32-bit integer
   - String: `0x03` followed by the length of the string followed by the data

This should be good enough to get the concept of data formats and how they might work differently than just encoding and decoding JSON. In the next two sections, we will see how we might implement an encoder and decoder utilizing streams.

Implementing the encoder

We are going to implement both the encoder and decoder utilizing transform streams. This will give us the most flexibility in terms of actually implementing the streams, and it already has a lot of the behavior that we need since we are technically transforming the data. First, we will need some generic helpers for both the encoding and decoding of our specific data types, and we will put all of these methods in a `helpers.js` helper file. The encoding functions will look like the following:

```
export const encodeString = function(str) {
    const buf = Buffer.from(str);
    const len = Buffer.alloc(4);
    len.writeUInt32BE(buf.byteLength);
    return Buffer.concat([Buffer.from([0x03]), len, buf]);
}
export const encodeNumber = function(num) {
    const type = Math.round(num) === num ? 0x01 : 0x02;
    const buf = Buffer.alloc(4);
    buf.writeInt32BE(num);
    return Buffer.concat([Buffer.from([type]), buf]);
}
```

Encoding the string takes in the string and outputs the buffer that will hold the information for the decoder to work on. First, we will change the string to the `Buffer` format. Next, we create a buffer to hold the length of the string. Then, we store the length of the buffer utilizing the `writeUInt32BE` method.

 For those that do not know byte/bit conversions, 8 bits of information (a bit is either a 1 or 0- the lowest form of data we can supply) makes up 1 byte. A 32-bit integer, what we are trying to write, is then made up of 4 bytes (32/8). The U portion of that method means it is unsigned. Unsigned means we only want positive numbers (lengths can only be 0 or positive in our case). With this information, we can see why we allocated 4 bytes for this operation and why we are utilizing this specific method. For more information on both the write/read portions for buffers, go to `https://nodejs.org/api/buffer.html` as it explains in depth the buffer operations we have access to. We will only explain the operations that we will be utilizing.

Once we have the string turned into the buffer format and the length of the string, we will write out a buffer that has `type` as the first byte, in our case the `0x03` byte; the length of the string, so we know how much of the incoming buffer is the string; and then finally, the string itself. This one should be the most complicated out of the two helper methods, but from a decoding perspective, it should make sense. When we are reading the buffer, we do not know how long a string is going to be. Because of this, we need some information in the prefix of this type to know how much to actually read. In our case, the `0x03` tells us that the type is a string and we know, based on our data type protocol that we established previously, that the next 4 bytes will be the length of the string. Finally, we can use this information to read so far ahead in the buffer to grab the string and decode it back to a string.

The `encodeNumber` method is much easier to understand. First, we check whether the rounding of the number equals itself. If it does, then we know that we are dealing with a whole number, otherwise, we treat it as a floating-point number. For those that are unaware, in most cases, knowing this information does not matter too much in JavaScript (though there are certain optimizations that the V8 engine utilizes when it knows that it is dealing with whole numbers), but if we want to use this data format with other languages, then the difference matters.

Next, we allocated 4 bytes since we are only going to write out 32-bit signed integers. Signed means they will support both positive and negative numbers (again, we won't go into the big difference between the two, but for those that are curious, we actually limit the maximum value we can store in here if we utilize signed integers since we have to utilize one of the bits to tell us whether the number is negative or not). We then write out the final buffer, which consists of our type and then the number in buffer format.

Now, with the helper methods and the following constants in the `helper.js` file, proceed as follows:

```
export const CONSTANTS = {
    object : 0x04,
    number : 0x01,
    floating : 0x02,
    string : 0x03,
    header : 0x10,
    body : 0x11
}
```

We can create our `encoder.js` file:

1. Import the necessary dependencies and also create the shell of our `SimpleSchemaWriter` class:

   ```
   import { Transform } from 'stream';
   import { encodeString, encodeNumber } from './helper.js';

   export default class SimpleSchemaWriter extends Transform {
   }
   ```

2. Create the constructor and make sure that `objectMode` is always turned on:

   ```
   // inside our SimpleSchemaWriter class
   constructor(opts={}) {
       opts.writableObjectMode = true;
       super(opts);
   }
   ```

3. Add a private `#encode` helper function that will do the underlying data check and conversion for us:

```
// inside of our SimpleSchemaWriter class
#encode = function(data) {
    return typeof data === 'string' ?
            encodeString(data) :
            typeof data === 'number' ?
            encodeNumber(data) :
            null;
}
```

4. Write the main `_transform` function for our `Transform` stream. Details of this stream will be explained as follows:

```
_transform(chunk, encoding, callback) {
    const buf = [];
    buf.push(Buffer.from([0x10]));
    for(const key of Object.keys(chunk)) {
        const item = this.#encode(key);
        if(item === null) {
            return callback(new Error("Unable to parse!"))
        }
        buf.push(item);
    }
    buf.push(Buffer.from([0x10]));
    buf.push(Buffer.from([0x11]));
    for(const val of Object.values(chunk)) {
        const item = this.#encode(val);
        if(item === null) {
            return callback(new Error("Unable to parse!"))
        }
        buf.push(item);
    }
    buf.push(Buffer.from([0x11]));
    this.push(Buffer.concat(buf));
    callback();
}
```

Overall, the `transform` function should look familiar to previous `_transform` methods we have implemented, with some exceptions:

1. Our first portion of the encoding is wrapping our headers (the keys of the object). This means that we need to write out our delineator for headers, which is the `0x10` byte.

Chapter 8

2. We will run through all of the keys of our object. From here, we will utilize the `private` method, `encode`. This method will check the data type of the key and return the encoding utilizing one of the helper methods that we discussed previously. If it does not get a type that it understands, it will return `null`. We will then give back an `Error` since our data protocol does not understand the type.

3. Once we have run through all of the keys, we will write out the `0x10` byte again, stating that we are done with the headers, and write out the `0x11` byte to tell the decoder that we are starting with the body of our message. (We could have utilized the constants from the `helpers.js` file here and we probably should, but this should help with understanding the underlying protocol. The decoder will utilize these constants to showcase better programming practices.)

4. We will now run through the values of the object and run them through the same encoding system that we did with the headers, and also return an `Error` if we do not understand the data type.

5. Once we are finished with the body, we will push the `0x11` byte again to say that we are done with the body. This will be the signal to the decoder to stop converting this object and to send out the object it has been converting. We will then push all of this data to the `Readable` portion of our `Transform` stream and use the callback to say that we are ready to process more data.

There are some problems with the overall structure of our encoding scheme (we shouldn't be using singular bytes for our wrappers since they can easily be misconstrued by our encoder and decoder) and we should support more data types, but this should give a nice understanding as to how an encoder can be built for more generally used data formats.

Right now, we will not be able to test this, other than that it spits out the correct encoding, but once we have the decoder up and running, we will be able to test to see whether we get the same object on both sides. Let's now take a look at the decoder for this system.

Implementing the decoder

The decoder has quite a bit more state to it than the encoder and this is usually true of data formats. When dealing with raw bytes, trying to parse the information out of it is usually more difficult than writing the data out as that raw format.

Let's take a look at the helper methods that we will use to decode the data types we support:

```
import { CONSTANTS } from './helper.js';

export const decodeString = function(buf) {
    if(buf[0] !== CONSTANTS.string) {
        return false;
    }
    const len = buf.readUInt32BE(1);
    return buf.slice(5, 5 + len).toString('utf8');
}
export const decodeNumber = function(buf) {
    return buf.readInt32BE(1);
}
```

The decodeString method showcases how we could handle errors in the case of incorrectly formatted data, the decodeNumber method does not showcase this. For the decodeString method, we need to grab the length of the string from the buffer and we know this is the second byte of the buffer that would be passed in. Based on this, we know we can grab the string by starting at the fifth byte in the buffer (the first byte is the one that tells us that this is a string; the next four are the length of the string), and we grab everything until we get to the length of the string. We then run this buffer through the toString method.

decodeNumber is quite simple since we only have to read the 4 bytes after the first byte telling us it is a number (again, we should do a check here, but we are keeping it simple). This showcases the two main helper methods that we need to decode the data types that we support. Next, we will take a look at the actual decoder. It will look something like the following.

As stated previously, the decoding process is a bit more involved. This is for a number of reasons, as follows:

- We are working directly on the bytes so we have to do quite a bit of processing.
- We are dealing with a header and body section. If we created a non-schema-based system, we may be able to write a decoder without as much state as we have in this one.
- Again, since we are dealing with the buffers directly, all of the data may not come in at once, so we need to handle this case. The encoder does not have to worry about this since we are operating the Writable stream in object mode.

With this in mind, let's run through the decoding stream:

1. We will set up our decode stream with all of the same types of setup that we
   have done with `Transform` streams in the past. We will set up a few private
   variables to track the state as we move through the decoder:

```
import { Transform } from 'stream'
import { decodeString, decodeNumber, CONSTANTS } from './helper.js'

export default class SimpleSchemaReader extends Transform {
    #obj = {}
    #inHeaders = false
    #inBody = false
    #keys = []
    #currKey = 0
}
```

2. Next, we are going to utilize an index throughout the decoding process. We are
   not able to simply read a byte at a time since the decoding process runs through
   the buffer at different speeds (when we read a number, we are reading 5 bytes;
   when we read a string, we read at least 6 bytes). Because of this, a `while` loop
   will be better:

```
#decode = function(chunk, index, type='headers') {
    const item = chunk[index] === CONSTANTS.string ?
        decodeString(chunk.slice(index)) :
        decodeNumber(chunk.slice(index, index + 5));
    if( type === 'headers' ) {
        this.#obj[item] = null;
    } else {
        this.#obj[this.#keys[this.#currKey]] = item;
    }
    return chunk[index] === CONSTANTS.string ?
        index + item.length + 5 :
        index + 5;
}
constructor(opts={}) {
    opts.readableObjectMode = true;
    super(opts);
}
_transform(chunk, encoding, callback) {
    let index = 0; //1
    while(index <= chunk.byteLength ) {
    }
}
```

3. Now, we do a check on the current byte to see whether it is a header or body delineation mark. This will let us know whether we are working on the object keys or on the object values. If we detect the headers flag, we will set the #inHeaders Boolean stating that we are in the headers. If we are in the body, we have more work to do:

```
// in the while loop
const byte = chunk[index];
if( byte === CONSTANTS.header ) {
    this.#inHeaders = !this.#inHeaders
    index += 1;
    continue;
} else if( byte === CONSTANTS.body ) {
    this.#inBody = !this.#inBody
    if(!this.#inBody ) {
        this.push(this.#obj);
        this.#obj = {};
        this.#keys = [];
        this.#currKey = 0;
        return callback();
    } else {
        this.#keys = Object.keys(this.#obj);
    }
    index += 1;
    continue;
}
if( this.#inHeaders ) {
    index = this.#decode(chunk, index);
} else if( this.#inBody ) {
    index = this.#decode(chunk, index, 'body');
    this.#currKey += 1;
} else {
    callback(new Error("Unknown state!"));
}
```

4. Next, the paragraphs that follow will explain the process of getting the headers and the values of each JSON object.

First, we will change our body Boolean to the opposite of what it is currently at. Next, if we are going from inside the body to outside of the body, this means that we are done with this object. Because of this, we can push out the object that we are currently working on and reset all of our internal state variables (the temporary object, `#obj`; the temporary set of `#keys` that we get from the header; and the `#currKey` to know which key we are working on when we are in the body). Once we have this, we can run the callback (we are returning here so we don't run through more of our main body). If we do not do this, we will keep going through the loop and we will be in a bad state.

Otherwise, we have gone through the headers of our payload and have reached the values for each object. We will set our private `#keys` variable to the keys of the object (since, at this point, the headers should have grabbed all of the keys from the headers). We can now start to see the decoding process.

If we are in the headers, we will run our private `#decode` method and not utilize the third argument since the default is to run the method as if we are in headers. Otherwise, we will run it like we are in the body and pass a third argument to state that we are in the body. Also, if we are in the body, we will increment our `#currKey` variable.

Finally, we can take a look at the heart of the decoding process, the `#decode` method. We grab the item based on the first byte in the buffer, which will tell us which decoding helper method we should run. Then, if we are running this method in header mode, we will set a new key for our temporary object, and we will set its value to null since that will be filled in once we get to the body. If we are in body mode, we will set the value of the key corresponding to the `#currKey` index in our `#keys` array that we are looping through once we are in the body.

With that code explanation, the basic process that is happening can be summed up in a few basic steps:

1. We need to go through the headers and set the object's keys to these values. We are temporarily setting the values for each of these keys to null since they will be filled in later.
2. Once we move out of the header section and we go to the body section, we can grab all of the keys from the temporary object, and the decode run we do at that time should correspond to the key at the current key's index in the array.
3. Once we are out of the body, we reset all of the temporary variables for the state and send out the corresponding object since we are finished with the decoding process.

This may seem confusing, but all we are doing is lining up the header at some index with the body element at that same index. It would be similar to the following code if we wanted to put an array of keys and values together:

```
const keys = ['item1', 'item2', 'item3'];
const values = [1, 'what', 2.2];
const tempObj = {};
for(let i = 0; i < keys.length; i++) {
    tempObj[keys[i]] = null;
}
for(let i = 0; i < values.length; i++) {
    tempObj[keys[i]] = values[i];
}
```

This code is almost exactly the same as what we were doing with the preceding buffer, except we have to work with the raw bytes instead of higher-level items such as strings, arrays, and objects.

With both the decoder and the encoder finished, we can now run an object through our encoder and decoder to see whether we get the same value out. Let's run the following test harness code:

```
import encoder from './encoder.js'
import decoder from './decoder.js'
import json from './test.json'

const enc = new encoder();
const dec = new decoder();
enc.pipe(dec);
dec.on('data', (obj) => {
    console.log(obj);
});
enc.write(json);
```

We'll use the following test object:

```
{
    "item1" : "item",
    "item2" : 12,
    "item3" : 3.3
}
```

We will see that we will spit the same object out as we pipe the data through the encoder into the decoder. Now, it's great that we created our own encoding and decoding scheme, but how does it hold up to the transfer size compared to JSON (since we are trying to do better than just stringifying and parsing)? With this payload, we are actually increasing the size! If we think about it, this makes sense. We have to add in all of our special encoding items (all of the information other than the data such as the `0x10` and `0x11` bytes), but we now start to add more numerical items to our list that are quite large. We will see that we start to beat the basic `JSON.stringify` and `JSON.parse`:

```
{
    "item1" : "item",
    "item2" : 120000000,
    "item3" : 3.3,
    "item4" : 120000000,
    "item5" : 120000000,
    "item6" : 120000000
}
```

This is happening because stringified numbers are turned into just that, string versions of the numbers, so when we get numbers that are larger than 5 bytes, we are starting to save on bytes (1 byte for the data type and 4 bytes for the 32-bit number encoding). With strings, we will never see savings since we are always adding an extra 5 bytes of information (1 byte for the data type and 4 bytes for the length of the string).

In most encoding and decoding schemes, this is the case. The way they handle data has trade-offs depending on the type of data that is being passed. In our case, if we are sending large, highly numerical data over the wire, our scheme will probably work better, but if we are sending strings across, we are not going to benefit at all from this encoding and decoding scheme. Keep this thought in mind as we take a look at some data formats that are used quite heavily out in the wild.

 Remember, this encoding and decoding scheme is not meant to be used in actual environments as it is riddled with issues. However, it does showcase the underlying theme of building out data formats. While most of us will never have to build data formats, it is nice to understand what goes on when building them out, and where data formats may have to specialize their encoding and decoding schemes based on the type of data that they are primarily working with.

A look at data formats

Now that we have looked at our own data format, let's go ahead and take a look at some fairly popular data formats that are currently out there. This is not an exhaustive look at these, but more an introduction to data formats and what we may find out in the wild.

The first data format that we will look at is a schema-less format. As stated previously, schema-based formats either send ahead of time the schema for data, or they will send the schema with the data itself. This allows, usually, a more compact form of the data to come in, while also making sure both endpoints agree on the way the data will be received. The other form is schema-less, where we send the data in a new form, but all of the information to decode it is done through the specification.

JSON is one of these formats. When we send JSON, we have to encode it and then decode it once we are on the other side. Another schema-less data format is XML. Both of these should be quite familiar to web developers as we utilize JSON extensively and we use a form of XML when putting together our frontends (HTML).

Another popular format is MessagePack (https://msgpack.org/index.html). MessagePack is a format that is known for producing smaller payloads than JSON. What is also nice about MessagePack is the number of languages that have the library written natively for them. We will take a look at the Node.js version, but just note that this could be used on both the frontend (in the browser) and on the server. So let's begin:

1. We will npm install the what-the-pack extension by utilizing the following command:

   ```
   > npm install what-the-pack
   ```

2. Once we have done this, we can start to utilize this library. With the following code, we can see how easy it is to utilize this data format over the wire:

   ```
   import MessagePack from 'what-the-pack';
   import json from '../schema/test.json';

   const { encode, decode } = MessagePack.initialize(2**22);
   const encoded = encode(json);
   const decoded = decode(encoded);
   console.log(encoded.byteLength,
   Buffer.from(JSON.stringify(decoded)).byteLength);
   console.log(encoded, decoded);
   ```

What we see here is a slightly modified version of the example that is on the page for `what-the-pack` (`https://www.npmjs.com/package/what-the-pack`). We import the package and then we initialize the library. One way this library is different is that we need to initialize a buffer for the encoding and decoding process. This is what the `2**22` is doing in the `initialize` method. We are initializing a buffer that is 2 to the power of 22 bytes large. This way, it can easily slice the buffer and copy it without having expensive array-based operations. Another thing keen observers will note is that the library is not based on streaming. They have most likely done this to be compatible between the browser and Node.js. Other than these small issues, the overall library works just like we think it would.

The first console log shows us that the encoded buffer is 5 bytes less than the JSON version. While this does showcase that the library gives us a more compact form, it should be noted that there are cases where `MessagePack` may not be smaller than the corresponding JSON. It also may run slower than the built-in `JSON.stringify` and `JSON.parse` methods. Remember, everything is a trade-off.

There are plenty of schema-less data formats out there and each of them has their own tricks to try to make the encoding/decoding time faster and to make the over-the-wire data smaller. However, when we are dealing with enterprise systems, we will most likely see a schema-based data format being used.

There are a couple of ways to define a schema but, in our case, we will use the proto file format:

1. Let's go ahead and create a **proto** file to simulate the `test.json` file that we had. The schema could look something like the following:

```
package exampleProtobuf;
syntax = "proto3";

message TestData {
    string item1 = 1;
    int32  item2 = 2;
    float  item3 = 3;
}
```

What we are declaring here is that this message called `TestData` is going to live in a package called `exampleProtobuf`. The package is mainly there to group like items (this is heavily utilized in languages such as Java and C#). The syntax tells our encoder and decoder that the protocol we are going to use is `proto3`. There were other versions of the protocol and this one is the most up-to-date stable version.

We then declare a new message called `TestData` that has three entries. One will be called `item1` and will be of type `string`, one will be a whole number called `item2`, and the final one will be a floating-point number called `item3`. We are also giving them IDs as this makes it easier for things such as indexing and for self-reference types (also because it is mandatory for `protobuf` to work). We will not go into exactly what this does, but note that it can help with the encoding and decoding process.

2. Next, we can write some code that can use this to create a `TestData` object in our code that can specifically handle these messages. This would look like the following:

```
protobuf.load('test.proto', function(err, root) {
    if( err ) throw err;
    const TestTypeProto =
     root.lookupType("exampleProtobuf.TestData");
    if( TestTypeProto.verify(json) ) {
        throw Error("Invalid type!");
    }
    const message2 = TestTypeProto.create(json);
    const buf2 = TestTypeProto.encode(message2).finish();
    const final2 = TestTypeProto.decode(buf2);
    console.log(buf2.byteLength,
     Buffer.from(JSON.stringify(final2)).byteLength);
    console.log(buf2, final2);
});
```

Notice that this is similar to most of the code we have seen except for some verification and creation processes. First, the library needs to read in the proto file that we have and make sure it is actually correct. Next, we create the object based on the namespace and name we gave it. Now, we verify our payload and create a message from this. We then run it through the encoder specific to this data type. Finally, we decode the message and test to make sure that we got the same data that we put in.

Two things should be noticeable from this example. First, the data size is quite small! This is one advantage that schema-based/protobuf has over schema-less data formats. Since we know ahead of time what the types should be, we do not need to encode that information into the message itself. Second, we will see that the floating-point number did not come back out as 3.3. This is due to precision errors and it is something that we should be on the lookout for.

3. Now, if we do not want to read in proto files like this, we could build the message in the code like the following:

```
const TestType = new protobuf.Type("TestType");
TestType.add(new protobuf.Field("item1", 1, "string"));
TestType.add(new protobuf.Field("item2", 2, "int32"));
TestType.add(new protobuf.Field("item3", 3, "float"));
```

This should resemble the message that we created in the proto file, but we will go over each line to show that it is the same `protobuf` object. We are first creating a new type called `TestType` in this case (instead of `TestData`). Next, we add three fields, each with their own label, an index number, and the type of data that is stored in it. If we run this through the same type of verification, create, encode, decode process, we will get the same results as before.

While this has not been a comprehensive overview of different data formats, it should help to recognize when we might use schema-less (when we don't know what the data may look like) and when to use schemas (when communicating between unknown systems or we need a decrease in payload size).

Summary

While most of our starting applications will be done utilizing JSON to pass data between different servers, or even different parts of our applications, it should be noticeable where we may not want to use it. By utilizing other data formats, we can make sure that we get as much speed out of our application as possible.

We have seen what building our own data format could entail and then we took a look at other popular formats that are currently out there. This should be the last piece of information that we need to build highly performant server applications in Node.js. While we will use some libraries for data formats, we should also note that we have really only used the vanilla libraries that come with Node.js.

We will next take a look at a practical example of a static server that caches information. From here, we will utilize all of the previous concepts to create a highly available and speedy static server.

Practical Example - Building a Static Server

9

We have looked at Node.js and what it has to offer in the past few chapters. While we have not gone over every module or everything that Node.js has to offer, we have all the pieces to put together a static content/generator site. This means that we will set up a server to listen for requests and build pages off of that request.

To implement this server, we will need to understand how site generation works, and how we might implement this as an on-the-fly operation. On top of this, we will look at caching so that we do not have to recompile every single time a page is requested. Overall, in this chapter, we will look at and implement the following:

- Understanding static content
- Setting up our server
- Adding caching and clustering

Technical requirements

- A text editor or **integrated development environment** (IDE), preferably VS Code
- An operating system that supports Node.js
- The code for this chapter can be found at the following URL: `https://github.com/PacktPublishing/Hands-On-High-Performance-Web-Development-with-JavaScript/tree/master/Chapter09/microserve`.

Understanding static content

Static content means exactly that: content that does not change. This can be HTML pages, JavaScript, images, and so on. Anything that does not need to run through a database or some external system for processing can be considered as static content.

While we will not be implementing a static content server directly, we will be implementing an on-the-fly static content generator. For those that do not know, a static content generator is a system that builds the static content and then serves that content up. The content is usually built by some type of templating system.

Some common templating systems that are out there include Mustache, Handlebars.js, and Jade. These template engines look for some sort of tags and replace the content based on some variables. While we will not be looking at any of these templating engines directly, know that they are out there and that they can be quite useful for things such as code documentation generation, or even creating JavaScript files based off of some API specification.

Instead of using one of these common formats, we will implement our own version of a templating system to see how templating works. We will try to keep it as simple as possible since we want to use a minimal amount of dependencies for our server. The one dependency that we will be utilizing is a Markdown to HTML converter called `Remarkable`: `https://github.com/jonschlinkert/remarkable`. It depends on two libraries and each of those depends on one library, so we will be importing a total of five libraries.

While creating all of the pages on-the-fly will allow us to make changes quite easily, we would not want to keep doing this unless we were in a development environment. To make sure that we do not keep building the HTML files over and over again, we will implement an in-memory cache to store the files that have been requested the most.

With all of this, let's go ahead and get started with building out our application, by setting up our server and getting a response sent out.

Starting our application

First, let's go ahead and set up our project by creating our `package.json` file in a folder of our choosing. We can start with the following basic `package.json` file:

```
{
    "version" : "0.0.1",
    "name"    : "microserver",
```

```
    "type"    : "module"
}
```

This should be fairly straightforward now. The main thing is that the type is set to module so we can utilize modules inside of Node.js. Next, let's go ahead and add the Remarkable dependency by running npm install remarkable inside the folder in which we put our package.json file. With that, we should now have remarkable listed as a dependency in our package.json file. Next, let's go ahead and get our server set up. To do so, create a main.js file and do the following:

1. Import the http2 and fs modules, since we will use them to start our server and read our private key and certificate files, as follows:

   ```
   import http2 from 'http2'
   import fs from 'fs'
   ```

2. Create our server and read in our key and certificate files. We will generate these after setting up our main file, like this:

   ```
   const server = http2.createSecureServer({
       key: fs.readFileSync('selfsignedkey.pem'),
       cert: fs.readFileSync('selfsignedcertificate.pem')
   });
   ```

3. Respond to the error event by just crashing our server (we should probably handle this better, but for now, this will work). We will also handle an incoming request by just responding with a simple message and a status of 200 (which means all good), like this:

   ```
   server.on('error', (err) => {
       console.error(err);
       process.exit();
   });
   server.on('stream', (stream, headers) => {
       stream.respond({
           'content-type': 'text/html',
           ':status': 200
       });
       stream.end("A okay!");
   });
   ```

4. Finally, we will start listening in on port 50000 (a random port number can be used here).

Now, if we do try to run this, we should be greeted by a nasty error message similar to the following:

```
Error: ENOENT: no such file or directory, open 'selfsignedkey.pem'
```

We have not generated our self-signed private key and certificate yet. Remember from Chapter 6, *Message Passing – Learning about the Different Types*, that we cannot serve any content over an unsecured channel (HTTP); instead, we have to utilize HTTPS. To do this, we need to either get a certificate from a certificate authority or we need to generate one ourselves. From Chapter 6, *Message Passing – Learning about the Different Types*, we should have the openssl application installed on our computers.

5. Let's go ahead and generate that by running the following command and just pressing *Enter* through the Command Prompts:

```
> openssl req -newkey rsa:2048 -nodes -keyout selfsignedkey.pem -
x509 -days 365 -out selfsignedcertificate.pem
```

We should now have both of those files in our current directory, and now, if we try running our application, we should have a server listening on port 50000. We can check this by going to the following address: 127.0.0.1:50000. If everything worked correctly, we should see the message **A okay**!

While having variables such as the port, private key, and certificate hardcoded is okay for development purposes, we should still move these to our package.json file so another user could make the changes to them in a single place, instead of having to go into the code and make the changes. Let's go ahead and make these changes right now. Inside of our package.json file, let's add the following fields:

```
"config" : {
    "port" : 50000,
    "key"  : "selfsignedkey.pem",
    "certificate" : "selfsignedcertificate.pem",
    "template" : "template",
    "body_files" : "publish"
},
"scripts" : {
    "start": "node --experimental-modules main.js"
}
```

The `config` section will allow us to pass in various variables that we will let the user of the package set, either with the `package.json config` section, or when running our file by using the `npm config set tinyserve:<variable>` command. The `scripts` section, as we saw from Chapter 5, *Switching Contexts – No DOM, Different Vanilla*, allows us access to these variables and allows the user of our package to now just use `npm start`, instead of using `node --experimental-modules main.js`. With this, we can change our `main.js` file by declaring all of these variables near the top of our file, like so:

```
const ENV_VARS = process.env;
const port = ENV_VARS.npm_package_config_port || 80;
const key  = ENV_VARS.npm_package_config_key || 'key.pem';
const cert = ENV_VARS.npm_package_config_certificate || 'cert.pem';
const templateDirectory = ENV_VARS.npm_package_config_template ||
'template';
const publishedDirectory = ENV_VARS.npm_package_config_bodyFiles || 'body';
```

All of the configuration variables can be found on our `process.env` variable, so we declare a shortcut to it at the top of our file. We can then get access to the various variables, as we have seen in Chapter 5, *Switching Contexts – No DOM, Different Vanilla*. We also set defaults, just in case the user does not run our file using the `npm start` script that we declared. Users will also notice that we have declared a few extra variables. These are variables that we will talk about later, but they deal with where we hyperlink to and whether we want to enable the caching or not (the development variable). Next, we will take a look at how we will access the templating system that we want to set up.

Setting up our templating system

We are going to use Markdown for the various content we want to host, but there are going to be certain sections of our files that we will want to use across all of the articles. These will be things such as the header, footer, and the sidebar of our pages. Instead of having to have these inserted into all of the Markdown files that we will create for our articles, we can template these in.

We will put these sections in a folder that will be known at runtime, by using the `templateDirectory` variable that we declared. This will also allow users of our package to change out the look and feel of our static site server without having to do anything too crazy. Let's go ahead and create the directory structure for the template section. This should look like the following:

- **Template**: Where we should look for the static content across all pages
  - **HTML**: Where all of our static HTML code will go
  - **CSS**: Where our stylesheets will live

With this directory structure, we can now create some basic header, footer, and sidebar HTML files, and also some basic **Cascading Style Sheets** (**CSS**), to get a page structure that should be familiar to everyone. So, let's begin, as follows:

1. We will write the `header` HTML, like so:

```
<header>
    <h1>Our Website</h1>
    <nav>
        <a href="/all">All Articles</a>
        <a href="/contact">Contact Us</a>
        <a href="/about">About Us</a>
    </nav>
</header>
```

With this basic structure, we have the name of our website, and then a couple of links that most blog sites will have.

2. Next, let's create the `footer` section, like this:

```
<footer>
    <p>Created by: Me</p>
    <p>Contact: <a href="mailto:me@example.com">Me</a></p>
</footer>
```

3. Again, fairly self-explanatory. Finally, we will create the sidebar, as follows:

```
<nav>
    <% loop 5
    <a href="article/${location}">${name}</a>
    %>
</nav>
```

This is where our templating engine comes into play. First, we are going to use `<% %>` character pattern to denote that we want to replace this with some static content. Next, `loop <number>` will let our templating engine know that we plan on looping through the next piece of content a certain amount of times before stopping the engine. Finally, the `<a href="article/${location}">${name}</a>` pattern will tell our templating engine that this is the content we want to put in, but we will want to replace the `${ }` tags with variables in an object that we pass in our code.

Next, let's go ahead and create the basic CSS for our page, as follows:

```css
*, html {
    margin : 0;
    padding : 0;
}
:root {
    --main-color : "#003A21";
    --text-color : "#efefef";
}
/* header styles */
header {
    background : var(--main-color);
    color      : var(--text-color);
}
/* Footer styles */
footer {
    background : var(--main-color);
    color   : var(--text-color);
}
```

Most of the CSS file has been cut since a majority of it is boilerplate code. The only piece that is worth mentioning is the custom variables. With CSS, we can declare our own custom variables by using the pattern `--<name> : <content>`, and then we can use it later in the CSS file by using the `var()` declaration. This allows us to reuse variables such as colors and heights without having to use a preprocessor such as **Syntactically Awesome Style Sheets (SASS)**.

CSS variables are scoped. This means if you define the variable for the `header` section, it will only be available in the `header` section. This is why we decided to put our colors at the `:root` pseudo element level since it will be available across our entire page. Just remember that CSS variables have scope similar to the `let` and `const` variables we declare in JavaScript.

With our CSS laid out, we can now write our main HTML file in our `template` file. We will move this outside of the HTML folder since this is the main file that we will want in order to put everything together. It will also let users of our package know that this is the main file that we will use to put together all of the pieces and that if they want to change it up, they should do it here. For now, let's create a `main.html` file that looks like the following:

```
<!DOCTYPE html>
<html>
    <head>
        <link rel="stylesheet" type="text/css" href="css/main.css" />
    </head>
    <body>
        <% from html header %>
        <% from html sidebar %>
        <% from html footer %>
    </body>
</html>
```

The top section should look familiar, but we now have a new template type. The `from` directive lets us know that we are going to source this file from somewhere else. The next statement says it is an HTML file, so we will look inside the HTML folder. Finally, we see the name of the file, so we know that we want to bring in the `header.html` file.

With all of this, we can now write the templating system that we are going to use to build our pages. We will be implementing our templating system utilizing a `Transform` stream. While we could utilize something like a `Writable` stream, it makes more sense to utilize a `Transform` stream since we are changing the output based on some input criteria.

To implement the `Transform` stream, we will need to keep track of a few things so, that way, we can process our keys correctly. First, let's get us reading and sending off the proper chunks to be processed. We can do this by implementing the `transform` method and spitting out the chunks that we are going to replace. To do this, we will do the following:

1. We will extend a `Transform` stream and set up the basic structure, as we did in Chapter 7, *Streams – Understanding Streams and Non-Blocking I/O*. We will also create a custom class to hold the start and end locations of a buffer. This will allow us to know if we got the start of the pattern matcher in the same loop. We will need this later. We will also set up some private variables for our class, such as the `begin` and `end` template buffers, on top of state variables such as the `#pattern` variable, as follows:

   ```
   import { Transform } from 'stream'
   class Pair {
       start = -1
   ```

```
        end = -1
    }
export default class TemplateBuilder extends Transform {
    #pattern = []
    #pair = new Pair()
    #beforePattern = Buffer.from("<%")
    #afterPattern = Buffer.from("%>")
    constructor(opts={}) {
        super(opts);
    }
    _transform(chunk, encoding, cb) {
        // process data
    }
}
```

2. Next, we will have to check if we have data held in our #pattern state variable. If we do not, then we know to look for the beginning of a template. Once we do the check for the beginning of a template statement, we can check to see if it is actually in this chunk of data. If it is, we set the start property of #pair to this location so our loop can keep going; otherwise, we have no template in this chunk and we can start to process the next chunk, as shown here:

```
// inside the _transform function
if(!this.#pattern.length && !this.#pair.start) {
    location = chunk.indexOf(this.#beforePattern, location);
    if( location !== -1 ) {
        this.#pair.start = location;
        location += 2;
    } else {
        return cb();
    }
}
```

3. To handle the other condition (we are looking for the end of a template), we have quite a bit more state to deal with. First, if our #pair variable's start is not -1 (we set it), we know we are still processing a current chunk. This means we need to check if we can find the end template buffer in the current chunk. If we do, then we can process the pattern and reset our #pair variable. Otherwise, we just push the current chunk from the start member location of #pair to our #pattern holder at the end of the chunk, as follows:

```
if( this.#pair.start !== -1 ) {
    location = chunk.indexOf(this.#afterPattern, location);
    if( location !== -1 ) {
        this.#pair.end = location;
this.push(processPattern(chunk.slice(this.#pair.start,this.#pair.en
```

```
    d)));
            this.#pair = new Pair();
    } else {
            this.#pattern.push(chunk.slice(this.#pair.start));
    }
}
```

4. Finally, if `start` member of `#pair` is set, we check for the `end` template pattern. If we do not find it, we just push the entire chunk to the `#pattern` array. If we do find it, we slice the chunk from the beginning of it to where we found our `end` template string. We then concatenate all this together and process it. We will then also reset our `#pattern` variable back to holding nothing, like this:

```
location = chunk.indexOf(this.#afterPattern, location);
if( location !== -1 ) {
    this.#pattern.push(chunk.slice(0, location));
    this.push(processPattern(Buffer.concat(this.#pattern)));
    this.#pattern = [];
} else {
    this.#pattern.push(chunk);
}
```

5. All of this will be wrapped in a do/while loop since we want to run this piece of code at least once, and we will know that we are finished when our `location` variable is −1 (this is what is returned from an `indexOf` check when it does not find what we want). After the do/while loop, we run the callback to tell our stream that we are ready to process more data, as follows:

```
do {
    // transformation code
} while( location !== -1 );
cb();
```

With all of this put together, we now have a `transform` loop that should handle almost all of the conditions to grab our templating system. We can test this by passing in our `main.html` file and putting the following code inside of our `processPattern` method, like this:

```
console.log(pattern.toString('utf8'));
```

6. We can create a test script to run our `main.html` file through. Go ahead and create a `test.js` file and put the following code in it:

```
import TemplateStream from './template.js';
const file = fs.createReadStream('./template/main.html');
const tStream = new TemplateStream();
file.pipe(tStream);
```

With this, we should get a nice printout with the template syntax that we were looking for, such as `from html header`. If we ran our `sidebar.html` file through it, it should look something like the following:

```
loop 5
    <a href="article"/${location}">${name}</a>
```

Now that we know our `Transform` stream's template-finding code works, we just need to write our process chunk system to handle the preceding cases we have.

To now process the chunks, we will need to know where to look for the files. Remember from before, when we declared various variables inside of our `package.json` file? Now, we will utilize the `templateDirectory` one. Let's go ahead and pass that in as an argument for our stream, like so:

```
#template = null
constructor(opts={}) {
    if( opts.templateDirectory ) {
        this.#template = opts.templateDirectory;
    }
    super(opts);
}
```

Now, when we call `processPattern`, we can pass in the chunk and the `template` directory as arguments. From here, we can now implement the `processPattern` method. We will handle two cases: when we find a `for` loop and when we find a `find` statement.

To process a `for` loop and a `find` statement, we will proceed as follows:

1. We will build out an array of buffers that will be what the template held, other than the `for` loop. We can do this with the following code:

```
const _process = pattern.toString('utf8').trim();
const LOOP = "loop";
const FIND = "from";
const breakdown = _process.split(' ');
switch(breakdown[0]) {
    case LOOP:
```

```
                    const num = parseInt(breakdown[1]);
                    const bufs = new Array(num);
                    for(let i = 0; i < num; i++) {
                        bufs[i] = Buffer.from(breakdown.slice(2).join(''));
                    }
                    break;
            case FIND:
                    console.log('we have a find loop', breakdown);
                    break;
            default:
                    return new Error("No keyword found for processing! " +
                    breakdown[0]);
        }
```

2. We will look for the loop directive and then take the second argument, which should be a number. If we print this out, we will see that we have buffers that are all filled with the same exact data.

3. Next, we will need to make sure that we are filling in all of the templated string locations. These look like the pattern `${<name>}`. To do this, we will add another argument to this loop that will give the name of the variable we want to use. Let's go ahead and add this to the `sidebar.html` file, as follows:

```
<% loop 5 articles
    <a href="article/${location}">${name}</a>
%>
```

4. With this, we should now pass in a list of variables that we are going to want to use for our templating system—in this case, one named `articles` that is an array of objects that have a `location` and `name` key. This could look like the following:

```
const tStream = new TemplateStream({
    templateDirectory,
    templateVariables : {
        sidebar : [
            {
                location : temp1,
                name       : 'article 1'
            }
        ]
    }
}
```

With enough to satisfy our `for` loop condition, we can now head back to the `Transform` stream and add this as an item we will process in our constructor, and send it to our `processPattern` method. Once we have added these items here, we will update our loop case with the following code inside of the `for` loop:

```
const num = parseInt(breakdown[1]);
const bufs = new Array(num);
const varName = breakdown[2].trim();
for(let i = 0; i < num; i++) {
    let temp = breakdown.slice(3).join(' ');
    const replace = /\${([0-9a-zA-Z]+)}/
    let results = replace.exec(temp);
    while( results ) {
        if( vars[varName][i][results[1]] ) {
            temp = temp.replace(results[0], vars[varName][i][results[1]]);
        }
        results = replace.exec(temp);
    }
    bufs[i] = Buffer.from(temp);
}
return Buffer.concat(bufs);
```

Our temporary string holds all of the data that we consider a template, and the `varName` variable tells us where to look in our object that we pass into `processPattern` to do our replacement strategy. Next, we will use a regular expression to pull out the name of the variable. This specific regular expression says to look for the `${<name>}` pattern while also saying to capture whatever is in the `<name>` section. This allows us to easily get to the name of the variable. We will also keep looping through the template to see if there are more regular expressions that pass these criteria. Finally, we will replace that templated code with the variable we have stored.

Once all of this is done, we will concatenate all of these buffers together and return all of them. That is a lot for that piece of code; luckily, the `from` section of our template is quite a bit easier to handle. The `from` section of our templating code will just look for a file with that name from our `templateDirectory` variable and will return the buffer form of it.

It should look something like the following:

```
case FIND: {
    const type = breakdown[1];
    const HTML = 'html';
    const CSS  = 'css';
    if(!(type === HTML || type === CSS)) return new Error("This is not a
      valid template type! " + breakdown[1]);
    return fs.readFileSync(path.join(templateDirectory, type,
  `${breakdown[2]}.${type}`));
}
```

We first grab the type of file from the second argument. If it is not an HTML or CSS file, we will reject it. Otherwise, we will try reading the file in and sending it to our stream.

Some of you may be wondering how we will handle the templating in the other files. Right now, if we run our system on the main.html file, we will get all the separate chunks, but our sidebar.html file is not filled out. This is one weakness of our templating system. One way around this is to create another function that will call our Transform stream a certain amount of times. This will make sure we get the templating done for these separate pieces. Let's go ahead and create that function right now.

 This is not the only way to handle this. Instead, we could utilize another system: when we see template directives in a file, we add that buffer to the list of items needed for processing. This would allow our stream to process the directives instead of looping through the buffers again and again. This leads to its own problems since someone could write an infinitely recursing template and would cause our stream to break. Everything is a trade-off, and right now, we are going for ease of coding over ease of use.

First, we will need to import the once function from the events module and the PassThrough stream from the stream module. Let's update those dependencies now, like this:

```
import { Transform, PassThrough } from 'stream'
import { once } from 'events'
```

Next, we will create a new `Transform` stream that will bring in the same information as before, but now, we will also add in a loop counter. We will also respond to the `transform` event and push it onto a private variable until we have read in the entire starting template, as follows:

```
export class LoopingStream extends Transform {
    #numberOfRolls = 1
    #data = []
    #dir = null
    #vars = null
    constructor(opts={}) {
        super(opts);
        if( 'loopAmount' in opts ) {
            this.#numberOfRolls = opts.loopAmount
        }
        if( opts.vars ) {
            this.#vars = opts.vars;
        }
        if( opts.dir) {
            this.#dir = opts.dir;
        }
    }
    _transform(chunk, encoding, cb) {
        this.#data.push(chunk);
        cb();
    }
    _flush(cb) {
    }
}
```

Next, we will make our `flush` event `async` since we will utilize an async `for` loop, like so:

```
async _flush(cb) {
    let tData = Buffer.concat(this.#data);
    let tempBuf = [];
    for(let i = 0; i < this.#numberOfRolls; i++) {
        const passThrough = new PassThrough();
        const templateBuilder = new TemplateBuilder({ templateDirectory :
        this.#dir, templateVariables : this.#vars });
        passThrough.pipe(templateBuilder);
        templateBuilder.on('data', (data) => {
            tempBuf.push(data);
        });
        passThrough.end(tData);
        await once(templateBuilder, 'end');
        tData = Buffer.concat(tempBuf);
        tempBuf = [];
    }
```

```
        this.push(tData);
        cb();
    }
```

Essentially, we will put all of the initial template data together. Then, we will run this data through our `TemplateBuilder`, building a new template for it to run over. We utilize the `await once(templateBuilder, 'end')` system to let us treat this code synchronously. Once we have gone through the counter, we will spit out the data.

We can test this with our old test harness. Let's go ahead and set it up to utilize our new `Transform` stream, along with spitting the data out to a file, as follows:

```
const file = fs.createReadStream('./template/main.html');
const testOut = fs.createWriteStream('test.html');
const tStream = new LoopingStream({
    dir : templateDirectory,
    vars : { //removed for simplicity sake },
    loopAmount : 2
});
file.pipe(tStream).pipe(testOut);
```

If we now run this, we will notice that the `test.html` file holds our fully built-out `template` file! We now have a functioning template system we can use. Let's hook this up to our server.

Setting up our server

With our templating system working, let's go ahead and hook all of this up to our server. Instead of now responding with a simple message of **A okay!**, we will respond with our template all put together. We can do this easily by running the following code:

```
stream.respond({
        'content-type': 'text/html',
        ':status': 200
    });
    const file = fs.createReadStream('./template/main.html');
    const tStream = new LoopingStream({
        dir: templateDirectory,
        vars : { //removed for readability }
    },
        loopAmount : 2
    })
    file.pipe(tStream).pipe(stream);
});
```

This should look almost exactly like our test harness. If we now head to `https://localhost:50000`, we should see a very basic HTML page, but we have our templated file created! If we now head into the development tools and look at the sources, we will see something odd. The CSS states that we loaded in our `main.css` file, but the contents of the file look exactly like our HTML file!

Our server is responding to every request with our HTML file! What we need to do is some extra work so our server can respond to the requests correctly. We will do this by mapping the URL of the request to the files that we have. For simplicity's sake, we will only respond to HTML and CSS requests (we will not be sending any JavaScript across), but this system can easily be added upon to add in return types for images, and even files. We will add all of this by doing the following:

1. We will set up a lookup table for our file endings, like this:

```
const FILE_TYPES = new Map([
    ['.css', path.join('.', templateDirectory, 'css')],
    ['.html', path.join('.', templateDirectory, 'html')]
]);
```

2. Next, we will use this map to pull the files based off of `headers` of the request, like this:

```
const p = headers[':path'];
for(const [fileType, loc] of FILE_TYPES) {
    if( p.endsWith(fileType) ) {
        stream.respondWithFile(
            path.join(loc, path.posix.basename(p)),
            {
                'content-type': `text/${fileType.slice(1)}`,
                ':status': 200
            }
        );
        return;
    }
}
```

The basic idea is to loop through our supported file types to see if we have them. If we do, then we will respond with the file and also tell the browser whether it is an HTML or CSS file through the `content-type` header.

3. Now, we need a way to tell if a request is bad or not. Currently, we can go to any URL and we will just get the same response over and over again. We will utilize a `publishedDirectory` environment variable for this. Based on the name of the files in there, those will be our endpoints. For every sub-URL pattern, we will look for subdirectories that follow the same pattern. This is illustrated as follows:

```
https:localhost:50000/articles/1 maps to
<publishedDirectory>/articles/1.md
```

The `.md` extension means that it is a Markdown file. This is how we will write out pages.

4. For now, let's get this mapping working. To do this, we will put the following code below our `for` loop:

```
try {
    const f = fs.statSync(path.join('.', publishedDirectory, p));
    stream.respond({
        'content-type': 'text/html',
        ':status': 200
    });
    const file = fs.createReadStream('./template/main.html');
    const tStream = new LoopingStream({
        dir: templateDirectory,
        vars : { },
        loopAmount : 2
    })
    file.pipe(tStream).pipe(stream);
} catch(e) {
    stream.respond({
        'content-type': 'text/html',
        ':status' : 404
    });
    stream.end('File Not Found! Turn Back!');
    console.warn('following file requested and not found! ', p);
}
```

We wrap our method for finding the file (`fs.statSync`) inside of a `try/catch` block. With this, if we error out, this will usually mean that we did not find the file, and we will send a `404` message to the user. Otherwise, we will just send what we have been sending: our example `template`. If we now run our server, we will be greeted with the following message: **File Not Found! Turn Back!**. We have nothing in that directory!

Let's go ahead and create the directory, and add a file called `first.md`. If we add this directory and the file and rerun our server, we will still get the error message if we head to `https://localhost:50000/first`! We are getting this because we did not tack on the Markdown file extension when checking for the file! Let's go ahead and add this to the `fs.statSync` check, as follows:

```
const f = fs.statSync(path.join('.', publishedDirectory, `${p}.md`));
```

Now, when we rerun our server, we will see the normal template that we had before. If we add content to the `first.md` file, we will not get that file. We now need to add this addition to our templating system.

Remember at the start of the chapter we added the npm package `remarkable`? We will now add the Markdown renderer, `remarkable`, and a new keyword that our templating language will look for to render the Markdown, as follows:

1. Let's add `Remarkable` as an import to our `template.js` file, like this:

   ```
   import Remarkable from 'remarkable'
   ```

2. We will look for the following directive to include that Markdown file into `<% file <filename> %>` template, like this:

   ```
   const processPattern = function(pattern, templateDir, publishDir,
   vars=null) {
       const process = pattern.toString('utf8').trim();
       const LOOP = "loop";
       const FIND = "from";
       const FILE = "file";
       const breakdown = process.split(' ');
       switch(breakdown[0]) {
         // previous case statements removed for readability
           case FILE: {
               const file = breakdown[1];
               return fs.readFileSync(path.join(publishDir, file));
           }
           default:
               return new Error("Process directory not found! " +
               breakdown[0]);
       }
   }
   ```

3. We will now need to add the `publishDir` variable to our `Transform` stream's possible options in the constructor, as follows:

```
export default class TemplateBuilder extends Transform {
    #pattern = []
    #publish = null
    constructor(opts={}) {
        super(opts);
        if( opts.publishDirectory ) {
            this.#publish = opts.publishDirectory;
        }
    }
    _transform(chunk, encoding, cb) {
        let location = 0;
        do {
            if(!this.#pattern.length && this.#pair.start === -1 ) {
                // code from before
            } else {
                if( this.#pair.start !== -1 ) {
this.push(processPattern(chunk.slice(this.#pair.start,
this.#pair.end), this.#template, this.#publish, this.#vars)); //add
publish to our processPattern function
                }
            }
        } while( location !== -1 );
    }
}
```

Remember: Quite a bit of code has been removed from these examples to make them easier to read. For the full examples, head on over to the book's code repository.

4. Create a `LoopingStream` class that will loop and run the `TemplateBuilder`:

```
export class LoopingStream extends Transform {
    #publish = null
    constructor(opts={}) {
        super(opts);
        if( opts.publish ) {
            this.#publish = opts.publish;
        }
    }
    async _flush(cb) {
        for(let i = 0; i < this.#numberOfRolls; i++) {
            const passThrough = new PassThrough();
            const templateBuilder = new TemplateBuilder({
```

```
                    templateDirectory : this.#dir,
                    templateVariables : this.#vars,
                    publishDirectory  :this.#publish
                });
            }
            cb();
        }
    }
```

5. We will need to update our template with the following templated line:

```
<!DOCTYPE html>
<html>
    <head>
        <link rel="stylesheet"  type="text/css" href="css/main.css"
/>
    </head>
    <body>
        <% from html header %>
        <% from html sidebar %>
        <% file first.md %>
        <% from html footer %>
    </body>
</html>
```

6. Finally, we need to pass in the `publish` directory to our stream from the server. We can do this with the following code addition:

```
const tStream = new LoopingStream({
        dir: templateDirectory,
        publish: publishedDirectory,
        vars : {
}});
```

With all of this, we should get something back from the server that is not just our base template. If we added some Markdown to the file, we should just see that Markdown with our template. We now need to make sure that this Markdown gets processed. Let's head back to our transformation method and call the `Remarkable` method so that it processes the Markdown and gives us back HTML, as shown in the following code block:

```
const MarkdownRenderer = new Remarkable.Remarkable();
const processPattern = function(...) {
    switch(breakdown[0]) {
        case FILE: {
            const file = breakdown[1];
            const html =
MarkdownRenderer.render(fs.readfileSync(path.join(publishDir, file)
```

```
).toString('utf8'));
            return Buffer.from(html);
        }
    }
}
```

With this change, we now have a generic Markdown parser that enables us to take our template files and send them back with our `main.html` file. The final change we will need to make in order to have a functioning templating system and static server is to make sure that instead of the `main.html` file having the exact template, it has the directive state that we want in order to put a file there and have our templating system put the file that is declared in our stream constructor. We can do this easily with the following changes:

1. In our `template.js` file, we will utilize a unique variable called `fileToProcess`. We get this the same way we get the variables that we want to process for the `sidebar.html` file, through the `vars` that we pass through. We will utilize the file we have in the second part of the `template` directive if we do not have the file from the `fileToProcess` variable, as shown in the following code block:

    ```
    case FILE: {
        const file = breakdown[1];
        const html =
        MarkdownRenderer.render(fs.readFileSync(path.join(publishDir,
        vars.fileToProcess || file)).toString('utf8'));
        return Buffer.from(html);
    }
    ```

2. We will need to pass this variable from our server to the stream, like this:

    ```
    const p = headers[':path'];
    const tStream = new LoopingStream({
        dir: templateDirectory,
        publish: publishedDirectory,
        vars : {
            articles : [ ],
            fileToProcess : `${p}.md`
        },
        loopAmount : 2
    });
    ```

3. The final change we will make is to change the `html` file, to have a new base Markdown file for pages that we do not have. This could allow us to have a base page for the root URL. We will not be implementing this, but this is a way for us to do that:

```
<body>
    <% from html header %>
    <% from html sidebar %>
    <% file base.md %>
    <% from html footer %>
</body>
```

With this change, if we now run our server, we have a fully functioning templating system with Markdown support! This is an amazing achievement! However, we will need to add two features to our server so that it will be able to handle more requests and process the same requests quickly. These features are caching and clustering.

Adding caching and clustering

First, we will start by adding a cache to our server. We do not want to constantly recompile pages that we have already compiled before. To do this, we will implement a class that surrounds a map. This class will keep track of 10 files at a time. We will also implement the timestamp when the file was last used. When we reach the eleventh file, we will see that it is not in the cache and that we have hit the maximum number of files we can hold in the cache. We will replace the compiled page with the earliest timestamped file.

This is known as a **Least Recently Used (LRU)** cache. There are many other types of caching strategies out there, such as a **Time To Live (TTL)** cache. This type of cache will eliminate files that have been in the cache for too long. This is a great type of cache for when we keep using the same files over and over again, but we eventually want to free up space when the server has not been hit for a while. An LRU cache will always keep these files in place, even if the server has not been hit for hours. We could always implement both caching strategies, but we will just implement the LRU cache for now.

First, we will create a new file called `cache.js`. Inside of here, we will do the following:

1. Create a new class. We don't need to extend any other class since we are just writing a wrapper around the `Map` data structure built into JavaScript, as shown in the following code block:

```
export default class LRUCache {
    #cache = new Map()
}
```

2. We will then have a constructor that will take in the number of files that we want to store in the cache before we use our strategy to replace one of the files, like this:

```
#numEntries = 10
constructor(num=10) {
    this.#numEntries = num
}
```

3. Next, we will add the `add` operation to our cache. It will take in the buffer form of our page and the URL that we hit to get it. The key will be the URL, and the value will be the buffer form of our page, as shown in the following code block:

```
add(file, url) {
    const val = {
        page : file,
        time : Date.now()
    }
    if( this.#cache.size === this.#numEntries ) {
        // do something
        return;
    }
    this.#cache.set(url, val);
}
```

4. Then, we will implement the `get` operation, whereby we try to grab a file based on the URL. If we do not have it, we will return `null`. If we do retrieve a file, we will update the time, since this would be considered the latest page grab. This is illustrated as follows:

```
get(url) {
    const val = this.#cache.get(url);
    if( val ) {
        val.time = Date.now();
        this.#cache.set(url, val);
        return val.page;
    }
    return null;
}
```

5. Now, we can update our `add` method's `if` statement. If we are at the limit, we will iterate through our map and see what the shortest time is. We will remove that file and replace it with the newly created one, like this:

```
if( this.#cache.size === this.#numEntries ) {
    let top = Number.MAX_VALUE;
    let earliest = null;
```

```
    for(const [key, val] of this.#cache) {
        if( val.time < top ) {
            top = val.time;
            earliest = key;
        }
    }
    this.#cache.delete(earliest);
}
```

We now have a basic LRU cache in place for our files. To attach this to our server, we will need to put it in the middle of our pipeline:

1. Let's head back into the main file and import this file:

```
import cache from './cache.js'
const serverCache = new cache();
```

2. We will now change a bit of the logic in our stream handler. If we notice the URL is something that we have in the cache, we will just grab the data and pipe it into our response. Otherwise, we will compile the template, set it in our cache, and stream the compiled version down, like this:

```
const cacheHit = serverCache.get(p);
if( cacheHit ) {
    stream.end(cacheHit);
} else {
    const file = fs.createReadStream('./template/main.html');
    const tStream = new LoopingStream({
        dir: templateDirectory,
        publish: publishedDirectory,
        vars : { /* shortened for readability */ },
        loopAmount : 2
    });
    file.pipe(tStream);
    tStream.once('data', (data) => {
        serverCache.add(data, p);
        stream.end(data);
    });
}
```

If we try to run the preceding code, we will now see that we grab files from the cache if we hit the same page twice; and if we hit them for the first time, it will compile through our template stream and then set it in the cache.

3. To make sure that our replace strategy works, let's go ahead and set the size of the cache to only 1, and see if we constantly replace the file if we hit a new URL, as follows:

```
const serverCache = new cache(1);
```

If we now log our cache when each method is hit, we will now see that we are replacing the file when we hit a new page, but if we stay on the same page, we are just sending the cached file back.

Now that we have added caching, let's add one more piece to our server so, that way, we can handle a lot of connections. We will be adding in the cluster module, just as we did in Chapter 6, *Message Passing – Learning about the Different Types*. We'll proceed as follows:

1. Let's import the cluster module in the main.js file:

```
import cluster from 'cluster'
```

2. We will now have the initialization of the server in our main process. For our other processes, we will process the requests.

3. Now, let's change our strategy to handle the incoming requests inside of our child processes, like this:

```
if( cluster.isMaster ) {
    const numCpus = os.cpus().length;
    for(let i = 0; i < numCpus; i++) {
        cluster.fork();
    }
    cluster.on('exit', (worker, code, signal) => {
        console.log(`worker ${worker.process.pid} died`);
    });
} else {
    const serverCache = new cache();
    // all previous server logic
}
```

With this single change, we are now handling the requests between four different processes. Just as we learned in Chapter 6, *Message Passing – Learning about the Different Types*, we can share a single port for our cluster module.

Summary

While there is one piece left to add (hooking our sidebar up to point to real files), this should be a great general-purpose templating server. All that needs to be done is modifying our FILE template and hooking it into the sidebar of our templating system. With everything we have learned about Node.js, we should be able to handle almost any type of server-side application. We should also be able to understand how implementations of web servers such as Express are created from these basic building blocks.

From here, we will head back into the browser and take some of the concepts we learned from this part of the book and apply them to the web over the next couple of chapters. We will start by looking at worker threads in the browser, known as dedicated workers. We will then take a look at shared workers, and how we can benefit from being able to offload work to these workers, but still be able to grab the data from them. Finally, we will take a look at service workers, and see how they can help us with various optimizations, such as caching in the browser.

10
Workers - Learning about Dedicated and Shared Workers

In the past few chapters, we have focused on Node.js and how we can write backend applications utilizing the same language as the frontend. We have seen various ways of creating servers, offloading tasks, and streaming. In this part, we will focus on the offloading tasks aspect of the browser.

Eventually, as we have seen in Node.js, we need to offload some computationally intensive tasks from the main thread to a separate thread, or process, to make sure that our application stays responsive. While the effects of having a server not respond can be quite jarring, the effects of our user interface not working are downright off-putting to most users. Therefore, we have the Worker API.

In this chapter, we will specifically look at two kinds of workers, dedicated and shared. Overall, we will do the following:

- Learn to offload heavy processing to a worker thread via the Worker API.
- Learn how to talk with workers via the `postMessage` and `BroadcastChannel` APIs.
- Talk about `ArrayBuffer` and the `Transferrable` property so we can quickly move data between workers and the main thread.
- Look at `SharedWorker` and the Atomics API to see how we can share data between multiple tabs of our application.
- Take a look at a partial implementation of a shared cache utilizing the knowledge from the previous sections.

Technical requirements

The following items are needed to complete this chapter:

- A text editor or IDE, preferably VS Code
- Access to Chrome or Firefox
- Some knowledge of parallelization in computing
- The code found at https://github.com/PacktPublishing/Hands-On-High-Performance-Web-Development-with-JavaScript/tree/master/Chapter10.

Offloading work to a dedicated worker

Workers give us the ability to offload long-running, computationally-intensive tasks to the background. Instead of having to make sure our event loop is not filled with some type of heavy task, we can offload that task to a background thread.

In other languages/environments, this might look like the following (this is only pseudo-code and is not really tied to any language):

```
Thread::runAsync((data) -> {
    for(d : data) { //do some computation }
});
```

While this works well in those environments, we have to start thinking about topics such as deadlock, zombie threads, read after write, and so on. All of these can be quite hard to comprehend and are usually some of the most difficult bugs that can be encountered. Instead of JavaScript giving us the capability of utilizing something like the preceding, they gave us workers, which give us another context to work in where we don't face the same issues.

 For those that are interested, a book on operating systems or Unix programming can help shed light on the preceding issues. These topics are out of the scope of this book, but they are quite interesting and there are even languages that are trying to address these issues by building the workarounds into the languages. Some examples of these are Go (https://golang.org/), which uses a technique of message passing, and Rust (https://www.rust-lang.org/), which utilizes the concept of borrow checking and such to minimize these issues.

To start off with an example of work being done in the background, we are going to spawn a `Worker` and have it compute a sum over 1 million numbers. To do this:

1. We add the following `script` section to our HTML file:

```
<script type="text/javascript">
    const worker = new Worker('worker.js');
    console.log('this is on the main thread');
</script>
```

2. We create a JavaScript file for our `Worker` and add the following:

```
let num = 0;
for(let i = 0; i < 1000000; i++) {
    num += i;
}
```

If we launch Chrome, we should see two messages printed – one that says it was run on the main thread and another with the value **499999500000**. We should also see that one was logged by the HTML file and the other was logged by the worker. We have just spawned a worker and got it to do some work for us!

Remember that if we want to run JavaScript files from our filesystem and not a server, we will need to close out of all instances of Chrome and then relaunch it from the command line using `chrome.exe --allow-file-access-from-files`. This will give us access to launch our external JavaScript files from the filesystem and not need a server.

Let's go ahead and do something a little more complex that the user may want to do. One interesting math problem is getting the prime factorization for a number. This means that, when given a number, we will try to find all of the prime numbers (numbers that are only divisible by one and itself) that make up that number. An example would be the prime factorization of 12, which is 2, 2, and 3.

This problem leads to the interesting field of cryptography and how public/private keys work. The basic understanding is that, given two relatively large prime numbers, multiplying them is easy, but finding those two numbers from that product of them is infeasible due to time constraints.

Back to the task at hand, what we will do is spawn a `worker` after the user inputs a number into an input box. We will compute that number and log it to the console. So let's begin:

1. We add an input to our HTML file and change the code to spawn a `worker` on the change event for that input box:

```html
<input id="in" type="number" />
<script type="text/javascript">
document.querySelector("#in").addEventListener('change', (ev) => {
    const worker = new Worker('worker.js', {name :
     ev.target.value});
});
</script>
```

2. Next, we will grab our name in the `worker` and use that as the input. From there, we will run the prime factorization algorithm found at https://www.geeksforgeeks.org/print-all-prime-factors-of-a-given-number/, but transposed to JavaScript. Once we are done, we will turn off the `worker`:

```javascript
let numForPrimes = parseInt(self.name);
const primes = [];
console.log('we are looking for the prime factorization of: ',
numForPrimes);
while( numForPrimes % 2 === 0 ) {
    primes.push(2);
    numForPrimes /= 2;
}
for(let i = 3; i <= Math.sqrt(numForPrimes); i+=2) {
    while( numForPrimes % i === 0 ) {
        primes.push(i);
        numForPrimes /= i;
    }
}
if( numForPrimes > 2 ) {
    primes.push(numForPrimes);
}
console.log('prime factorization is: ', primes.join(" "));
self.close();
```

If we now run this application in the browser, we will see that after each input we get the console log message in the console. Notice that there is no factor for the number 1. There is a mathematical reason for this, but just note that there is no prime factorization for the number 1.

We can run this for a bunch of inputs, but if we put in a relatively large number such as `123,456,789`, it will still compute it in the background as we do things on the main thread. Now, we are currently passing data to the worker through the name of the worker. There has to be a way to pass data between the worker and the main thread. This is where the `postMessage` and `BroadcastChannel` APIs come into play!

Moving data in our application

As we have seen in the `worker_thread` module inside of Node.js, there is a way to communicate with our workers. This is through the `postMessage` system. If we take a look at the method signature, we will see that it requires a message that can be any JavaScript object, even those with cyclical references. We also see another parameter called transfer. We will go into depth on that in a bit but, as the name suggests, it allows us to actually transfer the data instead of copying the data to the worker. This is a much faster mechanism for transferring data, but there are some caveats when utilizing it that we will discuss later.

Let's take the example that we have been building on and respond to messages sent from the frontend:

1. We will swap out creating a new `worker` each time a change event occurs and just create one right away. Then, on a change event, we will send the data to the `worker` via the `postMessage`:

```
const dedicated_worker = new Worker('worker.js', {name : 'heavy
lifter'});
document.querySelector("#in").addEventListener('change', (ev) => {
    dedicated_worker.postMessage(parseInt(ev.target.value));
});
```

2. If we now tried this example, we would not receive anything from the main thread. We have to respond to the `onmessage` event that comes on the worker's global descriptor called `self`. Let's go ahead and add our handler to that and also remove the `self.close()` method since we want to keep this around:

```
function calculatePrimes(val) {
    let numForPrimes = val;
    const primes = [];
    while( numForPrimes % 2 === 0 ) {
        primes.push(2);
        numForPrimes /= 2;
    }
    for(let i = 3; i <= Math.sqrt(numForPrimes); i+=2) {
        while( numForPrimes % i === 0 ) {
```

```
                    primes.push(i);
                    numForPrimes /= i;
            }
        }
        if( numForPrimes > 2 ) {
            primes.push(numForPrimes);
        }
        return primes;
    }
    self.onmessage = function(ev) {
        console.log('our primes are: ', calculatePrimes(ev.data).join('
'));
    }
```

As we can see from this example, we have moved the calculation of the primes to a separate function and when we get a message, we grab the data and pass it to the `calculatePrimes` method. Now, we are working with the messaging system. Let's go ahead and add another feature to our example. Instead of printing to the console, let's give the user some feedback based on what they input:

1. We will add a paragraph tag below the input that will hold our answer:

```
<p>The primes for the number is: <span id="answer"></span></p>
<script type="text/javascript">
    const answer = document.querySelector('#answer');
    // previous code here
</script>
```

2. Now, we will add to the `onmessage` handler of `worker`, just like we did inside of the `worker`, to listen for events from the `worker`. When we get some data, we will populate the answer with the values returned:

```
dedicated_worker.onmessage = function(ev) {
    answer.innerText = ev.data;
}
```

3. Finally, we will change our `worker` code to send the data utilizing the `postMessage` method to send the primes back to the main thread:

```
self.onmessage = function(ev) {
    postMessage(calculatePrimes(ev.data).join(' '));
}
```

This also showcases that we do not need to add the `self` piece to call methods that are on the global scope. Just like the window is the global scope for the main thread, `self` is the global scope for the worker threads.

With this example, we have explored the `postMessage` method and seen how we can send data between a worker to the thread that spawned it, but what if we had multiple tabs that we wanted to communicate with? What if we had multiple workers that we wanted to send messages to?

One way of dealing with this is to just keep track of all of the workers and loop through them, sending the data out like the following:

```
const workers = [];
for(let i = 0; i < 5; i++) {
    const worker = new Worker('test.js', {name : `worker${i}`});
    workers.push(worker);
}
document.querySelector("#in").addEventListener('change', (ev) => {
    for(let i = 0; i < workers.length; i++) {
        workers[i].postMessage(ev.target.value);
    }
});
```

In the `test.js` file, we just console log the message and say which worker we are referencing by name. This can easily get out of hand since we would need to keep track of which workers are still alive and which ones have been removed. Another way of handling this would be to broadcast the data out on a channel. Luckily, we have an API for that, called the `BroadcastChannel` API.

As the document on the MDN site states (`https://developer.mozilla.org/en-US/docs/Web/API/Broadcast_Channel_API`), all we need to do is create a `BroadcastChannel` object by passing a single argument into its constructor, the name of the channel. Whoever calls it first creates the channel and then anyone can listen in on it. Sending and receiving data is as simple as our `postMessage` and `onmessage` examples have been. The following takes our previous code for our test interface and, instead of needing to keep track of all the workers, just broadcasts the data out:

```
const channel = new BroadcastChannel('workers');
document.querySelector("#in").addEventListener('change', (ev) => {
    channel.postMessage(ev.target.value);
});
```

Then, in our `workers`, all we need to do is listen in on `BroadcastChannel` instead of listening in on our own message handler:

```
const channel = new BroadcastChannel('workers');
channel.onmessage = function(ev) {
    console.log(ev.data, 'was received by', name);
}
```

We have now simplified the process of sending and receiving a message between multiple workers and even multiple tabs that have the same host. What makes this system great is that we can have some workers based on some criteria listen in on one channel and others listen in on another. We could then have a global channel to send commands that any of them could respond to. Let's go ahead and make a simple adjustment to our primes program. Instead of sending the data to a single dedicated worker, we will have four workers; two of them will handle even numbers and the other two will handle odd numbers:

1. We update our main code to launch four workers. We will name them based on whether the number is even or not:

    ```
    for(let i = 0; i < 4; i++) {
        const worker = new Worker('worker.js',
            {name : `worker ${i % 2 === 0 ? 'even' : 'odd'}`}
        );
    }
    ```

2. We change what happens upon an input, sending the even numbers to the even channel and the odd numbers to the odd channel:

    ```
    document.querySelector("#in").addEventListener('change', (ev) => {
        const value = parseInt(ev.target.value);
        if( value % 2 === 0 ) {
            even_channel.postMessage(value);
        } else {
            odd_channel.postMessage(value);
        }
    });
    ```

3. We create three channels: one for the even numbers, one for the odd numbers, and one for a global send to all workers:

    ```
    const even_channel = new BroadcastChannel('even');
    const odd_channel = new BroadcastChannel('odd');
    const global = new BroadcastChannel('global');
    ```

4. We add a new button to kill all of the workers and hook it up to broadcast on the global channel:

    ```
    <button id="quit">Stop Workers</button>
    <script type="text/javascript">
    document.querySelector('#quit').addEventListener('click', (ev) => {
        global.postMessage('quit');
    });
    </script>
    ```

5. We change our worker to handle messages based on its name:

```
const mainChannelName = name.includes("odd") ? "odd" : "even";
const mainChannel = new BroadcastChannel(mainChannelName);
```

6. When we do get a message on one of these channels, we respond just like we have been:

```
mainChannel.onmessage = function(ev) {
    if( typeof ev.data === 'number' )
        this.postMessage(calculatePrimes(ev.data));
}
```

7. If we receive a message on the global channel, we check to see whether it is the quit message. If it is, then kill the worker:

```
const globalChannel = new BroadcastChannel('global');
globalChannel.onmessage = function(ev) {
    if( ev.data === 'quit' ) {
        close();
    }
}
```

8. Now, back on the main thread, we will listen in on the even and odd channels for data. When there is data, we handle it almost exactly like before:

```
even_channel.onmessage = function(ev) {
    if( typeof ev.data === 'object' ) {
        answer.innerText = ev.data.join(' ');
    }
}
odd_channel.onmessage= function(ev) {
    if( typeof ev.data === 'object' ) {
        answer.innerText = ev.data.join(' ');
    }
}
```

One thing to note is how our workers and the main thread handle data coming in on the odd and even channels. Since we are broadcasting, we need to make sure it is the data that we want. In the case of the workers, we only want numbers and, in the case of our main thread, we only want to see arrays.

 The BroadcastChannel API only works with the same origin. This means that we cannot communicate between two different sites, only with pages under the domain.

While this is an overly complex example of the `BroadcastChannel` mechanism, it should showcase how we can easily decouple workers from their parents and make them easy to send data to without looping through them. Now, we will return to the `postMessage` method and look at that `transferrable` property and what it means for sending and receiving data.

Sending binary data in the browser

While message passing is a great way to send data, there are some problems when it comes to sending very large objects across the channel. For instance, let's say we have a dedicated worker that makes requests on our behalf and also adds some data to the worker from a cache. It could potentially have thousands of records. While the worker would already be taking up quite a bit of memory, as soon as we utilize `postMessage` we will see two things:

- The amount of time it takes to move the object is going to be long
- Our memory is going to increase dramatically

The reason for this is the structured clone algorithm that browsers use to send the data. Essentially, instead of just moving the data across the channel, it is going to serialize and deserialize our object, essentially creating multiple copies of it. On top of this, we have no idea when the garbage collector is going to run as we know it is non-deterministic.

We can actually see the copying process in the browser. If we create a worker called `largeObject.js` and move a giant payload, we can measure the time it takes by utilizing the `Date.now()` method. On top of this, we can utilize the record system in the developer's tools, as we learned in Chapter 1, *Tools for High Performance on the Web*, to profile the amount of memory that we use. Let's set this test case up:

1. Create a new worker and assign it a large object. In this case, we are going to use a 100,000-element array that is storing objects inside of it:

```
const dataToSend = new Array(100000);
const baseObj = {prop1 : 1, prop2 : 'one'};
for(let i = 0; i < dataToSend.length; i++) {
    dataToSend[i] = Object.assign({}, baseObj);
    dataToSend[i].prop1 = i;
    dataToSend[i].prop2 = `Data for ${i}`;
}
console.log('send at', Date.now());
postMessage(dataToSend);
```

2. We now add to our HTML file some code to launch this worker and listen for the message. We will mark when the message arrives and then we will profile the code to see the increase in memory:

```
const largeWorker = new Worker('largeObject.js');
largeWorker.onmessage = function(ev) {
    console.log('the time is', Date.now());
    const obj = ev.data;
}
```

If we now load this up into our browser and profile our code, we should see results similar to the following. The message took anywhere between 800 ms to 1.7 s, and the heap size was anywhere between 80 MB and 100 MB. While this case is definitely out of the bounds of most people, it showcases some issues with this type of message passing.

A solution to this is to use the transferrable portion of the `postMessage` method. This allows us to *send* a binary data type across the channel and, instead of copying it, the channel actually just transfers the object. This means that the sender no longer has access to it, but the receiver does. A way to think about this is that the sender puts the data in a holding location and tells the receiver where it is at. At this point, the sender can no longer access it. The receiver receives all of the data and notices that it has a location to look for data. It goes to this location and grabs it, thereby fulfilling the data transfer mechanism.

Let's go ahead and code a simple example. Let's take our heavy worker and populate it with a bunch of data, in this case, a list of numbers from 1 to 1,000,000:

1. We create an `Int32Array` with 1,000,000 elements. We then add all of the numbers 1 through 1,000,000 in it:

```
const viewOfData = new Int32Array(1000000);
for(let i = 1; i <= viewOfData.length; i++) {
    viewOfData[i-1] = i;
}
```

2. We will then send that data by utilizing the transferrable portion of `postMessage`. Note that we have to get the underlying `ArrayBuffer`. We will discuss this shortly:

```
postMessage(viewOfData, [viewOfData.buffer]);
```

3. We will receive the data on the main thread and write out the length of that data:

```
const obj = ev.data;
console.log('data length', obj.byteLength);
```

We will notice that the time it took to transfer this large chunk of data was almost unnoticeable. This is because of the preceding theory where it just boxes the data and puts it to the side for the received.

An aside is needed for typed arrays and `ArrayBuffers`. The `ArrayBuffers` can be thought of as buffers in Node.js. They are the lowest form of storing data and directly hold the bytes of some data. But, to truly utilize them, we need to put a *view* on the `ArrayBuffer`. This means that we need to give meaning to that `ArrayBuffer`. In our case, we are saying that it stores signed 32-bit integers. We can put all sorts of views over `ArrayBuffer`, just like how we can interpret buffers in Node.js in different ways. The best way to think about this is that `ArrayBuffer` is the low-level system that we really don't want to utilize and that the views are the system that gives meaning to the underlying data.

With this in mind, if we check out the byte length of the `Int32Array` on the worker side, we will see that it is zero. We no longer have access to that data, just as we said. To further utilize this feature before heading on to `SharedWorkers` and `SharedArrayBuffers`, we will modify our factorization program to utilize this transferrable property to send the factors across:

1. We will utilize almost the exact same logic, except instead of sending over the array that we have, we will send over `Int32Array`:

```
if( typeof ev.data === 'number' ) {
    const result = calculatePrimes(ev.data);
    const send = new Int32Array(result);
    this.postMessage(result, [result.buffer]);
}
```

2. Now we will update our receiving end code to handle `ArrayBuffers` being sent instead of just an array:

```
if( typeof ev.data === 'object' ) {
    const data = new Int32Array(ev.data);
    answer.innerText = data.join(' ');
}
```

If we test this code out, we will see that it works just the same, but we are no longer copying the data across, we are just giving it to the main thread, thereby making the message passing faster and making it utilize less memory.

The main idea is that, if we are just sending results or we need to be as quick as possible, we should try to utilize the transferrable system for sending data. If we have to use the data in the worker after sending it, or there is not a simple way to send the data (we have no serialization technique), we can utilize the normal `postMessage` system.

 Just because we can use the transferrable system to reduce memory footprint, it could cause times to increase based on the amount of data transformation we need to apply. If we already have binary data, this is great, but if we have JSON data that needs to be moved, it may be better to just transfer it in that form instead of having to go through many intermediary transformations.

With all of these ideas, let's take a look at the `SharedWorker` system and `SharedArrayBuffer` system. Both of these systems, especially the `SharedArrayBuffer`, have led to some issues in the past (we will discuss this in the following section), but if we utilize them carefully we will be able to leverage their capability of being a good message-passing and data-sharing mechanism.

Sharing data and workers

While most of the time we want to keep the boundaries up between our workers and tabs of our applications, there will be times when we want to just share the data or even the worker among every instance. When this is the case, we can utilize two systems, `SharedWorker` and `SharedArrayBuffer`.

`SharedWorker` is just what it sounds like, when one spins up, just like `BroadcastChannel`, and someone else makes the same call to create a `SharedWorker`, it will just connect to the already created instance. Let's go ahead and do just this:

1. We will create a new file for the `SharedWorker` JavaScript code. Inside of here, put some general computing functions such as adding and subtracting:

```
const add = function(a, b) {
    return a + b;
}
const mult = function(a, b) {
    return a * b;
}
const divide = function(a, b) {
    return a / b;
}
const remainder = function(a, b) {
```

```
        return a % b;
    }
```

2. Inside of one of our current workers' code, start up `SharedWorker`:

```
const shared = new SharedWorker('shared.js');
shared.port.onmessage = function(ev) {
    console.log('message', ev);
}
```

We will already see a problem. Our system states that `SharedWorker` is not found. To utilize `SharedWorker`, we have to start it in a window. So now, we will have to move that start code to our main page.

3. Move the start code into the main page and then pass the port to one of the workers:

```
const shared = new SharedWorker('shared.js');
shared.port.start();
for(let i = 0; i < 4; i++) {
    const worker = new Worker('worker.js',
        {name : `worker ${i % 2 === 0 ? 'even' : 'odd'}`}
    );
    worker.postMessage(shared.port, [shared.port]);
}
```

We now run into another problem. Since we wanted to pass the port to the worker and not have access to it in the main window, we utilized the transferrable system. However, since we only had a single reference at that time, once we send it to one worker, we can't send it again. Instead, let's start one worker and turn our `BroadcastChannel` system off.

4. Comment out our `BroadcastChannel`s and all of our looping code. Let's only start a single worker up in this window:

```
const shared = new SharedWorker('shared.js');
shared.port.start();
const worker = new Worker('worker.js');
document.querySelector("#in").addEventListener('change', (ev) => {
    const value = parseInt(ev.target.value);
    worker.postMessage(value);
});
document.querySelector('#quit').addEventListener('click', (ev) => {
    worker.postMesasge('quit');
});
```

5. With these changes, we will have to simplify our dedicated worker. We will just respond to events on our message channel like before:

```
let sharedPort = null;
onmessage = function(ev) {
    const data = ev.data;
    if( typeof data === 'string' ) {
        return close();
    }
    if( typeof data === 'number' ) {
        const result = calculatePrimes(data);
        const send = new Int32Array(result);
        return postMessage(send, [send.buffer]);
    }
    // handle the port
    sharedPort = data;
}
```

6. Now we have the `SharedWorker` port in a single worker, but what did all of this solve for us? Now, we can have multiple tabs open at the same time and get the data to every single one of them. To see this, let's hook a handler up to `sharedPort`:

```
sharedPort.onmessage = function(ev) {
    console.log('data', ev.data);
}
```

7. Finally, we can update our `SharedWorker` to respond once a connection happens, like the following:

```
onconnect = function(e) {
    let port = e.ports[0];
    console.log('port', port);
    port.onmessage = function(e) {
        port.postMessage('you sent data');
    }
    port.postMessage('you connected');
}
```

With this, we will see a message come back to our workers. We now have our `SharedWorker` up and running and communicating directly with our `DedicatedWorker`! However, there is still one problem: why did we not see the log from our `SharedWorker`? Well, our `SharedWorker` lives in a different context than our `DedicatedWorker` and our main thread. To get access to our `SharedWorker`, we can go to the URL `chrome://inspect/#workers` and then locate it. Right now, we did not call it anything so it should be called `untitled`, but when we click the `inspect` option underneath it, we now have a debug context for the worker.

We have connected our `SharedWorker` to the DOM context, and we have connected every `DedicatedWorker` to that `SharedWorker`, but we need to be able to send messages to each `DedicatedWorker`. Let's go ahead and add this code:

1. First, we will need to keep track of all of the workers that connected to us through the `SharedWorker`. Add the following code to the bottom of our `onconnect` listener:

   ```
   ports.push(port);
   ```

2. Now, we will add some HTML to our document so we can send the `add`, `multiply`, `divide`, and `subtract` requests along with two new number inputs:

   ```
   <input id="in1" type="number" />
   <input id="in2" type="number" />
   <button id="add">Add</button>
   <button id="subtract">Subtract</button>
   <button id="multiply">Multiply</button>
   <button id="divide">Divide</button>
   ```

3. Next, we will pass this information through the `DedicatedWorker` to the `SharedWorker`:

   ```
   if( typeof data === 'string' ) {
       if( data === 'quit' ) {
           close();
       } else {
           sharedPort.postMessage(data);
       }
   }
   ```

4. Finally, our `SharedWorker` will run the corresponding operation and pass it back to the `DedicatedWorker`, which will log the data to the console:

```
port.onmessage = function(e) {
    const _d = e.data.split(' ');
    const in1 = parseInt(_d[1]);
    const in2 = parseInt(_d[2]);
    switch(_d[0]) {
        case 'add': {
            port.postMessage(add(in1, in2));
            break;
        }
        // other operations removed since they are the same thing
    }
}
```

With all of this, we can now have multiple tabs of our application open that are all sharing the same preceding math system! This is overkill for this type of application, but it could be useful when we need to perform complex operations in our application that span multiple windows or tabs. This could be something that utilizes the GPU and we only want to do this once. Let's go ahead and wrap this section up with an overview of `SharedArrayBuffer`. However, one thing to remember is that a `SharedWorker` is a single thread held by all tabs, whereas a `DedicatedWorker` is a thread per tab/window. While sharing a worker can be beneficial for some tasks explained previously, it can also slow down other tasks if multiple tabs are utilizing it at the same time.

`SharedArrayBuffer` allows all of our instances to share the same block of memory. Just as a transferrable object can have different owners based on passing the memory to another worker, a `SharedArrayBuffer` allows different contexts to share the same piece. This allows for updates to propagate across all of our instances and has almost instant updates for some types of data, but it also has many pitfalls associated with it.

This is as close as we will most likely get to `SharedMemory` in other languages. To properly utilize `SharedArrayBuffer`, we will need to utilize the Atomics API. Again, not diving directly into the detail behind the Atomics API, it makes sure that operations happen in the correct sequence and that they are guaranteed to update what they need to without anyone overriding them during their update.

Again, we are starting to get into details where it can be hard to fully understand what is happening. One good way to think of the Atomics API is a system where many people are sharing a piece of paper. They all take turns writing on it and reading what others wrote down.

However, one of the downfalls is that they are only allowed to write a single character at a time. Because of this, someone else may write something in their location while they are still trying to finish writing their word, or someone may read their incomplete phrase. We need a mechanism for people to be able to write the entire word that they want, or read the entire section, before someone starts writing. This is the job of the Atomics API.

SharedArrayBuffer does suffer from issues related to browsers not supporting it (currently, only Chrome supports it without a flag), to issues where we might want to use the Atomics API (SharedWorker cannot send it to the main thread or the dedicated workers due to security issues).

To set up a basic example of SharedArrayBuffer in action, we will share a buffer between the main thread and a worker. When we send a request to the worker, we will update the number that is inside that worker by one. Updating this number should be visible to the main thread since they are sharing the buffer:

1. Create a simple worker and using the onmessage handler check whether it received a number or not. If it is, we will increment the data in the SharedArrayBuffer. Otherwise, the data is the SharedArrayBuffer coming from the main thread:

```
let sharedPort = null;
let buf = null;
onmessage = function(ev) {
    const data = ev.data;
    if( typeof data === 'number' ) {
        Atomics.add(buf, 0, 1);
    } else {
        buf = new Int32Array(ev.data);
    }
}
```

2. Next, on our main thread, we are going to add a new button that says `Increment`. When this is clicked, it will send a message to the dedicated worker to increment the current number:

```
// HTML
<button id="increment">Increment</button>
<p id="num"></p>

// JavaScript
document.querySelector('#increment').addEventListener('click', ()
=> {
    worker.postMessage(1);
});
```

3. Now, when the worker updates the buffer on its side, we will constantly be checking `SharedArrayBuffer` if there is an update. We will always just put the number inside of the number paragraph element that we showed in the previous code snippet:

```
setInterval(() => {
    document.querySelector('#num').innerText = shared;
}, 100);
```

4. Finally, to kick all of this off, we will create a `SharedArrayBuffer` on the main thread and send it to the worker once we have launched it:

```
let shared = new SharedArrayBuffer(4);
const worker = new Worker('worker_to_shared.js');
worker.postMessage(shared);
shared = new Int32Array(shared);
```

With this, we can see that our value is now incrementing even though we are not sending any data from the worker to the main thread! This is the power of shared memory. Now, as stated previously, we are quite limited with the Atomics API since we cannot use the `wait` and `notify` systems on the main thread and we cannot use `SharedArrayBuffer` inside of a `SharedWorker`, but it can be useful for systems that are only reading data.

In these cases, we may update the `SharedArrayBuffer` and then send a message to the main thread that we updated it, or it may already be a Web API that takes `SharedArrayBuffers` such as the WebGL rendering context. While the preceding example is not very useful, it does showcase how we might be able to use the shared system in the future if the ability to spawn and use `SharedArrayBuffer` in a `SharedWorker` is available again. Next, we will focus on building a singular cache that all the workers can share.

Building a simple shared cache

With everything that we have learned, we are going to focus on a use case that is quite prevalent in reporting systems and most types of operation GUIs—a large chunk of data that needs to have other data added to it (some call this decorating the data and others call this attribution). An example of this is that we have the buy and sell orders for a list of customers.

This data may come back in the following manner:

```
{
    customerId : "<guid>",
    buy : 1000000,
    sell : 1000000
}
```

With this data, we may want to add some context that the customer ID is associated with. We could go about this in two ways:

- First, we could have a join operation done in the database that adds the required information for the user.
- Second, and the one we will be illustrating here, is adding this data on the frontend when we get the base-level query. This means when our application starts, we would fetch all of this attribution data and store it in some background cache. Next, when we make a request, we will also make a request to the cache for the corresponding data.

For us to achieve the second option, we will implement two of the technologies that we learned previously, the `SharedWorker` and the `postMessage` interface:

1. We create a base-level HTML file that has a template for each row of data. We will not go into a deep dive of creating a web component as we did in Chapter 3, *Vanilla Land – Looking at the Modern Web*, but we will use it to create our table rows on demand:

```html
<body>
    <template id="row">
        <tr>
            <td class="name"></td>
            <td class="zip"></td>
            <td class="phone"></td>
            <td class="email"></td>
            <td class="buy"></td>
            <td class="sell"></td>
        </tr>
```

```
        </template>
        <table id="buysellorders">
        <thead>
            <tr>
                <th>Customer Name</th>
                <th>Zipcode</th>
                <th>Phone Number</th>
                <th>Email</th>
                <th>Buy Order Amount</th>
                <th>Sell Order Amount</th>
            </tr>
        </thead>
        <tbody>
        </tbody>
        </table>
    </body>
```

2. We set up some pointers to our template and table so we can do quick inserts. On top of this, we can create a placeholder for the `SharedWorker` that we are about to create:

```
const tableBody = document.querySelector('#buysellorders > tbody');
const rowTemplate = document.querySelector('#row');
const worker = new SharedWorker('<fill in>', {name : 'cache'});
```

3. With this basic setup, we can create our `SharedWorker` and give it some base-level data. To do this, we are going to use the website `https://www.mockaroo.com/`. This will allow us to create a bunch of random data without having to think of it ourselves. We can change the data to whatever we want but, in our case, we will go with the following options:

- `id`: Row number
- `full_name`: Full name
- `email`: Email address
- `phone`: Phone
- `zipcode`: Digit sequence: ######

4. With these options filled in, we can change the format to JSON and save by clicking **Download Data**. With this done, we can build out our `SharedWorker`. Similar to our other `SharedWorker`, we will take the `onconnect` handler and add an `onmessage` handler for the port that comes in:

```
onconnect = function(e) {
    let port = e.ports[0];
```

```
        port.onmessage = function(e) {
            // do something
        }
    }
```

5. Next, we launch our `SharedWorker` back in our HTML file:

```
const worker = new SharedWorker('cache_shared.js', 'cache');
```

6. Now, when our `SharedWorker` is launched, we will load the file by utilizing `importScripts`. This allows us to load in outside JavaScript files, just like we would do in HTML, with the `script` tag. To do this, we will need to modify the JSON file to point the object to a variable and rename it to a JavaScript file:

```
let cache = [{"id":1,"full_name":"Binky
Bibey","email":"bbibey0@furl.net","phone":"370-576-9587","zipcode":
"640069"}, //rest of the data];

// SharedWorker.js
importScripts('./mock_customer_data.js');
```

7. Now that we have brought the cache of data in, we will respond to messages sent from the ports. We will expect only arrays of numbers. These will correspond to the ID that is associated with a user. For now, we will loop through all of the items in our dictionary to see whether we have them. If we do, we will add them to an array that we will respond with:

```
const handleReq = function(arr) {
    const res = new Array(arr.length)
    for(let i = 0; i < arr.length; i++) {
        const num = arr[i];
        for(let j = 0; j < cache.length; j++) {
            if( num === cache[j].id ) {
                res[i] = cache[j];
                break;
            }
        }
    }
    return res;
}
onconnect = function(e) {
    let port = e.ports[0];
    port.onmessage = function(e) {
        const request = e.data;
        if( Array.isArray(request) ) {
            const response = handleReq(request);
            port.postMessage(response);
```

```
            }
        }
    }
```

8. With this, we will need to add the corresponding code inside of our HTML file. We will add a button that is going to send 100 random IDs to our `SharedWorker`. This will simulate when we make a request and get back the IDs associated with the data. The simulation function looks like this:

```
// developer.mozilla.org/en-US/docs/Web/JavaScript/Reference/
// Global_Objects/Math/random

const getRandomIntInclusive = function(min, max) {
    return Math.floor(Math.random() * (max - min + 1)) + min;
}
const simulateRequest = function() {
    const MAX_BUY_SELL = 1000000;
    const MIN_BUY_SELL = -1000000;
    const ids = [];
    const createdIds = [];
    for(let i = 0; i < 100; i++) {
        const id = getRandomIntInclusive(1, 1000);
        if(!createdIds.includes(id)) {
            const obj = {
                id,
                buy : getRandomIntInclusive(MIN_BUY_SELL,
                 MAX_BUY_SELL),
                sell : getRandomIntInclusive(MIN_BUY_SELL,
                 MAX_BUY_SELL)
            };
            ids.push(obj);
        }
    }
    return ids;
}
```

9. With the preceding simulation, we can now add in our input for a request and then send that to our `SharedWorker`:

```
requestButton.addEventListener('click', (ev) => {
    const res = simulateRequest();
    worker.port.postMessage(res);
});
```

10. Now, we are currently posting the wrong data to our `SharedWorker`. We only want to post the IDs, but how are we going to tie our request to the responses from our `SharedWorker`? We will need to slightly modify the structure that we have for our `request` and `response` methods. We will now tie an ID to our message so we can have the `SharedWorker` post that back to us. This way, we can have a map on the frontend of requests and the IDs associated with them. Make the following changes:

```
// HTML file
const requestMap = new Map();
let reqCounter = 0;
requestButton.addEventListener('click', (ev) => {
    const res = simulateRequest();
    const reqId = reqCounter;
    reqCounter += 1;
    worker.port.postMessage({
        id : reqId,
        data : res
    });
});

// Shared worker
port.onmessage = function(e) {
    const request = e.data;
    if( request.id &&
        Array.isArray(request.data) ) {
        const response = handleReq(request.data);
        port.postMessage({
            id : request.id,
            data : response
        });
    }
}
```

11. With these changes, we still need to make sure we only pass the IDs to the `SharedWorker`. We can pull these off from the request before we send it:

```
requestButton.addEventListener('click', (ev) => {
    const res = simulateRequest();
    const reqId = reqCounter;
    reqCounter += 1;
    requestMap.set(reqId, res);
    const attribute = [];
    for(let i = 0; i < res.length; i++) {
        attribute.push(res[i].id);
    }
    worker.port.postMessage({
```

```
        id : reqId,
        data : attribute
    });
});
```

12. Now we need to handle the data coming back to us inside of our HTML file. First, we attach an `onmessage` handler to the port:

```
worker.port.onmessage = function(ev) {
    console.log('data', ev.data);
}
```

13. Finally, we grab the associated buy/sell order from our map and populate it with the returned cache data. Once we have done this, we just have to clone our row template and fill in the corresponding fields:

```
worker.port.onmessage = function(ev) {
    const data = ev.data;
    const baseData = requestMap.get(data.id);
    requestMap.delete(data.id);
    const attribution = data.data;
    tableBody.innerHTML = '';
    for(let i = 0; i < baseData.length; i++) {
        const _d = baseData[i];
        for(let j = 0; j < attribution.length; j++) {
            if( _d.id === attribution[j].id ) {
                const final = {..._d, ...attribution[j]};
                const newRow = rowTemplate.content.cloneNode(true);
                newRow.querySelector('.name').innerText =
                  final.full_name;
                newRow.querySelector('.zip').innerText =
                  final.zipcode;
                newRow.querySelector('.phone').innerText =
                  final.phone;
                newRow.querySelector('.email').innerText =
                  final.email;
                newRow.querySelector('.buy').innerText =
                  final.buy;
                newRow.querySelector('.sell').innerText =
                  final.sell;
                tableBody.appendChild(newRow);
            }
        }
    }
}
```

With the preceding example, we have created a shared cache that any page that has the same domain can use. While there are certain optimizations (we could store the data as a map and have the ID as the key), we are still going to run a bit faster than having to potentially wait on a database connection (especially when we are in places that have limited bandwidth).

Summary

This entire chapter has been focused on offloading tasks from the main thread to other threads of work. We have looked at dedicated workers that only a single page has. We have then taken a look at how we can broadcast messages between multiple workers without having to loop through the respective ports.

Then we saw how we can share a worker on the same domain utilizing `SharedWorker` and also looked at how we can share a data source utilizing `SharedArrayBuffer`. Finally, we took a practical look at creating a shared cache that anyone has access to.

In the next chapter, we will take this concept of caching and handling requests one step further by utilizing `ServiceWorker`.

11
Service Workers - Caching and Making Things Faster

So far, we have looked at dedicated and shared workers, which help throw computationally expensive tasks into the background. We have even created a shared cache that utilizes `SharedWorker`. Now, we will take a look at service workers and learn how they can be used to cache both resources (such as HTML, CSS, JavaScript, and so on) and data for us so that we don't have to make expensive round trips to our server.

In this chapter, we will cover the following topics:

- Understanding the ServiceWorker
- Caching pages and templates for offline use
- Saving requests for later

By the end of this chapter, we will be able to create offline experiences for our web applications.

Technical requirements

For this chapter, you will need the following:

- An editor or IDE, preferably VS Code
- Chrome
- An environment that can run Node.js
- This chapter's code, which can be found at `https://github.com/ PacktPublishing/Hands-On-High-Performance-Web-Development-with- JavaScript/tree/master/Chapter11`.

Understanding the ServiceWorker

A `ServiceWorker` is a proxy that sits between our web applications and the server. It catches requests that are made and checks if there is a pattern that matches it. If a pattern matches it, then it will run the code that fits that pattern. Writing code for a `ServiceWorker` is a bit different than it is for `SharedWorker` and `DedicatedWorker`, which we looked at previously. Initially, we set it up in some code and it downloads itself. We have various events that tell us the stage that the worker is in. These run in the following order:

1. **Download**: The `ServiceWorker` is downloading itself for the domain or subdomain.
2. **Install**: The `ServiceWorker` is attaching itself to the domain or subdomain where it is hosted.
3. **Activate**: The `ServiceWorker` is fully attached and is loaded up to intercept requests.

The install event is especially important. This is where we can listen for a `ServiceWorker` that is updated. Say that we want to push new code out for our `ServiceWorker`. If a user is still on a page when we decide to push that code out to the server, they will still have the old worker. There are ways to kill off this old worker and force them to update (as we will see in a bit), but it will still utilize the old cache.

On top of this, if we are utilizing a cache to store the resources that are being requested, they will be stored in the old cache. If we were to update these resources, then we want to make sure that we dump the previous cache and start with a new one. We will look at an example of this later, but it is good to know this upfront.

Finally, service workers will update themselves every 24 hours, so if we don't force the user to update the `ServiceWorker`, they will get this new copy on that 24-hour mark. These are all ideas to keep in mind as we go through the examples in this chapter. We will remind you of these when we write them out.

Let's start off with a very basic example. Follow these steps:

1. First, we need a static server so that we can work with service workers. To do this, run `npm install serve` and add the following code to the `app.js` file:

```
const handler = require('serve-handler');
const http = require('http');
const server = http.createServer((req, res) => {
    return handler(req, res, {
        public : 'source'
```

```
        });
    });
    server.listen(3000, () => {
        console.log('listening at 3000');
    });
```

2. Now, we can serve all of our content from the `source` directory. Create a basic HTML page and have it load in a `ServiceWorker` called `BaseServiceWorker.js`:

```
<!DOCTYPE html>
<html>
    <head>
        <!-- get some resources -->
    </head>
    <body>
        <script type="text/javascript">
navigator.serviceWorker.register('./BaseServiceWorker.js',
            { scope : '/'})
            .then((reg) => {
                console.log('successfully registered worker');
            }).catch((err) => {
                console.error('there seems to be an issue!');
            })
        </script>
    </body>
</html>
```

3. Create a basic `ServiceWorker` that will log to our console whenever a request is made:

```
self.addEventListener('install', (event) => {
    console.log('we are installed!');
});
self.addEventListener('fetch', (event) => {
    console.log('a request was made!');
    fetch(event.request);
});
```

We should see two messages appear in our console. One should be static, stating that we have installed everything correctly, while the other will state that we have successfully registered a worker! Now, let's add a CSS file to our HTML and service it.

4. Call our new CSS file `main.css` and add the following CSS to it:

```
*, :root {
    margin : 0;
    padding : 0;
    font-size : 12px;
}
```

5. Add this CSS file to the top of our HTML page.

With this, reload the page and see what it states in the console. Notice how it doesn't state that we have successfully made a request. If we keep hitting the reload button, we may see the message appear before the page reloads. If we want to see this message, we can head to the following link inside of Chrome and inspect the `ServiceWorker` that's there: `chrome://serviceworker-internals`.

 We may see other service workers being loaded in. Quite a few sites do this and it is a technique for caching certain pieces of a web page. We will look at this in more detail soon. This is why the first load can be quite a pain for some applications and why they seem to load up a lot faster afterward.

The top of the page should show an option for starting the dev tools when we start the `ServiceWorker`. Go ahead and check this option. Then, stop/start the worker. Now, a console should open that allows us to debug our `ServiceWorker`:

While this is great for debugging, if we take a look at the page where we initiate this behavior, we will see a little window that states something similar to the following:

```
Console: {"lineNumber":2,"message":"we are
installed!","message_level":1,"sourceIdentifier":3,"sourceURL":"http://loca
lhost:3000/BaseServiceWorker.js"}
```

It is getting the CSS file every single time we reload the page! If we reload it a few more times, we should have more of these messages. This is interesting, but we can definitely do a bit better than this. Let's go ahead and cache our main.css file. Add the following to our BaseServiceWorker.js file:

```
self.addEventListener('install', (event) => {
    event.waitUntil(
        caches.open('v1').then((cache) => {
            return cache.addAll([
                './main.css'
            ]);
        }).then(() => {
            console.log('we are ready!');
        })
    );
});
self.addEventListener('fetch', (event) => {
    event.respondWith(
        caches.match(event.request).then((response) => {
            return response || fetch(event.request);
        })
    )
});
```

With this, we have introduced a cache. This cache will fetch various resources for us. Along with this cache, we have introduced the waitUntil method of the event. This allows us to hold up the initialization of the ServiceWorker until we are done fetching all of the data we want from the server. Inside of our fetch handler, we are now checking to see if we have the resource in our cache. If we do, we will serve that file up; otherwise, we will just make the fetch request on the page's behalf.

Now, if we load the page, we will notice that we just have the we are ready message. Even though we have new code, the page was cached by Chrome, so it hasn't let go of our old service worker. To force the new service worker to be added, we can go into our developer console and head to the **Application** tab. Then, we can go to the left panel and head over to the ServiceWorker section. There should be a timeline stating that there is a ServiceWorker waiting to be activated. If we click the text next to it that says **skipWaiting**, we can activate the new code.

Go ahead and click on this option. It won't look like anything has happened, but if we head back to the `chrome://serviceworker-internals` page, we will see that there is a single message. If we keep reloading the page, we will see that we just have the one message. This means that we have loaded in our new code!

Another way to check that we have successfully cached our `main.css` file is to throttle the download speed of our application (especially since we are hosting it locally). Head back to the developer tools and click the **Network** tab. There should be a dropdown of network speeds near the **Disable cache** option. Currently, it should state that we are online. Go ahead and turn this to offline:

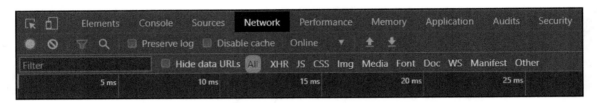

Well, we just lost our page! Inside of `BaseServiceWorker.js`, we should add the following:

```
caches.open('v1').then((cache) => {
    return cache.addAll([
        './main.css',
        '/'
    ]);
})
```

Now, we can turn our application online again and have this new `ServiceWorker` add itself to the page. Once it's been added, go ahead and turn our application offline. Now, the page works offline! We will explore this idea in more detail later, but this gives us a nice preview of this capability.

With this simple look at the `ServiceWorker` and caching mechanism, let's turn our attention to caching pages and adding some templating capabilities inside of our `ServiceWorker`.

Caching pages and templates for offline use

As we stated at the beginning of this chapter, one of the main uses for service workers is to cache page resources for future use. We saw this with our first simple `ServiceWorker`, but we should set up a more complicated page with more resources. Follow these steps:

1. Create a brand new `ServiceWorker` called `CacheServiceWorker.js` and add the following template code to it. This is what most of the `ServiceWorker` instances will use:

```
self.addEventListener('install', (event) => {
    event.waitUntil(
        caches.open('v1').then((cache) => {
            return cache.addAll([
                // add resources here
            ]);
        }).then(() => {
            console.log('we are ready!');
        })
    );
});
self.addEventListener('fetch', (event) => {
    event.respondWith(
        caches.match(event.request).then((response) => {
            return response || fetch(event.request);
        })
    )
});
```

2. Update our `index.html` file in order to utilize this new `ServiceWorker`:

```
navigator.serviceWorker.register('./CacheServiceWorker.js', { scope
: '/'})
    .then((reg) => {
        console.log('successfully registered worker');
    }).catch((err) => {
        console.error('there seems to be an issue!', err);
    })
```

3. Now, let's add some buttons and tables to our page. We will utilize these shortly:

```
<button id="addRow">Add</button>
<button id="remove">Remove</button>
<table>
    <thead>
        <tr>
            <th>Id</th>
```

```
            <th>Name</th>
            <th>Description</th>
            <th>Points</th>
        </tr>
    </thead>
    <tbody id="tablebody">
    </tbody>
</table>
```

4. Add a JavaScript file that will handle all of our interaction with the `interactions.js` page:

```
const add = document.querySelector('#addRow');
const remove = document.querySelector('#remove');
const tableBody = document.querySelector('#tablebody');
add.addEventListener('click', (ev) => {
    fetch('/add').then((res) => res.json()).then((fin) =>
    tableBody.appendChild(fin));
});
remove.addEventListener('click', (ev) => {
    while(tableBody.firstChild) {
        tableBody.removeChild(tableBody.firstChild);
    }
});
```

5. Add the JavaScript file to our `ServiceWorker` as a preload:

```
caches.open('v1').then((cache) => {
    return cache.addAll([
        '/',
        './interactions.js',
        './main.css'
    ]);
}).then(() => {
    console.log('we are ready!');
})
```

6. Add the JavaScript file to the bottom of our `index.html` file:

```
<script src="interactions.js" type="text/javascript"></script>
```

Now, if we load our page, we should see a simple table sitting there with a header row and some buttons. Let's go ahead and add some basic styling to our page to make it a bit easier to see. Add the following to that `main.css` file that we added when we were working with `BaseServiceWorker`:

```
table {
    margin: 15px;
```

```
    border : 1px solid black;
}
th {
    border : 1px solid black;
    padding : 2px;
}
button {
    border : 1px solid black;
    padding :5px;
    background : #2e2e2e;
    color : #cfcfcf;
    cursor : pointer;
    margin-left : 15px;
    margin-top : 15px;
}
```

This CSS gives us some basic styling to work with. Now, if we hit the **Add** button, we should see the following message:

```
The FetchEvent for "http://localhost:3000/add" resulted in a
network error response: the promise was rejected.
```

Since we haven't added any code to actually handle this, let's go ahead and intercept this message inside of our `ServiceWorker`. Follow these steps to do so:

1. Add the following dummy code to our `fetch` event handler for the `ServiceWorker`:

```
event.respondWith(
    caches.match(event.request).then((response) => {
        if( response ) {
            return response
        } else {
            if( event.request.url.includes("/add") ) {
                return new Response(new Blob(["Here is some data"],
                    { type : 'text/plain'}),
                    { status : 200 });
            }
            fetch(event.request);
        }
    })
)
```

2. Click the **Add** button. We should see a new error stating that it could not parse the JSON message. Change the `Blob` data to some JSON:

```
return new Response(new Blob([JSON.stringify({test : 'example',
stuff : 'other'})], { type : 'application/json'}), { status : 200
});
```

3. Click the **Add** button again. We should get something that states that what we just passed to our handler is not of the `Node` type. Parse the data that we got inside of our **Add** button's click handler:

```
fetch('/add').then((res) => res.json()).then((fin) =>  {
    const tr = document.createElement('tr');
    tr.innerHTML = `<td>${fin.test}</td>
                    <td>${fin.stuff}</td>
                    <td>other</td>`;
    tableBody.appendChild(tr);
});
```

Now, if we try to run our code, we will see something interesting: our JavaScript file is still the old code. The `ServiceWorker` is utilizing the old cache that we had. We could do one of two things here. First, we could just disable the `ServiceWorker`. Alternatively, we could remove the old cache and replace it with our new one. We will perform the second option. To do this, we will need to add the following code to our `ServiceWorker` inside the install listener:

```
event.waitUntil(
    caches.delete('v1').then(() => {
        caches.open('v1').then((cache) => {
            return cache.addAll([
                '/',
                './interactions.js',
                './main.css'
            ]);
        }).then(() => {
            console.log('we are ready!');
        });
    })
);
```

Now, we could have the template loaded in on the frontend code, but we're going to mimic a server-side rendered system here instead. There are a couple of applications for this, but the main one that comes to mind is a templating system that we are trying out in development.

Most template systems need to be compiled to their final HTML forms before we can use them. We could set up a *watch* type system where these templates are reloaded every single time we update them, but that can become tiresome, especially when we only want to focus on the frontend. Another way to do this is to load those templates into our `ServiceWorker` and let it render them. That way, when we want to make updates, we just have our cache be deleted through the `caches.delete` method and then reload it.

Let's go ahead and set up a simple example like the preceding one, but instead of the template being created in our frontend code, we will have it in our `ServiceWorker`. Follow these steps to do so:

1. Create a template file called `row.template` and fill it in with the following code:

```
<td>${id}</td>
<td>${name}</td>
<td>${description}</td>
<td>${points}</td>
```

2. Remove the templating code inside of our `interactions.js` and replace it with the following:

```
fetch('/add').then((res) => res.text()).then((fin) => {
    const row = document.createElement('tr');
    row.innerHTML = fin;
    tableBody.appendChild(row);
});
```

3. Let's set up some basic templating code. We will do nothing close to what we did in `Chapter 9`, *Practical Example – Building a Static Server*. Instead, we will loop through the objects we get passed and fill in the parts of our template where our keys line up in the object:

```
const renderTemplate = function(template, obj) {
    const regex = /\${([a-zA-Z0-9]+)\}/;
    const keys = Object.keys(obj);
    let match = null;
    while(match = regex.exec(template)) {
        const key = match[1];
        if( keys.includes(key) ) {
            template = template.replace(match[0], obj[key]);
        } else {
            match = null;
        }
    }
    return template;
}
```

4. Change the response to the `/add` endpoint with the following code:

```
if( event.request.url.includes('/add') ) {
    return fetch('./row.template')
        .then((res) => res.text())
        .then((template) => {
            return new Response(new Blob([renderTemplate(template,
                add)],{type : 'text/html'}), {status : 200});
        })
} else if( response ) {
    return response
} else {
    return fetch(event.request);
}
```

Now, we will grab the template we want from the server (in our case, the `row.template` file) and fill it with whatever data we have (again, in our case we will use stub data). Now, we have templating inside of our `ServiceWorker` and can easily set up endpoints to go through this templating system.

This can also be beneficial when we want to personalize the error pages of our site. If we want to have a random image appear and incorporate it in our 404 page, we could have this done in the `ServiceWorker` instead of hitting this server. We could even do this for an offline state. We would just need to implement the same type of templating that we did here.

With these concepts in mind, it should be easy to see the power we have when intercepting requests and how we can make our web applications work offline. One final technique that we will learn about is storing our requests when we are offline and running them when we go back online. This type of technique can be used for saving or loading files from the browser. Let's take a look.

Saving requests for later

So far, we've learned how to intercept requests and either return or even enhance the response from our local system. Now, we will learn how to save requests when we are in offline mode and then send the calls to the server once we appear online.

Let's go ahead and set up a new folder for just this. Follow these steps:

1. Create a folder called `offline_storage` and add the following files to it:

   - `index.html`
   - `main.css`
   - `interactions.js`
   - `OfflineServiceWorker.js`

2. Add the following boilerplate code to `index.html`:

```
<!DOCTYPE html>
<html>
    <head><!-- add css file --></head>
    <body>
        <h1>Offline Storage</h1>
        <button id="makeRequest">Request</button>
        <table>
            <tbody id="body"></tbody>
        </table>
        <p>Are we online?: <span id="online">No</span>
        <script src="interactions.js"></script>
        <script>
            let online = false;
            const onlineNotification =
             document.querySelector('#online');
            window.addEventListener('load', function() {
                const changeOnlineNotification = function(status) {
                    onlineNotification.textContent = status ? "Yes"
                     : "No";
                    online = status;
                }
                changeOnlineNotification(navigator.onLine);
                 navigator.serviceWorker.register('.
                 /OfflineCacheWorker.js', {scope : '/'})
                window.addEventListener('online', () => {
                 changeOnlineNotification(navigator.onLine) });
                window.addEventListener('offline', () => {
                 changeOnlineNotification(navigator.onLine) });
            });
        </script>
    </body>
</html>
```

3. Add the following boilerplate code to `OfflineServiceWorker.js`:

```javascript
self.addEventListener('install', (event) => {
    event.waitUntil(
     // normal cache opening
    );
});
self.addEventListener('fetch', (event) => {
    event.respondWith(
        caches.match(event.request).then((response) => {
            // normal response handling
        })
    )
});
```

4. Finally, add the following boilerplate code to `interactions.js`:

```javascript
const requestMaker = document.querySelector('#makeRequest');
const tableBody = document.querySelector('#body');
requestMaker.addEventListener('click', (ev) => {
    fetch('/request').then((res) => res.json()).then((fin) => {
        const row = document.createElement('tr');
        row.innerHTML = `
        <td>${fin.id}</td>
        <td>${fin.name}</td>
        <td>${fin.phone}</td>
        <td><button id=${fin.id}>Delete</button></td>
        `
        row.querySelector('button').addEventListener('click', (ev)
         => {
            fetch(`/delete/${ev.target.id}`).then(() => {
                tableBody.removeChild(row);
            });
        });
        tableBody.appendChild(row);
    })
})
```

With all of this code in place, let's go ahead and change our Node.js server so that it points to this new folder location. We'll do this by stopping our old server and changing the `app.js` file so that it points to our `offline_storage` folder:

```
const server = http.createServer((req, res) => {
    return handler(req, res, {
        public : 'offline_storage'
    });
});
```

With this, we can rerun our server by running `node app.js`. We may experience our old page showing up. If this is the case, we can go to the **Application** tab in our developer tools and click the **Unregister** option under the **Service workers** section. Once we reload the page, we should see the new `index.html` page show up. Our handlers aren't working at the moment, so let's add some stub code inside of our `ServiceWorker` that will handle the two fetch cases that we added in `interactions.js`. Follow these steps to do so:

1. Add the following support inside the fetch event handler for the request:

```
caches.match(event.request).then((response) => {
    if( event.request.url.includes('/request') ) {
        return handleRequest();
    }
})
// below in the global scope of the ServiceWorker
let counter = 0;
let name = 65;
const handleRequest = function() {
    const data = {
        id : counter,
        name : String.fromCharCode(name),
        phone : Math.round(Math.random() * 10000)
    }
    counter += 1;
    name += 1;
    return new Response(new Blob([JSON.stringify(data)], {type :
     'application/json'}), {status : 200});
}
```

2. Let's make sure this code handles the response correctly by making sure that it adds a row to our table. Reload the page and make sure a new row is added when we click the **Request** button:

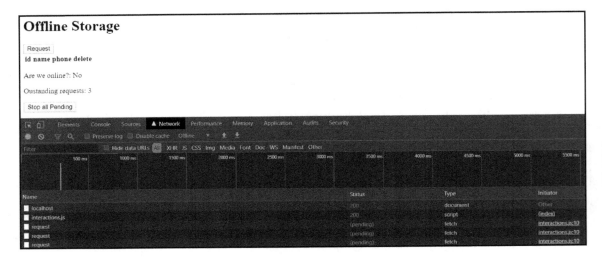

3. Now that we have made sure that that handler is working, let's go ahead and add the other handler for our delete request. We will mimic a delete for a database on the server in our ServiceWorker:

```
caches.match(event.request).then((response) => {
    if( event.request.url.includes('/delete') ) {
        return handleDelete(event.request.url);
    }
})
// place in the global scope of the Service Worker
const handleDelete = function(url) {
    const id = url.split("/")[2];
    return new Response(new Blob([id], {type : 'text/plain'}),
    {status : 200});
}
```

4. With this, let's go ahead and test it to make sure that our rows are deleting when we click the **Delete** button. If all of this is working, we will have a functioning application that can work online or offline.

Now, all we need to do is add support for requests that are going to go out but can't because we are currently offline. To do this, we will store requests in an array, and once we detect that we are back online in our `ServiceWorker`, we will send all the requests out. We will also add some support to let our frontend know that we are waiting on so many requests and that if we want, we can cancel them out. Let's add this now:

> In Chrome, switching from offline to online will trigger our **online** handler, but switching from online to offline doesn't seem to trigger the event. We can test the offline-to-online system functionality, but testing the other way around can be a bit more difficult. Just note that this limitation could be in place on many development systems and that trying to account for this can be quite difficult.

1. First, move most of our `caches.match` code to a standalone function, like so:

```
caches.match(event.request).then((response) => {
    if( response ) {
        return response
    }
    return actualRequestHandler(event);
})
```

2. Code the standalone function, as follows:

```
const actualRequestHandler = function(req) {
    if( req.request.url.includes('/request') ) {
        return handleRequest();
    }
    if( req.request.url.includes('/delete') ) {
        return handleDelete(req.request.url);
    }
    return fetch(req.request);
}
```

3. We will handle requests by polling them to see if we are back online. Set up a poll timer that will work every 30 seconds and change our `caches.match` handler like so:

```
const pollTime = 30000;
self.addEventListener('fetch', (event) => {
    event.respondWith(
        caches.match(event.request).then((response) => {
            if( response ) {
                return response
            }
```

```
if(!navigator.onLine ) {
    return new Promise((resolve, reject) => {
        const interval = setInterval(() => {
            if( navigator.onLine ) {
                clearInterval(interval);
                resolve(actualRequestHandler(event));
            }
        }, pollTime)
    })
} else {
    return actualRequestHandler(event);
}
})
)
});
```

What we have just done is set up a return for a promise. If we can't see the system online, we will keep polling every 30 seconds to see if we are back online. Once we are back online, our promise will clear the interval and actually handle the request in the resolve handler. We could set a system of so many attempts before we cancel the request. All we would have to do is add a reject handler after so many times through the interval.

Finally, we will add a way to stop all currently outstanding requests. To do this, we will need a way of keeping track of whether we have requests outstanding and a way to abort them in the ServiceWorker. This will be quite simple since we can easily keep track of what is still pending in the frontend. We can add this by doing the following:

1. First, we will add a display that shows how many outstanding requests we have in the frontend. We will put this right after our online status system:

```
// inside of our index.html
<p>Oustanding requests: <span id="outstanding">0</span></p>

//inside our interactions.js
const requestAmount = document.querySelector('#outstanding');
let numRequests = 0;
requestMaker.addEventListener('click', (ev) => {
    numRequests += 1;
    requestAmount.textContent = numRequests;
    fetch('/request').then((res) => res.json()).then((fin) => {
        // our previous fetch handler
        numRequests -= 1;
        requestAmount.textContent = numRequests;
    });
    // can be setup for delete requests also
});
```

2. Add a button that will cancel all outstanding requests to our `index.html` file. Also, add the corresponding JavaScript code to our `interactions.js` file:

```
//index.html
<button id="stop">Stop all Pending</button>

//interactions.js
const stopRequests = document.querySelector('#stop');
stopRequests.addEventListener('click', (ev) => {
    fetch('/stop').then((res) => {
        numRequests = 0;
        requestAmount.textContent = numRequests;
    });
});
```

3. Add the corresponding handler to our `ServiceWorker` for the stop request:

```
caches.match(event.request).then((response) => {
    if( response ) {
        return response
    }
    if( event.request.url.includes('/stop') ) {
        controller.abort();
        return new Response(new Blob(["all done"], {type :
        'text/plain'}), {status : 200});
    }
    // our previous handler code
})
```

Now, we will utilize something called an `AbortController`. This system allows us to send signals to things such as fetch requests so that we can say that we want to stop the pending request. While this system is mainly for stopping fetch requests, we can actually utilize the signal in order to stop any asynchronous requests. We do this by creating an `AbortController` and grabbing the signal from it. Then, inside of our promise, we listen for the abort event on the signal and reject the promise.

4. Add the `AbortController`, as follows:

```
const controller = new AbortController();
const signal = controller.signal;
const pollTime = 30000;
self.addEventListener('fetch', (event) => {
    event.respondWith(
        caches.match(event.request).then((response) => {
            if( response ) {
                return response
```

```
        }
        if( event.request.url.includes('/stop') ) {
            controller.abort();
            return new Response(new Blob(["all done"], {type :
            'text/plain'}), {status : 200});
        }
        if(!navigator.onLine ) {
            return new Promise((resolve, reject) => {
                const interval = setInterval(() => {
                    if( navigator.onLine ) {
                        clearInterval(interval);
                        resolve(actualRequestHandler(event));
                    }
                }, pollTime)
                signal.addEventListener('abort', () => {
                    reject('aborted');
                })
            });
        } else {
            return actualRequestHandler(event);
        }
    })
    )
});
```

Now, if we go into our system and ready up some requests in offline mode and then click the Cancel button, we will see that all of our requests get canceled! We could have put the `AbortController` on the fetch request in our frontend `interactions.js` file, but once we go back online, all of the promises would have still run, so we wanted to make sure that nothing was running. This is why we put it in the `ServiceWorker`.

By doing this, we have seen how we can not only handle requests by caching data for them but that we can also store those requests when we have spotty locations. On top of this, we have seen how we can utilize the `AbortController` to stop pending promises and how to utilize them besides just stopping fetch requests.

Summary

In this chapter, we learned how service workers can turn our applications from always being online to systems where we can create truly *always working* applications. By saving the state, handling requests locally, enriching requests locally, and even saving requests for offline use, we are able to handle the full state of our application.

Now that we have looked at creating rich web applications from both the client side and the server side with JavaScript, we will start to take a look at some advanced techniques that we can use to create highly performant applications that we only thought were possible through native application code. We can do this by utilizing C, C++, or Rust.

However, before we get to that, one piece of application development that is often overlooked by application developers is the deployment process. In the next chapter, we will look at a way of setting up **continuous integration and continuous development (CI/CD)** through a popular system called CircleCI.

12
Building and Deploying a Full Web Application

Now that we have seen both the server-side and the client-side code for JavaScript, we need to focus on another matter entirely; that is, building our code for deployment and deploying that code to a server.

While we have run our servers locally, we have never actually run them in a remote environment such as Amazon's AWS or Microsoft's Azure. Deploying today is not like it used to be 5 years ago. Before, we could move our application onto a server through the **File Transfer Protocol** (**FTP**). Now, even for small applications, we use a system of Continuous Deployment.

In this chapter, we will explore the following topics:

- Understanding Rollup
- Integrating into CircleCI

These topics will allow us to develop almost any application and get it deployed in a typical development environment. By the end of this chapter, we will be able to implement a typical build-and-deploy environment for a web application.

Let's get started.

Technical requirements

For this chapter, you'll need the following:

- A machine that can run Node.js
- A text editor or IDE, preferably VS Code
- A web browser
- A user account for GitHub
- This chapter's code, which can be found at `https://github.com/PacktPublishing/Hands-On-High-Performance-Web-Development-with-JavaScript/tree/master/Chapter12`.

Understanding Rollup

RollupJS is a build tool that allows us to prepare our applications in different ways, depending on the environment. There have been many tools before it (Grunt, Gulp), many that are competing with it (Webpack, Parcel), and many that will be built in the future. We will focus on RollupJS for our specific use case (getting our static server application built in `Chapter 9`, *Practical Example – Building a Static Server*), but just note that most build tools are similar in terms of their architecture.

What RollupJS gives us is a way to have *hooks* into different parts of the build life cycle. Most applications have the following states during a build process:

- Build start
- Dependency injection
- Compilation
- Post compilation
- Build end

Each of these states may go by different names in different build systems, and some may even have more than just these (as we will see, RollupJS does), but this is the typical build system.

In most cases, we will need to do the following things for our JavaScript applications:

- Bring in any dependencies that our Node/browser side needs
- Compile our JavaScript to a single file (if targeting HTTP/1) or compile it to an earlier version (if we are targeting wider browser support)
- Compile CSS to a single file, move images around, and so on

In the case of our application, we will make this quite easy. Here, we will learn how to do the following:

- Build our Node.js code into a single distributable
- Prepare our static assets, such as CSS/images
- Add Rollup to our npm build process

Building our static server into a single distributable

To start off, we will need to create a folder that we're ready to work with. To do this, either work in the folder that we worked in Chapter 9, *Practical Example – Building a Static Server*, or pull down the code from this book's GitHub repository. With this, run the npm install -g rollup command. This will put the rollup system into our global path so that we can utilize the command line if we want to by running the rollup command. Next, we are going to create a configuration file. To do this, we will add a rollup.config.js file to the base of our directory (the exact same location as our package.json file) and add the following code to it:

```
module.exports = {
    input: "./main.js",
    output: {
        file: "./dist/build.js",
        format: "esm"
    }
}
```

We have told Rollup that the starting point of our application is in the main.js file. Rollup will follow this starting point and run through it to see what it depends on. Whatever it depends on, it will try to put it into a single file and remove any unwanted dependencies along the way (this is called tree-shaking). Once it's done, it will put the file in dist/build.js.

If we try to run this, we will run into a problem. Here, we are utilizing private variables for classes, and Rollup does not support this, along with other features of ESNext that we are utilizing. We will also need to change anywhere that had member variables set outside of a function. This means we will need to change cache.js to the following:

```
export default class LRUCache {
    constructor(num=10) {
        this.numEntries = num;
        this.cache = new Map();
```

```
    }
  }
```

We will also need to replace all of the constructors in `template.js`, just like we did with `LRUCache`.

After making the preceding changes, we should see that `rollup` is happy with us and is now compiling. If we go into the `dist/build.js` file, we will see that it put all of the files together. Let's go ahead and put another option in our configuration file. Follow these steps:

1. Run the following command to add the minifier and code uglifier plugin to Rollup as a dev dependency:

   ```
   > npm install -D rollup-plugin-terser
   ```

2. With this installed, add the following lines to our `config.js` file:

   ```
   import { terser } from 'rollup-plugin-terser';
   module.exports = {
       input: "./main.js",
       output: {
           file: "./dist/build.js",
           format: "esm",
           plugins: [terser()]
       }
   }
   ```

Now, if we take a look at our `dist/build.js` file, we will see a file that is barely noticeable. This is all we need for the Rollup configuration for our application, but there are many more configuration options and plugins that can help with the compilation process. Next, we will take a look at some options that can help us put our CSS files into a smaller format, and also look at what would happen if we used Sass and how we could compile that with Rollup.

Adding other file types to our distribution

Currently, we are only bundling up our JavaScript files, but most application developers know that any frontend work also needs to be bundled up. Take Sass (`https://sass-lang.com/`), for example. It allows us to write CSS in a way that allows maximum reusability.

Let's go ahead and turn the CSS that we had for this project into a Sass file. Follow these steps:

1. Create a new folder called `stylesheets` and add `main.scss` to it.
2. Add the following code to our Sass file:

```scss
$main-color: "#003A21";
$text-color: "#efefef";
/* header styles */
header {
    // removed for brevity
    background : $main-color;
    color      : $text-color;
    h1 {
        float : left;
    }
    nav {
        float : right;
    }
}
/* Footer styles */
footer {
    // removed for brevity
    h2 {
        float : left;
    }
    a {
        float : right;
    }
}
```

The previous code showcases two features of Sass that make it easier to use:

- It allows us to nest styling. Instead of having to have a separate `footer` and `h2` section, we can just nest them.
- It allows the use of variables (yes, we have them in CSS).

 With HTTP/2, some standards for bundling files have gone by the wayside. Items such as sprite sheets are no longer advisable since the HTTP/2 standard added the concept of TCP multiplexing. It can actually be faster to download multiple smaller files than one large file. For those of you who are interested, the following link explains these concepts in more detail: `https://css-tricks.com/musings-on-http2-and-bundling/`
.

There is quite a bit more to Sass that what can be found on their website, such as mixins, but here, we want to focus on converting these files into the CSS that we know we can use on the frontend.

Now, we need to convert this into CSS and put it in our original folder. To do that, we will add `rollup-plugin-sass` to our configuration. We can do that by running `npm install -D rollup-plugin-sass`. With that added, we will add a new rollup configuration called `rollup.sass.config.js` and add the following code to it:

```
import sass from 'rollup-plugin-sass';
module.exports = {
    input: "./main-sass.js",
    output: {
        file: "./template/css/main.css",
        format: "cjs"
    },
    plugins: [
        sass()
    ]
}
```

Once we have made our rollup file, we will need to create the `main-sass.js` file that we have currently. Let's go ahead and do just that. Add the following code to that file:

```
import main_sass from './template/stylesheets/main.scss'
export default main_sass;
```

Now, let's run the following command:

```
> rollup --config rollup.sass.config.js
```

By doing this, we will see that the `css` directory inside of our template folder has been populated. By doing this, we can see how we can bundle everything up, not just our JavaScript files. Now that we've integrated Rollup's build system into our development pipeline, we will take a look at integrating Rollup into NPM's build pipeline.

Bringing rollup into Node.js commands

Now, we could just leave everything alone and run our rollup commands through the command line, but this may make things a bit harder when we bring continuous integration into our process (up next). Also, we may have other developers working on the same system and instead of having them run multiple commands, they can run a single `npm` command. Instead, we want to integrate rollup into various Node.js scripts.

We looked at this in `Chapter 9`, *Practical Example – Building a Static Server*, with the `microserve` package and the `start` command. But now, we want to integrate two new commands called `build` and `watch`.

First, we want the `build` command to run our rollup configurations. Follow these steps to make this happen:

1. Let's clean up our main directory and move our rollup configurations to a build directory.
2. With both of those moved, we will add the following line to our `package.json` file:

```
"scripts": {
        "start": "node --experimental-modules main.js",
        "build": "rollup --config ./build/rollup.config.js &&
rollup --config ./build/rollup.sass.config.js",
}
```

3. With this move, we can run `npm run build` and see everything built for us in a single command.

Second, we want to add a watch command. This will allow rollup to watch for changes and instantly run that script for us. We can easily add this into our `package.json` by adding the following line to our `scripts` section:

```
"watch": "rollup --config ./build/rollup.config.js --watch"
```

Now, if we type `npm run watch`, it will start rollup in watch mode. With that, as we make changes to our JavaScript files, we can see that rollup is automatically rebuilding our distribution file.

One final change that we need to make before we move onto continuous integration is to point our main entry point to our distribution file. To do this, we will change the start section in the `package.json` file so that it points to `dist/build.js`:

```
"start": "node --experimental-modules dist/build.js"
```

With that, let's go ahead and check to make sure that everything is still working correctly by running `npm run start`. We will see that some of our files aren't pointing to the correct location. Let's go ahead and fix this by making some changes to the `package.json` file:

```
"config": {
    "port": 50000,
    "key": "../selfsignedkey.pem",
    "certificate": "../selfsignedcertificate.pem",
```

```
        "template": "../template",
        "bodyfiles": "../publish",
        "development": true
    }
```

With this, we should be good to go! There are plenty of options with Rollup and there are even more when we want to integrate into the Node script system, but this should get us ready for the next section of this chapter, which is integrating into a CI/CD pipeline. Our system of choice is CircleCI.

Integrating into CircleCI

As we mentioned previously, development in the real world has dramatically shifted in the past couple of decades. From building everything locally and deploying from our development machines to complicated orchestration and dependency deployment trees, we have seen a rise in tools that help us rapidly develop and deploy.

One example of this is the CI/CD tools that we have available to us, such as Jenkins, Travis, Bamboo, and CircleCI. These tools pick up on various hooks, such as pushing code to a remote repository and instantly running a *build*. We will be utilizing CircleCI as our tool of choice. It is easy to set up and an easy-to-use development tool that has a nice free tier for developers.

In our case, this build is going to be doing the following three things:

1. Pulling in all of our project dependencies
2. Running our Node.js build script
3. Deploying those resources to our server, where we will be running the application

Getting all of this set up can be quite a frustrating experience, but it is well worth the payoff once our application is hooked up. We will be utilizing the following technologies to help us with this process:

- CircleCI
- GitHub

With this in mind, our first step will be to go to GitHub and create a profile, if we haven't done so already. This is as simple as going to `https://github.com/` and looking toward the top-right corner for the signup option. Once we have done this, we can start creating/forking repositories.

Since all of the code for this book is on GitHub, most of you should already have a GitHub account and know the basics of utilizing Git.

 For those of you who are struggling with Git or haven't utilized a version control system, the following resource may help: `https://try.github.io/`.

Now, we need to fork the repository that all of the code is in into our own repository. To do this, run through the following steps:

1. Go to this book's GitHub repository at `https://github.com/PacktPublishing/Hands-On-High-Performance-Web-Development-with-JavaScript` and click the top-right option to fork the entire repository.

   If we do not want to do that, we can clone the repository to our local computer. (This may be the better option since we only want the contents of the `Chapter12` directory.)

2. Whichever of the two options we choose, go ahead and move the `Chapter12` directory into another location on our local computer and change the folder name to something like `microserve`.
3. Go back into GitHub and create a new repository. Make this a private repository.
4. Finally, go back to our local machine and remove the `.git` file that is already there with the following command:

   ```
   > rf -rf .git
   ```

 For those of you who are on Windows, you can run these commands if you have the Windows 10 Linux subsystem. Alternatively, you can download the Cmder tool: `https://cmder.net/`.

5. Run the following commands to hook the local system up to the remote GitHub repository:

   ```
   > git init
   > git add .
   > git commit -m "first commit"
   > git remote add origin
     https://github.com/<your_username>/<the_repository>.git
   > git push -u origin master
   ```

6. The command line will ask for some credentials. Use the ones that we set up our profile with.

   Our local files should be hooked into GitHub. Now all we need to do is set up this system with CircleCI. To do this, we will need to create an account on CircleCI's website.

7. Go to `https://circleci.com/` and click on **Sign Up** and then **Sign up with GitHub**.

   Once our account is hooked up, we can log in. We should see the following screen:

8. Click **Set Up Project** for the repository we just set up.

   It should detect that we have a CircleCI file already in our repository, but we can always start from scratch if we want to. The directions that follow are going to be for setting CircleCI up from scratch. To do this, we can utilize the Node.js template that they have. However, the main thing we will need to do is create the .circleci directory and the config.yml file in that directory. We should have something basic that looks like this:

   ```
   version: 2
   jobs:
   ```

```
build:
  docker:
    - image: circleci/node:12.13
  working_directory: ~/repo
  steps:
    - checkout
    - restore_cache:
        keys:
          - v1-dependencies-{{ checksum "package.json" }}
          - v1-dependencies-
    - run: npm install
    - save_cache:
        paths:
          - node_modules
        key: v1-dependencies-{{ checksum "package.json" }}
```

The CircleCI configuration file executes in the following way:

1. We state that we want to utilize the `circleci/node:12.13` image from Docker

> We won't be discussing Docker here, but it is yet another technology that many companies use to deploy and host applications. More information on this technology can be found here: `https://docs.docker.com/`.

2. We want to run all of our commands in `~/repo`. This will be the case for almost all the basic projects we create.
3. Next, we check the repository into that `~/repo`.
4. Now, we need to set up a cache for this repository, if we don't have one already. This will make sure that we only pull down the repository when we need to.
5. We need to run the `npm install` command to pull in all of our dependencies.
6. Finally, we save the cache.

> This process is known as continuous integration because it will constantly run builds for us when we push code. We can add different settings inside our CircleCI profile if we want, but that is beyond the scope of this book. We will also get notifications via email when a build is complete. We can tune this if we want at the following location: `https://circleci.com/gh/organizations/<your_user>/settings`.

With this, we have created a basic CircleCI file! Now, if we go to our dashboard, it should run a build once we push this CircleCI configuration. It should also show all the steps that we laid out previously. This is great! Now, let's hook in our build process so that we can actually do something with our CI system.

Adding our build steps

With our CircleCI configuration, we can add many steps to the process and even add things called orbs. Orbs are essentially predefined packages and commands that can enhance our build process. In this section, we will be adding an orb that was published by Snyk: `https://snyk.io/`. This scans and looks for bad packages that are currently in the npm ecosystem. We will add this after we have set up our build.

To get our build running and packaged into something that we can deploy, we will add the following to our CircleCI configuration:

```
- run: npm install
- run: npm run build
```

With this, we will have our system building just as if we were running locally. Let's go ahead and try it out. Follow these steps:

1. Add our configuration file to our `git` commit:

   > **git add .circleci/config.yml**

2. Commit this to our local repository:

   > **git commit -m "changed configuration"**

3. Push this to our GitHub repository:

   > **git push**

As soon as we do that, CircleCI will start up a build. If we go to the project directory in CircleCI, we will see it building. If we click on the job, we will see it running all of our steps – we will even see it running through the steps we laid out in our file. Here, we will see our build failed!

This has happened because when we installed Rollup, we installed it as a global item. In this case, we need to add it as a dev dependency in our package.json file. If we add it to our package.json file, we should have a devDependency section that looks like this:

```
"devDependencies": {
    "rollup-plugin-sass": "^1.2.2",
    "rollup-plugin-terser": "^5.1.2",
    "rollup-plugin-uglify": "^6.0.3",
    "rollup": "^1.27.5"
}
```

Now, if we commit and push these files to our GitHub repository, we will see that our build passes!

With a passing build, we should add the Snyk orb to our configuration. If we head to https://circleci.com/orbs/registry/orb/snyk/snyk, we will see all of the commands and the configuration that we need to set up. Let's go ahead and change our `config.yml` file in order to bring the Snyk orb in. We will check our repository after we have built it. This should look like this:

```
version: 2.1
orbs:
  snyk: snyk/snyk@0.0.8
jobs:  build:
    docker:
      - image: circleci/node:12.13
    working_directory: ~/repo
    steps:
      - checkout
      - run: npm install
      - snyk/scan
      - run: npm run build
```

With the preceding configuration, we can go ahead and commit/push to our GitHub repository and see the new run of our build. It should fail because it will not allow us to run third-party orbs unless we explicitly state that we want to run them. We can do this by heading to our settings and going to the **Security** section. Once there, go ahead and state that we want to use third-party orbs. With this checked, we can do another build and we will see that we fail again!

We will need to sign up with Snyk to use their orb. Go ahead and head to snyk.io and sign up with a GitHub account. Then, go to the **Account settings** section. From there, grab the API token and head to the **Settings and contexts** section.

Create a new context and add the following environment variable:

```
SNYK_TOKEN : <Your_API_Key>
```

To utilize contexts, we will need to change up our `config.yml` file a bit. We will need to add in a workflows section and tell it to run our build job with that context. The file should look something like the following:

```
version : 2.1
orbs:
    snyk: snyk/snyk@0.0.8
jobs:
  build:
```

```
      docker:
        - image: circleci/node:12.13
      working_directory: ~/repo
      steps:
        - checkout
        - restore_cache:
            keys:
              - v1-dependencies-{{ checksum "package.json" }}
              - v1-dependencies-
        - run: npm install
        - snyk/scan
        - run: npm run build
        - save_cache:
            paths:
              - node_modules
            key: v1-dependencies-{{ checksum "package.json" }}
workflows:
  version: 2
  build_and_deploy:
    jobs:
      - build:
          context: build
```

With that change, we can go ahead and push it to the remote repository. We will see that the build passes with Snyk security scanning our packages!

 The idea of contexts is to hide API keys and secrets from the configuration file. We don't want to put those in our configuration files since anyone would be able to see them. Instead, we put them in something such as a context, where the administrators of a project will be able to see them. Every CI/CD system should have a concept like this, and this should be used whenever there are items like this.

With our project building and being scanned, all we need to do is deploy our application to a machine!

Deploying our build

To deploy our application, we will need to deploy to our own computers. There are many services out there, such as AWS, Azure, Netlify, and so on, which will have their own ways of deploying. In our case, we are going to deploy out to Heroku.

Follow these steps to do so:

1. We will need to get a Heroku account if we don't have one already. Head over to https://id.heroku.com/login and choose **Sign Up** at the bottom of the form.
2. Log in to the new account and click on the top-right button that states **New**.
3. In the dropdown, click **Create new app**.
4. We can call the app anything we want. Type in an application name.
5. Head back to our CircleCI dashboard and go back into the settings. Create a new context called **deploy**.
6. Add a new variable called HEROKU_APP_NAME. This is the app name that we set up in *step 3*.
7. Head back to Heroku and click on the user profile icon in the top right. From the dropdown, click on **Account Settings**.
8. You should see a section called **API Key**. Click the **Reveal** button and copy the key shown.
9. Head back to our CircleCI dashboard and create a new variable called HEROKU_API_KEY. The value should be the key we got in *step 8*.
10. Add a new job to our config.yml file. Our job should look something like the following:

```
version : 2.1
orbs:
  heroku: circleci/heroku@0.0.10
jobs:
  deploy:
    executor: heroku/default
    steps:
      - checkout
      - heroku/install
      - heroku/deploy-via-git:
          only-branch: master
workflows:
 version: 2
 build_and_deploy:
 jobs:
   - build:
       context: build
   - deploy
       context: deploy
       requires:
         - build
```

What we've done here is add a new job to our workflow, which is the `deploy` job. Here, the first step is to add the official Heroku orb to our workflow. Next, we created a job called `deploy` and we went through the steps set out by the Heroku orb. These can be found at `https://circleci.com/orbs/registry/orb/circleci/heroku`.

11. We need to deploy our build back to GitHub for Heroku to pick up the changes. To do this, we need to create a deploy key. Run the `ssh-keygen -m PEM -t rsa -C "<your_email>"` command in the command prompt. Make sure that you don't enter a password.
12. Copy the key that was just generated and head into the GitHub repository's **Settings**.
13. Click on **Deploy Keys** in the left navbar.
14. Click **Add a deploy key**.
15. Add a title and then paste the key that we copied in *step 12*.
16. Check the box that states **Allow write access**.
17. Head back into CircleCI and click on the project settings in the left-hand navbar.
18. Click on **SSH Permissions** and then **Add SSH Key**.
19. Add the private key we created in *step 11*. Make sure to add `github.com` in the **Hostname** section.
20. With this added, add the following lines to the `config.yml` file for our build job:

    ```
    steps:
      - add_ssh_keys:
          fingerprints:
            - "<fingerprint in SSH settings>"
    ```

21. At the end of our build, add the following step:

    ```
    - run: git push
    ```

One issue that we will have is that our application wants to work over HTTPS, but Heroku requires a pro license for this. Either opt in for this (this is a paid service) or change our application so that it only works with HTTP.

By doing this, we have successfully set up a CI/CD pipeline that can be utilized almost anywhere. We also added an additional security check to make sure that we are deploying safe code. With all of this under our belt, we are able to build and deploy web applications written in JavaScript!

Summary

In this chapter, we learned how applications can be built while utilizing build environments such as RollupJS. On top of this, we looked at how to add CI and CD through CircleCI.

The next chapter, and the final chapter of this book, will take a look at an advanced concept called WebAssembly. While the code will not be JavaScript, it will help us understand how we can take our web applications to the next level.

13
WebAssembly - A Brief Look into Native Code on the Web

The past few chapters have been all about how to leverage JavaScript in the modern web landscape. We have looked at frontend development, backend development, and even building and deploying applications through **continuous integration and continuous deployment (CI/CD)**. Now, we are going to take a step back and look at two topics that can help enhance our development with native speed code.

WebAssembly is a specification for assembly for the web. Assembly is a one-to-one mapping for the language that computers understand. WebAssembly, on the other hand, is a one-to-one mapping for a virtual computer that can run these instructions. In this chapter, we will explore WebAssembly and how we can port native applications to the browser.

Overall, we will explore the following topics:

- Understanding WebAssembly
- Setting up our environment to write WebAssembly
- Writing WebAssembly modules
- Porting C applications
- Taking a look at a major application

By the end of this chapter, we should be able to develop not only in the WebAssembly text format but also in C for the web. We will also be able to turn binary WebAssembly into its text format in order to diagnose possible issues with our ported applications.

Technical requirements

We will need the following tools for this chapter:

- An editor, such as VS Code.
- Access to build and compile programs on our computer. This may mean needing administrator privileges in some environments.
- This chapter's code, which can be found at `https://github.com/ PacktPublishing/Hands-On-High-Performance-Web-Development-with- JavaScript/tree/master/Chapter13`.

Understanding WebAssembly

WebAssembly is a specification for an instruction set that can be run on a machine. In our case, this machine is virtual. To comprehend how this translates into native speed applications and why the instructions are written the way they are, we need to have a basic understanding of how a program functions inside our computer. To understand WebAssembly, we will look at the following topics:

- Understanding the flow of a basic program
- Setting up our environment to code WebAssembly

Understanding a program

Let's take a look at a very basic C program:

```
#include <stdio.h>
int main() {
    printf("Hello, World!");
    return 0;
}
```

This program has an entry point. In our case, it is the `main` function. From here, we utilize a function that is declared in the `stdio` header file (a header file gives us function declarations so that we don't have to fully import all of the code into this file). We utilize the `printf` function to print out `Hello, World!` to the console and then we `return` with a `0` to signify that we have a successful program.

Since we won't be talking about the C/C++ code that we will be writing in depth, for those that are interested, a great resource is `https://www.learn-c.org/`.

While this is a program in a format that we, as programmers, generally understand, it needs to be turned into a format that the computer will actually understand. This means it needs to be compiled. This compilation process involves bringing in any external files (`stdio`, in this case) and linking them in. This also means we need to turn each of our instructions into one or more computer instructions.

Once the process of linking and compilation happens, we will usually get a binary file that can be read by our computer. If we opened this file in a byte reader, we would see a bunch of hexadecimal numbers. Each of these numbers corresponds to the instructions, data points, and so on, that we put in our file.

Now, this is just a basic understanding of how a program gets turned into something our computer understands and how the binary we created is understood by the computer. On most machines, a program runs as a stack of instructions and data. This means that it pulls instructions off of the top of the stack one at a time. These instructions can be anything from loading this number into a location or adding these two numbers together. As it peels these instructions off, it discards them.

We can store various pieces of data local to this stack, or we can store data at a global level. Those local to the stack are held on exactly that—the stack. Once that stack has been exhausted, we no longer have access to those variables.

The global ones are put into a location called the **heap**. The heap allows us to grab the data from anywhere in our system. Once the stack of our program has been exhausted, those heap objects can be left there if our program is still running.

Finally, we get a stack per function that we write. Because of this, we can treat each function as a mini-program. This means it will perform one task or a couple of tasks and then it will be exhausted, and we will go back to the stack of the function that called us. We can do two things when we exhaust this stack. The first thing we can do is go back to the stack of the function that called us with no data. Alternatively, we could give some data back (this is the `return` statement that we see in most languages).

Here, we can share data through these two mechanisms either by returning values from one of our subfunctions or by putting our results onto the heap so that others can access them. Putting it on the heap means that it will last for the duration of our program, but it also needs to be managed by us, whereas if we return values from the stack, it will be cleaned up as soon as the function that called us is exhausted. Most of the time, we will use simple data and return it through the stack. For complicated data, we will put it on the heap.

Before we look at WebAssembly, there's one final note you should know about: if we put data on the heap, we need to tell other parts of our program where to find that data. To do this, we pass a pointer to that location. This pointer is just an address that tells us where to find this data. We will be utilizing this in our WebAssembly code.

 The topic of computers and how programs work is quite interesting. For those of you who are interested, it may be beneficial to take a formal course at a community college. For those that like to self-learn, the following resource is of great help: https://www.nand2tetris.org/.

Now, let's set up our environment so that we can program in WebAssembly.

Setting up our environment

To program in WebAssembly, we need to get the wat2wasm program on our machine. The best way to do this is to download the repository for the WebAssembly suite of programs and get them compiled for our computer. Follow these steps to do so:

1. We need to get a program called CMake onto our system. For Linux/OS X, this just means going to https://cmake.org/download/ and running the installer. For those of you who are on Windows, this is a bit lengthier. Go to https://visualstudio.microsoft.com/vs/ and get Visual Studio. Make sure to get the C/C++ modules for it. With both CMake and Visual Studio on our machines, we can now move on and compile the WebAssembly suite of tools.

2. Head to https://github.com/WebAssembly/wabt and clone to an easily accessible location.

3. Open the CMake GUI tool. It should look similar to the following:

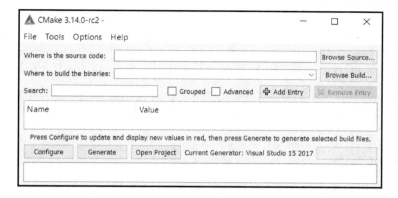

4. For the source code, go to the `wabt` folder that we downloaded from GitHub.
5. The location of the binaries should be in the `build` directory that we created in the `wabt` folder.
6. With this, we can hit the **Configure** button. This should populate the panel in the middle of the screen.
7. Now, just hit the **Generate** button. This should generate the files that we need to build our application.
8. Finally, we will go into Visual Studio and build the project.
9. Open **Visual Studio** and open the project from the **File** dropdown at the top left.
10. Once the project is in, we can hit **Build**. This should build all of the binaries that we need for working with WebAssembly. The screen should look something like this:

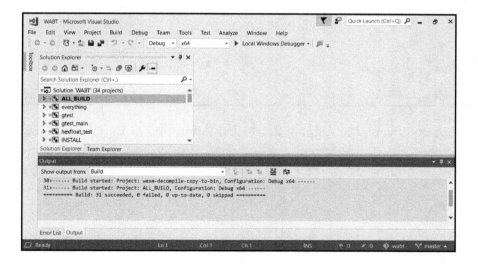

If you are having trouble, the repository at `https://github.com/WebAssembly/wabt` contains some excellent documentation on how to get the build done. The preceding instructions try to streamline the build process, but it can be difficult to get these projects up and running.

Now that we have built out our binaries, let's make sure that we put them on our path so that we have easy access to them. On Windows, we can do the following:

1. Go to the search bar and type `path variables`. The first option should allow us to set up our environment variables:

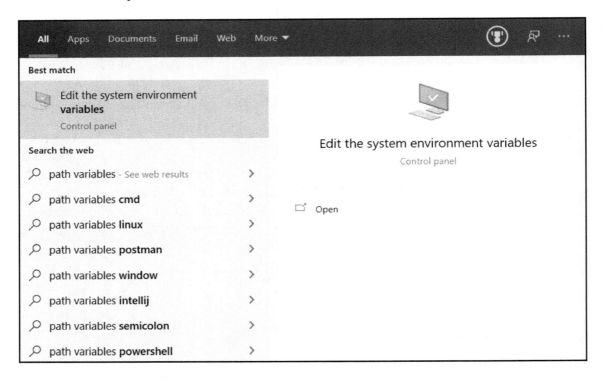

2. Click on the bottom right option called **Environment Variables...**:

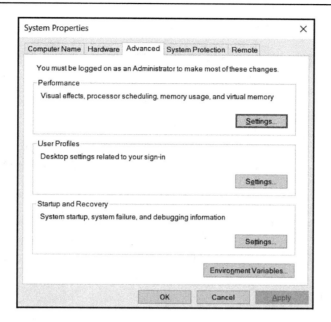

3. For the bottom box, find the **Path** variable and click **Edit...**:

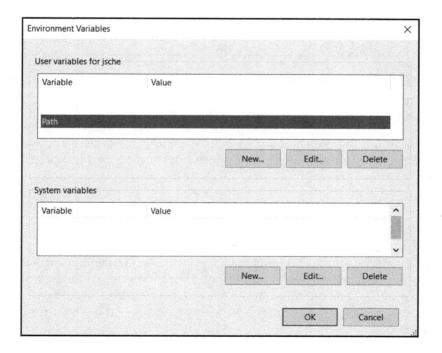

4. Click on **New** and find the directory where all of the binaries are being held:

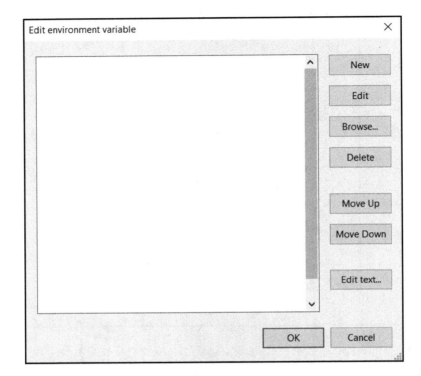

Once we've done this, we should be able to type `wat2wasm` into our command line and get the help documentation for the tool. Now, we are able to compile the text format of WebAssembly into a format that our browser expects!

Now that we've added the WebAssembly binary toolkit to our system and can compile/decompile WebAssembly programs, let's start writing our first program in WebAssembly!

Writing WebAssembly modules

A WebAssembly module is similar to a JavaScript module. We need to explicitly import anything we need from other WebAssembly/JavaScript modules. Whatever we write in our WebAssembly module can't be found by another WebAssembly module unless we explicitly export it. We can think of it as a JavaScript module – it is a sandboxed environment.

Let's start off with the most basic and useless version of a WebAssembly module:

```
(module)
```

With this, we can go to the command line and run the following command:

```
> wat2wasm useless.wat
```

This preceding code will spit out a file with the `wasm` extension. This is what we need to pass into the web browser to run WebAssembly. All this shows us is that WebAssembly, just like ESNext for JavaScript, wants to have everything declared in modules. It is easier to think of it like so, which is what happens when loading in JavaScript:

```
<script type="module"></script>
```

This means that all of the code loaded in the WebAssembly context can't spill into other WebAssembly modules that we set. Now, to load this `wasm` file into our browser, we need to utilize the static server that we utilized in `Chapter 9`, *Practical Example - Building a Static Server*.

Once you've loaded this up, follow these steps:

1. Create a basic `index.html` file that looks as follows:

```
<!DOCTYPE html>
<html>
    <head></head>
    <body>
        <script type="text/javascript">
        </script>
    </body>
</html>
```

2. Inside our `script` element, we will add the following code to load the module:

```
WebAssembly.instantiateStreaming(fetch('useless.wasm')).then(obj =>
{
    // nothing here
});
```

We have loaded our first WebAssembly module into the browser. The API is heavily promise-based and due to this, we need to utilize the Fetch interface. Once we've fetched the object, it's loaded in the WebAssembly context for the browser, which means this object is available to us. This is the WebAssembly module that we have just loaded up!

Let's go ahead and make a WebAssembly module that is a bit more useful. Let's take in two numbers and add them together. Follow these steps:

1. Create a file called `math.wat`.
2. Put the following code into the file:

```
(module
    (func $add (param $p1 i32) (param $p2 i32) (result i32)
        local.get $p1
        local.get $p2
        i32.add
    )
    (export "add" (func $add))
)
```

3. Compile this by running `wat2wasm math.wat`.
4. Load the new `wasm` file into the browser and add the following to the `then` body:

```
console.log(obj.instance.exports.add(100,200));
```

5. Make sure that the static server is running by going into the folder and running the `static-server` command.

 For those that have skipped ahead to this chapter, you can install a static server by running `npm install -g static-server`. This will install this static server globally. Then, all we need to do is run `static-server` in the folder that we want to deploy files from. Now that we've done this, we can hit our `index.html` file by going to `localhost:9080`.

If we launch our browser, go to `localhost:9080`, and open up the console, we will see that the number **300** has been printed out. We have just written our first accessible WebAssembly module!

Let's go over some of the concepts we covered in the preceding code. First, we defined a function. We stated that the name of this function is `$add` (all variables start with a dollar sign in WebAssembly). Then, we stated that it will take two parameters that we called `$p1` and `$p2`. Finally, we will output a result; that is, a 32-bit integer.

Now, we take the two parameters and store them on our stack. Finally, we add them together and use this as a result. Remember at the beginning of this chapter when we talked about how programs are stacks? This showcases the exact same concept. We loaded our two variables onto the stack. We popped them off so that we could use them in the `add` function, which put a new value onto the stack. Finally, we popped that value off of the stack and returned it to the main function body; in our case, the module.

Next, we exported the function so that our JavaScript code has access to it. This makes sure that our WebAssembly code is held in our sandbox, just like we want it to be. Now, as we mentioned previously, the object that is returned is the WebAssembly context. We grab the instance and look at the exports that are available. In our case, this is the `add` function, which we can now utilize in our JavaScript code.

Now that we have learned how we can export WebAssembly modules into the JavaScript context, you may be wondering if we can load JavaScript functions into the WebAssembly context. We can! Let's go ahead and add the following code to our `index.html` file:

```
const add = function(p1, p2) {
    return p1 + p2;
}
const importObject = { math : { add : add }};
WebAssembly.instantiateStreaming(fetch('math.wasm'), importObject).then(obj
=> {
    console.log(obj.instance.exports.add(100, 200));
    console.log(obj.instance.exports.add2(100, 200));
});
```

Here, we loaded in the `add` function we took from the JavaScript context and created an associated function that has the same function signature that our `add` function has in JavaScript. Now, we create a new `add` function called `$add2` that has a similar signature. We put our two parameters onto the stack and use the new `call` instruction. This instruction allows us to call other functions that have been declared in our context:

```
(func $add2 (param $p1 i32) (param $p2 i32) (result i32)
 local.get $p1
 local.get $p2
 call $externalAdd
 )
```

Finally, we export this function, just like we did with the other `add` function. Now, if we compile our code, go back into our browser, and reload the page, we will see that the number **300** is printed out twice.

Now, we know how to use WebAssembly functions in JavaScript and how to load JavaScript functions into WebAssembly. We are close to being able to write a program famous for being asked in an JavaScript coding interview. Before we do this, though, we will need to look at heap space and utilizing memory between JavaScript and WebAssembly.

Sharing memory between WebAssembly and JavaScript

So far, we have been working with one type of variable in WebAssembly. These are known as local variables, or stack variables. There is another type that will allow us to not only utilize them across our WebAssembly context but also share them between our JavaScript and our WebAssembly. But first, we will need to discuss the differences between the stack and the heap.

 There is a difference between global/local variables and the stack/heap. For now, we are going to keep things simple and treat global variables as if they are on the heap and local variables as if they are on the stack. Later, our application will have a global state that is not on the heap, but it is best to try to keep the idea of the local equivalent to the stack and the global equivalent to the heap.

We talked about the stack when we talked about how programs run on a typical computer. The best way to think of this is a stack of wood. We will always pull from the top and always add to the top. This is the same way in programming. We add to the top of the stack and then we pull from those top items. As an example, let's take the add function that we created.

We grabbed the two parameters and added them to the stack. First, parameter one and then parameter two. When we called $externalAdd or even if we called the add function built into WebAssembly, it takes those two items off the stack and replaces them with one item, the result. When we return from a function, we take that item off the local function stack and pop it on the top of the stack of the context for whoever called us.

A heap is just like what its name implies. We have the blob of things that can be grabbed, changed, and replaced from everywhere. Anyone can get to the heap, put items into it, and read from it. It's like a heap of clothes – we can search through it and find the item we need, or we can just add to it at the end of the day.

The main difference between the two is that the stack will get cleaned up. Any variables that we created inside it, once the function returns, are cleaned up. On the other hand, the heap stays there. Since anyone has access to it, we have to explicitly get rid of it; otherwise, it will be there permanently. In garbage-collected environments, the best way to think of this is that our environment doesn't know who else has items on it, so it doesn't know what needs to be cleaned up and what doesn't.

In WebAssembly, we don't have a garbage-collected environment, so we have to recollect the heap once we are done with it in our JavaScript or WebAssembly context. In our examples, we won't be doing this, so note that this is something we would want to do in a production-style environment. To do this, we could just set the memory object in JavaScript to null. This will let the garbage collector know that no one is utilizing it anymore.

Let's learn how to share memory between JavaScript and WebAssembly and how that is equivalent to the heap. Follow these steps:

1. Create a file named sharing_resources.wat.
2. Put the following code inside the file:

```
(module
    (import "js" "mem" (memory 1))
    (func $storeNumber
        (i32.store (i32.const 0) (i32.const 100))
    )
    (func $readNumber (result i32)
        (i32.load (i32.const 0))
    )
    (export "readNumber" (func $readNumber))
    (export "storeNumber" (func $storeNumber))
)
```

Our first function stores the number 100 at memory location 0. If we were storing an arbitrary amount of data, we would have to let whoever called us know how much we stored. However, in this case, we always know that it is just one number.

Our read function just reads that value from memory and returns it as a value.

3. Our script section inside the index.html file should look something like the following:

```
const memory = new WebAssembly.Memory({initial : 1});
const importObject = { js: {mem: memory}};
WebAssembly.instantiateStreaming(fetch('sharing_resources.wasm'),
importObject).then(obj => {
    obj.instance.exports.storeNumber();
    console.log(obj.instance.exports.readNumber());
});
```

The top section should look different. First, we are creating a piece of memory that both JavaScript and WebAssembly can share. We are going to create and load only one section of memory. In the context of WebAssembly, this is 64 KB worth of data.

Once our WebAssembly has loaded, we store the number and then read it out. Now, we can see that we have a global state in WebAssembly, but how would we share this with our JavaScript? Well, that starting section of the code tells us how. We have access to the memory object, so we should be able to get at it. Let's go ahead and change our script a bit so that we can read the memory directly inside JavaScript instead of calling a function that does this for us.

The following code should do this:

```
function readNumber() {
    const bytes = new Uint32Array(memory.buffer, 0, 1);
    console.log('The number that was put here is:', bytes[0]);
}
```

Now, we can add this to the body after our WebAssembly has loaded:

```
obj.instance.exports.storeNumber();
readNumber();
```

If we look inside our console, we should see the exact same output! The final test is to store something from JavaScript and grab it inside WebAssembly. We can achieve this by changing the script to the following:

```
const memory = new WebAssembly.Memory({initial : 1});
const storeByte = new Int32Array(memory.buffer, 0, 1);
storeByte[0] = 200;
const importObject = {js: {mem: memory}};
WebAssembly.instantiateStreaming(fetch('sharing_resources.wasm'),
importObject).then(obj => {
    console.log(obj.instance.exports.readNumber());
});
```

If we save this and go back to our console, we should see that the number **200** is printed out!

Now, we know how to share memory between two instances and how we can utilize this to do some cool stuff. Let's go ahead and put all of our skills to the test and create every programmer's favorite program: FizzBuzz.

Writing FizzBuzz in WebAssembly

FizzBuzz is a programming challenge that requires a user to take in a positive number loop from 1 to a chosen number and print out the results based on the following criteria:

- If the number is divisible by 3, then print *Fizz*
- If the number is divisible by 5, then print *Buzz*
- If the number is divisible by 15, then print *FizzBuzz*

Let's go ahead and kick this off by getting our JavaScript environment ready. The following code should look familiar, except for our new logging function:

```
const memory = new WebAssembly.Memory({initial : 1});
const storeByte = new Int32Array(memory.buffer, 0, 1);
function consoleLogString(offset, length) {
    const bytes = new Uint8Array(memory.buffer, offset, length);
    const string = new TextDecoder('utf8').decode(bytes);
    console.log(string);
}
const importObject = { console: {log: consoleLogString}, js: {mem:
memory}};
WebAssembly.instantiateStreaming(fetch('fizzbuzz.wasm'),
importObject).then(obj => {
    //obj.instance.exports.fizzbuzz(10);
});
```

This function takes in the offset of the memory and the length of the data and prints it out. As we mentioned previously, we need to know where the data is, as well as its length, to be able to read it from the heap. Now, we can get into the heart of the program. Follow these steps to do so:

1. Create a new file called `fizzbuzz.wat`.
2. We know that we will need to import both our memory and the `console` function, just like we have been importing other functions. We also know that we will be creating a function called `fizzbuzz` and that we will be exporting this so that our JavaScript context can utilize it:

```
(module
    (import "console" "log" (func $log (param i32 i32)))
    (import "js" "mem" (memory 1))
    (global $g (mut i32) (i32.const 0))
    (func $fizzbuzz (param $p i32)
        ;; content of the function
    )
```

```
(export "fizzbuzz" (func $fizzbuzz))
)
```

The only interesting piece of the preceding code is the global section. This is a global variable that can be thought of as the stack of our context. It isn't on the heap, so the JavaScript context doesn't have access to it. We can also see the mut keyword in front of the declaration. This tells us that we are going to be changing the global variable from the various parts of our WebAsembly code. We are going to utilize this so that it holds the length of our print out.

3. We will need to check for both conditions of FizzBuzz:

```
(func $checkFizz (param $p1 i32))
(func $checkBuzz (param $p1 i32))
```

Both of our functions will take a number. For the checkFizz function, we will test to see if it is divisible by 3. If it is, we will store the word *Fizz* in the memory heap where the global variable is and then update that global variable to the location after the word *Fizz*. For *Buzz*, we will do the exact same thing, except we will test to see if the number is divisible by 5. If this is true, we will put *Buzz* in the global pointer location and update it.

The following is the checkFizz function:

```
local.get $p1
i32.const 3
i32.rem_s
(if (i32.eq (i32.const 0))
    (then
        (i32.store8 (global.get $g) (i32.const 70))
        (i32.store8 (i32.add (global.get $g) (i32.const 1))
         (i32.const 105))
        (i32.store8 (i32.add (global.get $g) (i32.const 2))
         (i32.const 122))
        (i32.store8 (i32.add (global.get $g) (i32.const 3))
         (i32.const 122))
        (global.set $g (i32.add (global.get $g) (i32.const 4)))
    )
)
```

Here, we grab the number that was passed in. Then, we put 3 on the stack and run the remainder function. If the result is equal to 0, then we put the word *Fizz* into memory. Now, what's being put into memory may not look like the word *Fizz*, but if we look at the UTF8 decimal numbers for each of the letters, we will see that that is what we are putting into memory.

If we head back to our JavaScript code, we will see that we are utilizing a `TextDecoder`. This allows us to read these byte values and translate them into their string equivalent. Since WebAssembly only understands the concept of integers and floating-point numbers, this is how we have to deal with it for now.

Next is the `checkBuzz` function. It should look similar to the preceding code, except for the divisible, which is 5:

```
(func $checkBuzz (param $p1 i32)
    local.get $p1
    i32.const 5
    i32.rem_s
    (if (i32.eq (i32.const 0))
        (then
            (i32.store8 (global.get $g) (i32.const 66))
            (i32.store8 (i32.add (global.get $g) (i32.const 1))
            (i32.const 117))
            (i32.store8 (i32.add (global.get $g) (i32.const 2))
            (i32.const 122))
            (i32.store8 (i32.add (global.get $g) (i32.const 3))
            (i32.const 122))
            (global.set $g (i32.add (global.get $g) (i32.const 4)))
        )
    )
)
```

4. Now, we can write `fizzbuzz`. We will take in the integer and then loop from 1 to that value running our `checkFizz` and `checkBuzz` functions:

```
(func $fizzbuzz (param $p i32)
    (local $start i32)
    (local.set $start (i32.const 1))
    (block
        (loop
            (call $checkFizz (local.get $start))
            (call $checkBuzz (local.get $start))
            (br_if 1 (i32.eq (local.get $start) (local.get $p)))
            (local.set $start (i32.add (local.get $start)
            (i32.const 1)))
            (br 0)
        )
    )
    i32.const 0
    global.get $g
    call $log
)
```

The loop is fairly simple. `br_if` tests to see whether our `start` variable equals what we put in. If it does, it will equal `1` and it will break out of the loop. Otherwise, it will increment the `start` variable by one. (`br 0`) is what keeps the loop going.

Once we have finished the loop, we will get our global variable, wherever it finished up, and call the `log` function. Let's compile this and run the following test:

```
obj.instance.exports.fizzbuzz(10);
```

By doing this, we should get the following output:

FizzBuzzFizzFizzBuzz

We have just written a nontrivial program in pure WebAssembly! By now, you should have realized why most people don't write in pure WebAssembly since what should have been a simple program took us quite a bit of coding.

In the next section, we'll learn how to use a higher-level language, C, to write programs for the web.

Writing C/C++ for the web

So far, we have taken a look at writing the low-level instruction language of WebAssembly. While this can be a fun exercise to take on, most of our projects will be much grander in scale and we will want to utilize a high-level language to accomplish our goals. While there are languages out there that will compile to WebAssembly that are similar to JavaScript (`https://github.com/AssemblyScript/assemblyscript`), a good chunk of modules will be written while utilizing system languages such as C, C++, or Rust. In this section, we will take a look at writing C/C++ code for the browser.

The Rust language (`https://www.rust-lang.org/`) provides us with a safer alternative to C/C++. While utilizing it may be better in the long run, we are going to stick with C/C++ since this is what we will widely compile to WebAssembly for the foreseeable future since most programs are currently written in it.

For us to begin our C/C++ writing adventure, we will need to grab the Emscripten SDK to compile to WebAssembly. This can be found at https://emscripten.org/index.html. We will mostly be following the *Getting started* guide that Emscripten provides. Follow these steps:

1. First, we will clone the Emscripten SDK by running the following command:

    ```
    > git clone https://github.com/emscripten-core/emsdk.git
    ```

2. Head into the directory by using the following command:

    ```
    > cd emsdk
    ```

3. Pull the latest changes and the following commands:

    ```
    > git pull
    > emsdk latest install
    > emsdk activate latest
    > emsdk_env.bat
    ```

Now that we have the preceding commands to aid us, we are ready to start writing C and C++ for the web! Let's go ahead and start with an easy module:

```c
#include <stdio.h>
int main() {
    printf("Hello, World!\n");
    return 0;
}
```

This basic C program is everybody's favorite Hello World program. To compile this program, go ahead and run the following command:

```
> emcc hello_world.c
```

If everything has been installed correctly, we should get the following two files:

*   a.out.wasm
*   a.out.js

With these two files, we can utilize an index.html file and load them in, like so:

```html
<!DOCTYPE html>
<html>
    <head>
    </head>
    <body>
        <script type="text/javascript" src="a.out.js"></script>
```

```
    </body>
</html>
```

We should get a printout of **Hello World!** to our console! Let's go ahead and write another C program, just like the previous WebAssembly program we wrote – FizzBuzz:

```c
#include <stdio.h>
void fizzbuzz(int num) {
    for(int i = 1; i <= num; i++) {
        if(i%3 == 0) {
            printf("Fizz");
        }
        if(i%5 == 0) {
            printf("Buzz");
        }
    }
    printf("\n");
}
```

If we compile this and try to run it, we will see that nothing is found. The documentation states that it should be on the global `Module` variable, but if we check there, we will see that there is no `fizzbuzz` program to be found. Fortunately, Emscripten does dead code analysis for us and noticed that our C program doesn't have a `main` function and that it doesn't call the `fizzbuzz` function, so it eliminated it.

To handle this, we can add an argument to our `emcc` call:

```
> emcc -s "EXPORTED_FUNCTIONS=['_fizzbuzz']" fizzbuzz.c
```

 All of our functions will have an underscore before them. This helps us and the system differentiate what may be created in the JavaScript system and what is being created in the C/C++ context.

With this, we can go into the browser and our developer console and type the following:

```
Module._fizzbuzz(10);
```

We should see a printout! We have just compiled our first library function from C that can be used in our JavaScript code. Now, what if we want to try something a little more difficult? What if we want to run a JavaScript function inside our C/C++ code?

To do this, we will have to do the following:

1. We will need to put an `extern` declaration at the top of our file (Emscripten will look in the JS location first, but we can also pass a command-line flag to tell it where else to look):

```
#include <stdio.h>
extern int add(int, int);
int main() {
    printf("%d\n", add(100, 200));
    return 1;
}
```

2. Next, we will create an `external.js` file that will house our new function:

```
mergeInto(LibraryManager.library, {
    add: function(x, y) {
        return x + y;
    }
});
```

3. Now, we can compile our program with the following line of code:

```
> emcc -s extern.c --js-library external.js
```

   After, we can head back to the browser and see that it prints out **300**! Now, we know how to use external JavaScript in our C/C++ programs and we can grab our C/C++ code from the browser.

All this time, we have been overwriting our files, but is there another way for us to handle this? Of course – we can call the `emcc` system with the `emcc -o <file_name.js>` flag. Therefore, we can compile our `extern.c` file and call it `extern.js` by running the following command:

```
> emcc --help
```

Alternatively, we can go to their website: `https://emscripten.org/`.

Now that we are able to write and compile C code for our browser, we will turn our attention to utilizing this power. Let's implement a hamming code generator that we can utilize in JavaScript that is written in C and can be compiled to WebAssembly.

Writing a hamming code generator

Now, we are going to write a complicated piece of software. A hamming code generator creates a piece of data that should be able to be recovered when it is transmitted between two mediums. These mediums could be anything from a computer to another computer or even a process to another process (although we should hope that data transmission between processes does not get corrupted). The data that we will be adding to accomplish this is known as hamming codes.

To write this piece of software, we will need to understand how a hamming code is generated and how we can use a verifier to make sure that the data that does cross from one medium to another is correct. Specifically, we will be looking at the creation of hamming data and the verification process. We won't be looking at recovering the data as this is close to the reverse process of creating the data.

To understand how hamming data is created, we will need to look at data at the bit level. This means that if we want to transmit the number 100, we need to know what that looks like in terms of bits. Bits are the lowest data unit for a computer. A bit can only be a 0 or a 1. As we add more bits together, they represent the power of 2. The following table should help showcase this a bit:

Bit 3	Bit 2	Bit 1	Bit 0
8	4	2	1
2^3	2^2	2^1	2^0

As we can see, each bit location represents the next power of two. If we mix and match these bits together, we will find that we can represent all positive real numbers. There are also ways to represent negative and even floating-point numbers, but we will not be going into that here.

 For those that are curious, an article on floating-point representation can be found here: https://www.cprogramming.com/tutorial/floating_point/understanding_floating_point_representation.html.

So, if we wanted to see these numbers in their binary form, we could go through them one at a time. The following table shows the decimal notation on the left and the binary representation on the right (decimal is what we are used to):

0	0000
1	0001
2	0010
3	0011

4	0100
5	0101
6	0110
7	0111
8	1000

Hopefully, this clarifies how bits and binary representation works. Now, we are going to move on to how hamming codes actually work. Hamming codes work by adding what is known as parity bits to special locations in the data transmission process. These parity bits will either be a 1 or a 0, depending on the type of parity that we select.

The two types of parity that we can choose are even parity and odd parity. Even parity means that when we add up all of the bit locations for that parity bit, they need to be an even number. If we choose odd parity, we need to add up all the bits for that parity location and check to make sure they are odd. Now, we need to decide what bits correspond to each parity bit location and even where the parity bits go.

First, we will take a look at where the parity bits go. Parity bits will be at the bit location for each power of 2. Just as we saw in the preceding table, we will host our parity bits at the following bit locations: 1, 2, 4, 8, and 16. If we look at the preceding table, we will notice that these correspond to the bits where there is only a single bit set.

Now, we need to decide which data bit locations correspond to our parity bit locations. Well, we might be able to guess these based on where the parity bits are located. For each data bit, we will look at if they have the corresponding parity bit set there. This can be seen in the following table:

Number (Decimal Format)	Is It A Parity Bit?	Parity Bits That Use This Data
1	Yes	N/A
2	Yes	N/A
3	No	1, 2
4	Yes	N/A
5	No	1, 4
6	No	2, 4
7	No	1, 2, 4
8	Yes	N/A

The final piece that we need to know about is how to mesh our data with the parity data. The best way to look at this is through an example. Let's take the number 100 and turn it into its binary representation. We could do this by hand or we could pull up a programmer's calculator, which most operating systems have.

If we open up our calculator and type in 100, we should get the following binary representation of it: 1100100. Now, to add our parity bits, we will need to shift our data bits based on whether we place a parity bit there or not. Let's take this a step at a time:

1. Is the first bit used as a parity bit? Yes, so we will place a 0 there and shift our data to the left once. We now have 11001000.
2. Is the second bit used as a parity bit? Yes, so we will place a 0 there and shift our data to the left once. We now have 110010000.
3. Is the third bit used as a parity bit? No, so we can put our original first data bit there, which is a zero. Our data looks the same as before: 110010000.
4. Is the fourth bit used as a parity bit? Yes, so we will place a 0 there and shift our data to the left once. We now have 1100100000.
5. Is the fifth bit used as a parity bit? No, so we will place our original second data bit there, which is a zero. Our data looks the same as before: 1100100000.
6. Is the sixth bit used as a parity bit? No, so we will place our original third data bit there, which is a one. Our data looks the same as before: 1100100000.
7. Is the seventh bit used as a parity bit? No, so we will place our original fourth data bit there, which is a zero. Our data looks as follows: 1100100000.
8. Is the eight-bit used as a parity bit? Yes, so we will shift our data to the left one and place a zero there. Our data looks as follows: 11000100000.

For the rest of the numbers, they stay the same since we have no more parity bits to place. Now that we have our data, we have to set our parity bits. We will use even parity for our example and the code. The following table showcases the final number and the reason why we had to set a parity bit to one or zero:

Bit Location	Binary For Location	Do We Set It?	Count For Parity
1	00001	Yes	1
1	00010	Yes	3
0	00011	N/A	
1	00100	Yes	1
0	00101	N/A	
1	00110	N/A	
0	00111	N/A	
0	01000	No	2
0	01001	N/A	
1	01010	N/A	
1	01011	N/A	

As shown in the preceding table, we had to set the parity bits for the 1, 2, and 4 locations. Let's take a look at the second bit and go through the process. We will look for any bit locations where their binary representation has the second-bit set. If the bit is set at that location, we will count it. After adding up all of these numbers, if they add up to an odd number, we will need to set the parity bit location. For the second bit, we can see that the number 6, 10, and 11 locations have their second-bit set and that they have a 1 at them. This is why we have a count of three, which means we need to set our parity bit to make sure we have even parity.

This is a lot of information to take in, and rereading the preceding sections may help you understand how we got to this final parity number. If you want to find out more, go to https://www.geeksforgeeks.org/hamming-code-in-computer-network/.

Now, with all of this theory out of the way, let's go ahead and start writing our C program to be able to create parity data and also verify it.

First, let's create a file called hamming.c. We will create this as a pure library file, so we won't have the main function. Now, let's go ahead and stub out our functions just to get an idea of what we want to do. Follow these steps:

1. To create our data, we will need to read in the data and move the data bits to the proper locations, the same way that we did previously. Let's go ahead and call this function placeBits:

```
void placeBits(int data, int* parity) {
}
// creation of true data point with parity bits attached
int createData(int data) {
    int num = 0;
    placeBits(data, &num);
    return num;
}
```

We can see something interesting about the method signature of the placeBits function. It is taking in an int*. For JavaScript developers, this will be a new concept. We are passing in the location of the data instead of passing in the data itself. This is known as passing by reference. Now, the idea is similar to what it's like in JavaScript; that is, if we pass an object, we are passing the reference to it. This means that when we make changes to that data, we will see these changes in the original function. It is the same concept as the previous one, but we have a bit more control over this. If we don't pass by reference, it would pass by value, meaning we would get a copy of the preceding data and we wouldn't see the changes reflected in our createData function.

2. Now, we need to have a function that figures out if we set the parity bit for that location. We will call this `createParity`. It should have a method signature that looks like this:

```
void createParity(int* data)
```

Again, we are passing in a reference to the data instead of passing the data itself.

3. For our data checking algorithm, we will be going through each parity bit and checking the respective data locations for each. We will call this function `checkAndVerifyData` and it will have the following method signature:

```
int checkAndVerifyData(int data)
```

Now, instead of a Boolean, we will be passing back an `int`, where -1 means that the data is bad and 1 means that the data is good. In basic C, we don't have the concept of a Boolean, so we use numbers to represent the concepts of true or false (there is a Boolean in the `stdbool` header, but if we look at it, it utilizes the concept of 0 being `false` and 1 being `true`, so it still utilizes the numbers underneath). We can also make the system more robust by making each negative number mean a specific error code. In our case, we will just use -1, but this can be improved.

4. Now, we can begin filling out our functions. First, we will place our data in the correct locations and make sure we have room for our parity bits. This will look as follows:

```c
const int INT_SIZE = sizeof(int) * 8;
void placeBits(int data, int* parity) {
    int currentDataLoc = 1;
    int dataIterator = 0;
    for(int i = 1, j = 0; i < INT_SIZE; i++, j++) {
        if(ceil(log2(i)) == floor(log2(i))) continue; //we are at a
         parity bit section
        *parity |= ((data & (currentDataLoc << dataIterator)) << (j
         - dataIterator));
        dataIterator++;
    }
}
```

First, we created a constant known as `INT_SIZE`. This allows us to handle different types of environments (although WebAssembly is supposed to be a standardized environment to work in, this allows us to use this C program elsewhere). We are also utilizing three special functions: `ceil`, `floor`, and `log2`. All of these can be found in the math library that comes with the standard library for C.

We get this by importing the header file at the top of our file:

```
#include <math.h>
```

The iteration process works like so:

1. It checks to see if we are at a parity bit section. If we are, we will skip it and move on to the next section.

2. If we are not at a parity bit section, we will take the bit in our data at `dataIterator`. This counter keeps count of our location in the data that we passed in. All of the preceding operations are bit operations. The `|` tells us we are doing a bitwise or, which means that the bit will be set to a 1 if the left-hand side (the parity variable), the right-hand side (our equation), or both are 1; otherwise, it will be a 0.

3. We do a bitwise AND on our data with the bit set at our `dataIterator`. This will let us know if we have a bit set there. Finally, we need to make sure that we shift that bit by the number of parity bits that are already set (this is `j – dataIterator`).

4. If we reach the bottom of this `for` loop, then we check a data bit, so we need to increment our `dataIterator`.

 If bit operations are new to you, it would be a good idea to read up on them at https://developer.mozilla.org/en-US/docs/Web/JavaScript/ Reference/Operators/Bitwise_Operators.

Now, we can fill in our `createParity` method with the following code:

```
void createParity(int* data) {
    int parityChecks[4] = {1, 2, 4, 8};
    int bitSet[4] = {1, 2, 8, 128};
    for(int i = 0; i < 4; i++) {
        int count = 0;
        for(int j = 0; j < INT_SIZE; j++) {
            if((parityChecks[i] & (j+1)) != 0) {
                count += ((*data & (1 << j)) != 0) ? 1 : 0;
            }
        }
        if( count % 2 != 0 ) {
            *data |= bitSet[i];
        }
    }
}
```

This section can be a bit more complicated, but it is doing what we did by hand previously:

1. First, we are only going to handle a certain amount of bits for our data, so we will only use four parity bits. These parity bits correspond to the 0, 1, 2, and 4-bit locations, which are the decimal numbers 1, 2, 4, and 8.

2. Next, these bits are located at the 1, 2, 4, and 8-bit locations, which are represented as 1, 2, 8, and 128 in decimal form. This just makes it easier if we need to set the parity bit located there.

3. Now, we will loop through each of our parity checks and see if our newly moved data has a bit set there:

```
if((parityChecks[i] & (j+1)) != 0) {
    count += ((*data & (1 << j)) != 0) ? 1 : 0;
}
```

We are checking to make sure that the bit we are currently looking at is the data bit that we are worried about for that parity bit. If it is, we will add to the counter if the data bit is set there. We will do this by utilizing a bitwise AND with the data. If we don't get a zero, this means the bit is set, so we will add to the counter.

4. At the end of this `for` loop, if we don't have even parity, we will need to set the parity bit at this location to get even parity.

Now, let's compile our program with the following command-line operation:

```
> emcc -s "EXPORTED_FUNCTIONS=['_createData']" hamming.c
```

Next, we need to go to our `index.html` page in the browser and run the following command in our developer's tools:

```
Module._createData(100);
```

By doing this, we should get the following output: `1579`. If we put this decimal number into our programmer's calculator, we will get the following binary representation: `11000101011`. If we head back up and check when we did this by hand, we will see that we got the exact same thing! This means our hamming data generator is working. Now, let's make the verification tool. Follow these steps to do so:

1. Inside our `checkAndVerifyData` method, we will add the following code:

```
int checkAndVerifyData(int data) {
    int verify = 0;
    int parityChecks[4] = {1, 2, 8, 128};
    for(int i = 0; i < 4; i++) {
        verify = checkRow(&data, parityChecks[i]);
```

```
        if(verify != 0) { // we do not have even parity
            return -1;
        }
    }
    return 1;
}
```

Here, we have a `verify` variable that will tell us if the data is good or not. If it isn't good, it will output our error status, which is a −1. Otherwise, we'll have run through the data and seen it was good, so we'll return a 1. Next, we'll utilize the parity bits which, as we already know, are held at the decimal numbers 1, 2, 8, and 128. We will loop through these and check our hamming data with it by utilizing the `checkRow` method.

2. The `checkRow` method will utilize similar concepts to our creation process. This looks as follows:

```
int checkRow(int* data, int loc) {
    int count = 0;
    int verifier = 1;
    for(int i = 1; i < INT_SIZE; i++) {
        if((loc & i) != 0 ){
            count += (*data & (verifier << (i - 1))) != 0 ? 1 : 0;
        }
    }
    return count % 2;
}
```

Again, this should be very similar to our `createParity` method. We will run through the number and check to see if this is a parity bit number. If it is, we will utilize a bitwise AND operation at the location with a number we know has the bit set. If it is not equal to 0, then the bit is set and we update our counter. We will return our counter modded with 2 since this will tell us if we have even parity.

This should always return an even number (in our case, 0). If it doesn't, we instantly error out. Let's compile this with the following command:

```
> emcc -s "EXPORTED_FUNCTIONS=['_createData', '_checkAndVerifyData']"
hamming.c
```

Now, we can head into our browser and use the number we got from the `createData` method. Head into the developer console and run the following command:

```
Module._checkAndVerifyData(1579);
```

It should print out a 1, which means that we have good hamming data! Now, let's try it with an example that we haven't worked out by hand: the number 1000. Run the following commands; we should get the same results:

```
Module._createData(1000); // produces 16065
Module._checkAndVerifyData(16065); //produces 1
```

Now, we have a working hamming data creation method and a verification tool all written in C and running in the browser! This should help you understand how to port existing applications to the browser, but also how to utilize this powerful technology that allows you to run near-native speeds for computationally intensive applications.

The final section of this chapter will take a look at one of the ports that's being utilized today, and even take a look at some of the code that goes into it. This library is utilized by a lot of application developers and is known as SQLite.

A look at SQLite in the browser

SQLite is an embedded database that's used by thousands of applications. Instead of needing a server and a connection system like most databases, SQLite allows us to utilize it like any other library. But what's kept us from developing with this type of power in the browser has been a way to import this without needing native bindings. To utilize it in Node.js, we would need to utilize something like node-gyp and then create JavaScript bindings to the underlying C code.

We have a way of utilizing this database in the browser without needing these native bindings, thanks to WebAssembly. For a version that has already been compiled for us, go to https://github.com/kripken/sql.js/ and pull the repository into our local system. Let's go ahead and set up our static server to bring in all of the files for us. Follow these steps:

1. Create a new directory called sqlitetest.

2. Inside this directory, go ahead and run the following command to clone the repository from GitHub:

   ```
   > git clone https://github.com/kripken/sql.js.git
   ```

3. With this, we can create a basic index.html file and add the following code to it:

   ```html
   <!DOCTYPE html>
   <html>
       <head>
           <script src='sqljs/dist/sql-wasm.js'></script>
   ```

```
    </head>
    <body>
        <script type="module">
            initSqlJs({locateFile: () => `sqljs/dist/sql-wasm.wasm`
                }).then(function(SQL){
                    console.log("SQL", SQL);
                });
        </script>
    </body>
</html>
```

If we look inside our developer tools, we will see that we have the SQLite library up and running in our browser! Let's go ahead and create some tables and populate them with some data:

1. We are going to create a simple two-table database. These two tables will look as follows:

id	first_name	last_name	username
<auto_increment>	<text>	<text>	<text>

id	customer_id	op	timestamp
<auto_increment>	<foreign_key>	<text>	<integer>

Essentially, we will be simulating a remote procedure call server where, when customers make calls to it, we will log which operation they performed and the timestamp that they performed it at.

To make these tables in our SQLite database, we will run the following code:

```
initSqlJs({locateFile: () => `sqljs/dist/sql-wasm.wasm`
}).then(function(SQL){
    const db = new SQL.Database();
    db.run(`CREATE TABLE customer
        (id INTEGER PRIMARY KEY ASC,
        first_name TEXT,
        last_name TEXT,
        username TEXT UNIQUE)
    `);
    db.run(`CREATE TABLE rpc_operations
        (id INTEGER PRIMARY KEY ASC,
        customer_id INTEGER,
        op TEXT,
        timestamp INTEGER,
        FOREIGN KEY(customer_id) REFERENCES customer(id))`);
});
```

Now, we have a simple two-table database that has everything we need in it to get moving.

2. Let's go ahead and populate this with some data for each of the tables. We can do this with the following commands:

```
const insertCustomerData = `INSERT INTO customer VALUES (NULL, ?,
?, ?)`;
const insertRpcData = `INSERT INTO rpc_operations VALUES (NULL, ?,
?, time('now'))`;
const customers = [
    ['Morissa', 'Catford', 'mcatford0'],
    ['Aguistin', 'Blaxlande', 'ablaxlande1']
];
const ops = [
    ['1', 'add'],
    ['2', 'subtract']
]
for(let i = 0; i < customers.length; i++) {
    db.run(insertCustomerData, customers[i]);
}
for(let i = 0; i < ops.length; i++) {
    db.run(insertRpcData, ops[i]);
}
```

With this bit of code, we have entered our test data. Now, let's run the following command:

```
const statement = db.prepare("SELECT * FROM customer c JOIN
rpc_operations ro ON c.id = ro.customer_id WHERE c.username =
$username");
statement.bind({$username : 'mcatford0'});
while(statement.step()) {
    const row = statement.getAsObject();
    console.log(JSON.stringify(row));
}
```

We have successfully run a SQL database in our browser!

 For more information on how to utilize this, go to `https://github.com/kripken/sql.js/`. To get the SQLite reference documentation, go to `https://www.sqlite.org/lang.html`.

Now, being able to run a SQL engine in our browser is awesome, but let's take a look at how some of the underlying C code got turned into something that our browser understands. If we head to `https://www.sqlite.org/download.html` and download the latest release, we can pull up the `sqlite3.c` code base. Now that we have the code base, let's look for something that we might be able to see in the WebAssembly printout. Follow these steps:

We will utilize the `wasm2wat` tool that we received when we installed the wasm binary tools. Head into the `dist` folder of the `sqljs` folder and run the following command:

```
> wasm2wat sql-wasm-debug.wasm --output=sql-wasm.wat
```

Now, we can open that file to see the generated WebAssembly in a human-readable fashion. As we can see, it isn't that readable, but near the top, we can see a bunch of imports from Emscripten. We should realize that all of these are functions that Emscripten provides from their JavaScript API and that they are utilized to compile everything to WebAssembly and be usable.

Next, let's go to the bottom of the file. We'll notice that there are a bunch of exports that are named. Each of these should correspond to a function found in the c file. Let's go ahead and take a look at a semi-simple one: `sqlite3_data_count`. It should look as follows:

```
else
    i32.const 0
end
else
    i32.const 0
end)
```

We will see this return type in the C code if the pointer is NULL. If the result is NULL, we will return 0. This is how we can debug C programs that we are porting to the web. While this isn't easy, it can help us when we need to do this type of debugging.

This chapter covered just a taste of the libraries that have already been ported. Every day, more libraries are being ported, as well as languages, that can be compiled to WebAssembly.

 A final note on WebAssembly: while we are still in the very beginnings of this technology, we have already seen many advancements. From being able to utilize multiple threads to newly supported multiple return values, we are starting to see this technology really take off.

Summary

In this chapter, we learned how to read and write WebAssembly. We also gained an understanding of how programs are understood by typical computers. On top of this, we wrote a program that is able to utilize this near-native speed. Finally, we took a look at an existing WebAssembly program and how that relates to the code it was generated from.

By now, we have learned quite a bit about the web development landscape. We have looked at coding in the browser and how we can utilize all of the new features to create feature-rich web applications. On top of this, we have seen how JavaScript can be used as our server-side code utilizing Node.js. Finally, we took a look at how to build and deploy our applications. By now, we should be comfortable building scalable applications and utilizing many of the modern features to create blazing fast applications.

Thank you for reading and I hope that this information helps create the next generation of web applications! Keep up with the development of the modern web and build the next amazing application!

Further reading

For those that are interested, the following link showcases the work that Mozilla is doing with WebAsesmbly and how they are really driving the technology forward: `https://hacks.mozilla.org/`.

Other amazing projects that have been created with WebAssembly can be found at the following links:

- **Blazor**: `https://dotnet.microsoft.com/apps/aspnet/web-apps/blazor`
- **Unity**: `https://blogs.unity3d.com/2018/08/15/webassembly-is-here/`
- **Qt**: `https://doc.qt.io/qt-5/wasm.html`

Other Books You May Enjoy

If you enjoyed this book, you may be interested in these other books by Packt:

Clean Code in JavaScript

James Padolsey

ISBN: 978-1-78995-764-8

- Understand the true purpose of code and the problems it solves for your end-users and colleagues
- Discover the tenets and enemies of clean code considering the effects of cultural and syntactic conventions
- Use modern JavaScript syntax and design patterns to craft intuitive abstractions
- Maintain code quality within your team via wise adoption of tooling and advocating best practices
- Learn the modern ecosystem of JavaScript and its challenges like DOM reconciliation and state management
- Express the behavior of your code both within tests and via various forms of documentation

Mastering JavaScript Functional Programming, Second Edition
Federico Kereki

ISBN: 978-1-83921-306-9

- Simplify JavaScript coding using function composition, pipelining, chaining, and transducing
- Use declarative coding as opposed to imperative coding to write clean JavaScript code
- Create more reliable code with closures and immutable data
- Apply practical solutions to complex programming problems using recursion
- Improve your functional code using data types, type checking, and immutability
- Understand advanced functional programming concepts such as lenses and prisms for data access

Leave a review - let other readers know what you think

Please share your thoughts on this book with others by leaving a review on the site that you bought it from. If you purchased the book from Amazon, please leave us an honest review on this book's Amazon page. This is vital so that other potential readers can see and use your unbiased opinion to make purchasing decisions, we can understand what our customers think about our products, and our authors can see your feedback on the title that they have worked with Packt to create. It will only take a few minutes of your time, but is valuable to other potential customers, our authors, and Packt. Thank you!

Index

www.ingramcontent.com/pod-product-compliance
Lightning Source LLC
LaVergne TN
LVHW081514050326
832903LV00025B/1481